Governance and Administration: An Insider's View

GOVERNANCE AND ADMINISTRATION

An Insider's View

U.C. Agarwal

Indian Institute of Public Administration
in association with
KANISHKA PUBLISHERS, DISTRIBUTORS
NEW DELHI-110 002

KANISHKA PUBLISHERS, DISTRIBUTORS
4697/5-21 A, Ansari Road, Daryaganj
New Delhi-110 002
Phones : 2327 0497, 2328 8285
Fax : 011-2328 8285
E-mail: kanishka_publishing@yahoo.co.in

First Published 2010

ISBN 978-81-8457-249-0

PRINTED IN INDIA

Published by Madan Sachdeva for Kanishka Publishers, Distributors, 4697/5-21A, Ansari Road, Daryaganj, New Delhi-110 002, Typeset by Sunshine Graphics, Delhi, and Printed at Rajdhani Printers, Delhi.

DEDICATION

DEDICATED to the memory of my wife SAROJ who passed away recently. She had made our long journey of life together smooth and comfortable enough for me to remain usefully occupied in academic and civil service activities.

"Om asto ma satgamaya
Tamaso ma jyotirgamaya"

(Oh God lead me
from untruth to truth
and from darkness to light)

Brihdaranyak Upnishad–1:3:27

FOREWORD

I have read with interest Shri U.C. Agarwal's book *Governance and Administration: An Insider's View*. The book, as mentioned in the Introductory chapter by Shri Agarwal, is a compilation of some of his articles written from time to time. Since the articles, as mentioned by him, might seem outdated these had to be extensively reviewed, revised, modified and updated, which virtually imparts them a contemporary ring, relevance and meaning.

The twenty-one articles chosen by Shri Agarwal for inclusion in the book, I find are of sufficient current interest. The several important posts held by him (from the grassroot level field post of District Magistrate and Collector to senior level secretariat posts) under the State and Central Governments in diverse areas of administration give weight and credibility to the "Insider's view" part of the title of his book. It may be mentioned, at the very outset, that though seemingly a compendium of articles and pieces penned on different occasions, there is a consistent thread running through them due to the author's own thought process and personal view of life. His is a search for a governance system that could contribute more to the well-being of the common man. He has not lost sight of the citizen's perspective, nor other views from the outside. Moreover, we are all aware that in human affairs, problems arise, are attempted to be solved, but assume different complexions, quantitatively or qualitatively. Even attempts to find a solution may give rise to new problems with changing socio-economic environment. Time is in a flux, but it is also a continuum.

I have known Shri Agarwal very well and for long. I do not know of any other officer who held posts at all levels, i.e. from Under Secretary to Secretary in the Ministry of Personnel & Administrative Reforms dealing with civil services in his three tenures at the Centre. Before a separate ministry for civil services was set up in 1970, after the recommendations of the Administrative Reforms Commission headed by Shri Morarji Desai, these subjects were dealt with in the Home Ministry where Shri Agarwal had worked as Under Secretary and Deputy Secretary in his first central tenure. He was also the longest holder of the key civil service post of Establishment Officer (EO) and Additional Secretary to the Government of India in his second central tenure. His "insider's view" on various administrative matters at different times and under different political regimes could, therefore, stand well-substantiated. He had worked at senior levels of Joint Secretary and Additional Secretary during the regime of Smt. Indira Gandhi (1971-77), and during the Janata regime of Shri Morarji Desai (1977-78) and again was posted as Secretary, Ministry of Personnel & A.R. during Smt. Gandhi's and Shri Rajiv Gandhi's Congress regime (1981-85). He was later appointed as CVC (1985-88). This speaks sufficiently of him as a professional civil servant who was not affected by democratic policies of changing regimes. I find that in his state IAS cadre (Orissa) he had held senior posts both under the Congress regimes of Dr. Hare Krishna Mahtab and subsequently under the non-Congress Swatantra Party regime of Shri R.N. Singhdeo (former Maharaja of Bolangir). Throughout his official career Shri Agarwal exemplified, in his work and conduct, the strength of the concept of civil service neutrality. As a civil servant, all along, his endeavour had been to discharge whatever responsibilities he was entrusted with fairly and fearlessly, keeping in mind the requisite proprieties, rules and regulations; he followed the canons of fair-play, impartiality and public good and interests.

One can, therefore, well understand as to why Shri Agarwal was selected to be the Chairman of the Committee (fifteen years after his superannuation) set up in the year 2000 by the then NDA Government headed by Shri Atal Bihari Vajpayee at the Centre for division and allocation of All-India Service Officers between the newly reorganised states of UP-Uttrakhand; Bihar-Jharkhand and Madhya Pradesh-Chattisgarh–no simple task. As a former C&AG of India I remember having utilised the long civil service management experiences of Shri Agarwal of chairing a Committee in 1992 for the up-gradation of the training arrangements and courses for the Audit and Account Service Officers. In the matters of training, management, discipline, and functioning of civil services Shri Agarwal has commendable knowledge and experience. The expanded and revised version of his selected articles compiled in book form should therefore be of considerable value and interest in our on-going attempt of restructuring and reforming administration. As a matter of fact, the book is neither of the genre of memoirs nor a textbook in public administration. It represents the distillation of the experience, comprehension and observations of a civil servant with understanding and empathy for public aspirations and his role as a professional working within a political framework and constitutional parameters.

The main causes of the country's continuing backwardness as elaborated in the book undoubtedly are: corruption–political and administrative; emergence of vote-bank politics; lack of fiscal discipline leading to ever-growing fiscal deficit and heavy market borrowings each year; and increasing distance between the common man and the man on the chair, leading to tensions and law and order problems.

During the freedom movement led by Gandhiji there was largely a social and political consensus in the country about our aims and objectives. Top leaders and millions of other followers of Gandhiji were ready to make sacrifices for the country's liberation. After independence and after the erstwhile disciples of Gandhiji, started vacating the political space due to age or other factors, a different class of political leaders came to occupy the central stage of power and authority. Their motives, barring some honourable exceptions, came to be primarily to grab political power for self-aggrandisement and accumulation of huge private wealth. Serving the country and its people were of minor concern, if at all, for most of them. The lip homage to Gandhiji's ideals continue to be paid ad-nauseam. The election time slogans and rhetoric to serve the country, the farmers, the weak and the down-trodden, the dalits, the under-privileged and deprived etc. soon turned out to be hollow. Many programmes launched for the benefit of the poor due to malafide motives were ill-executed. The large sums of money allotted for such programmes were generally misappropriated through corrupt means by those executing the programmes or others holding positions of political power. There is common talk of the nexus of politicians, public servants, contractors, middlemen and criminals. And such nefarious activities remain unpunished and generate much of controversy and doubt in the public mind. Power also became the means of cultivating caste and communal forces at the cost of secularism and national unity. Thus, the social and political unity of the country and the cherished goals, visualised and forged during the freedom movement, started cracking.

Shri Agarwal's analysis and views on different aspects of the country's governance and administration have considerable validity. His observations on the poor quality of grassroots administration, based on his personal experience are noteworthy. Some of his suggestions for improvement also deserve serious consideration. The accusations and reasons for the Indian Bureaucracy being "most bureaucratic" have been well-explained, and his suggestions as to how to improve its functioning are worth serious consideration and action. The Indian administration has to be truly "Indian", in name and spirit for the *aam admi*. Shri Agarwal's discussion brings to focus the crying need for self-restraint and discipline at different levels in our democracy as well as the comprehension, conviction, and adherence to ethical dimensions in the conduct of public affairs. The rule of law must operate both in letter and spirit and must be credibly seen to be in operation. This hardly requires elaboration.

I think that Shri U.C. Agarwal has made a significant contribution to the ongoing debate on good governance, which is of primary concern to every citizen. He has carefully, perceptively and objectively analysed the many issues that impinge on the problem. It is neither possible nor necessary that everyone agrees with his diagnosis of the situation in full or with all of his suggestions for remedial action. What is important is that he stimulates thinking, and raises questions and misgivings which need adequate answers. Probably this has been the author's purpose and aim. As is said, eternal vigilance is the price of liberty. The constructive questioning by citizens who are the stakeholders as well as the guardians of good governance in democracy will keep our political masters and others exercising authority under control. Governance by implication, intention and aspiration connotes the governing system which has the approval, acceptance, appreciation and support of people. That is the basic thrust of Shri Agarwal's argument throughout the book. I need hardly reiterate that good governance has, therefore, to be a continuing quest of enlightened citizens.

I believe that Shri Agarwal's erudite volume will have the requisite response from thinking citizens, students of administration and scholars, persons working in different areas of administration and politicians with sensitivity to public good. It has been for me a rewarding experience to read it. I hope that others who have occasions to read it may share my feelings and reactions. I congratulate Shri U.C. Agarwal for his laudable endeavour. It is only fair and proper for me to add a personal note. It has been very kind, thoughtful and considerate on his part to ask me to write a foreword for his volume and introduce its thematic approach and basic purpose.

Shri Agarwal has taken a holistic and comprehensive look at issues in governance. Some chapters of the book dealing with different aspects of governance sufficiently highlight the present shortcomings of governance that require to be set right soon. The first chapter "Good Governance: Constitutional Goals, Achievements and Disappointments" by and large summarises Shri Agarwal's observations and views on post-independence administration and its various weak points that need to be addressed. He has explained as to how things were going on fairly well for about three decades after independence and how and why, thereafter, the country's governance and administration suffered perceptible qualitative setback leading to slowdown in its overall growth and development and rising public discontentment with governance.

Good governance and administration does not depend only on good laws, rules and procedures but more on the goodness of the human beings in-charge of implementing these laws, rules and procedures. Proper shaping and training of the administrative personnel who are the instruments of governance and administration deserve much greater attention. But persons manning administration are not to be looked upon mechanistically as tools as they constitute value in themselves. A conscious, confident and proud public service, which is not denigrated day in and day out, is an asset for any nation. The adage that a bad workman quarrels with his tools does hold true. But the callousness, indifference and rudeness towards the ***aam admi*** has to be removed through appropriate training and good examples set by the seniors. It has to be borne in mind by public servants that they exercise authority on behalf of the people and that authority is limited by time and space. They cannot be oblivious of the fact that they themselves are part and parcel of the citizenry.

Shri Agarwal has covered a very broad canvas of administrative, constitutional and political problems as they all have their direct or indirect relationship with the core issue of governance. He has explored issues such as the role of All-India Services in our federal set up, public perception of the police as it raises a host of questions, citizen and administration–interface or relationship, judicial delays and clamour for more judges, job reservations and so on. They are controversial issues and require cool and dispassionate thinking without ideological tilt or political considerations and pressures. He has given his attention to the need for fiscal discipline and social sector investment, to the importance of safeguarding autonomy of the Election Commission and the need for promotion of citizenship values as envisaged in our Constitution, as well as the role of administration in national integration. The concern about water resources may appear to be of peripheral nature, but its vital importance is being slowly realised in our country and all over the globe. He also does not ignore the issue of the secular character of the state and the positive role that the majority religion can play in promoting it. He has a small piece on Sardar Patel to exemplify the issues of administrative and political leadership–a matter of worldwide debate these days. In the context of monitoring complaints about venality in high public offices, his contribution on Ombudsman and Right to Information and Open Government have their own usefulness, especially in the background of the discussion on "Why and How to vote for Democracy." Our democracy has to be saved from unhealthy and undemocratic practices which have crept in.

In the chapter–"Caste-Census: Not only folly but Disaster", Shri Agarwal has made out a strong and convincing case against the proposed recording of castes of individuals during the 2011 census. This he says, with good reasons, would amount to taking official notice of caste and revitalizing casteism to hinder the goal of making India a truly secular and egalitarian state. However much "social reality" caste may be, it is undoubtedly a diminishing phenomenon and the state ought to play a positive role in ignoring and marginalizing caste in official activities like the ten-yearly census. No opportunity should be allowed for caste labels to be exploited for narrow political ends and perpetuate fissures in society. Spread of casteism and caste feelings ought to be discouraged by all possible means for social cohesion and national solidarity.

I have made at best some mention of the problems that Shri Agarwal analyses, only to point out the wide gamut of governance that he has explored in his book.

The politicians, in power or out of power, need to remember that for good governance civil service neutrality has to be protected and ensured to make administration apolitical and people friendly. Administration has to be above political partisanship if it is to achieve its cherished objective.

T.N. CHATURVEDI
Chairman
Indian Institute of Public Administration
New Delhi

ACKNOWLEDGEMENTS

In writing this book the help and encouragement received from Shri T.N. Chaturvedi, Chairman, Indian Institute of Public Administration, an esteemed senior colleague has been immense. He has a scholastic bent of mind and keeps it well nourished by remaining in close touch with the ever growing wealth of literature in diverse fields. As a member of the IAS Shri Chaturvedi had earned a name and reputation for his professionalism which made colleagues like me proud. My association with Shri Chaturvedi has been long and rewarding starting from the sixties. In the early eighties, when he as a senior member of the IAS, was the Union Home Secretary, I was Secretary, Ministry of Personnel & Administrative Reforms, both sitting in adjoining rooms of North Block. Shri Chaturvedi was elevated to the constitutional office of the Comptroller & Auditor General of India, he took premature retirement from the IAS to take up the constitutional assignment. On my superannuation from the service I was appointed as the Chairman of the Central Vigilance Commission. We have been in regular touch with each other and this has been quite rewarding for me.

After demitting the constitutional office of C&AG Shri T.N. Chaturvedi was elected to the Rajya Sabha twice but before the expiry of his second term in the Rajya Sabha he was persuaded by the powers that be to accept the office of the Governor of Karnataka necessitating his resignation from the Rajya Sabha. Even in these constitutional assignments of political nature Shri Chaturvedi enjoyed the reputation of being above all party politics. He carried out his responsibilities with due sense of justice, fair play and constitutional proprieties. As a state Governor he was rated by the national media to be among the best.

I am indeed very grateful to Shri Chaturvedi for the time he spared in reading the manuscript of the book and writing a comprehensive "foreword" which has undoubtedly added value to it.

I am also very thankful to Shri B.S. Baswan, the Director of the IIPA, for the academic and other facilities I received from the IIPA. Shri Baswan with his usual smiling face also made enquiries from time to time as to how my work was progressing and if he could be of any further assistance. Shri Baswan too is an old colleague with whom I had worked in the Ministry of Personnel & A.R. many years back. He was well-known for his positive and helpful attitude and I benefited from the same in full measure.

Shri Sunil Dutt, Assistant Editor, Indian Journal of Public Administration (IJPA), another valued colleague whom I came to know during my tenure as the Editor of the same Journal had motivated and prevailed upon me to compile several old articles of mine for publication in a book. He took the initiative to select some of the articles on important topics which he thought could be included in the book. After I finally selected the articles these were extensively revised, modified and updated to be of current interest. Shri Sunil Dutt helped in giving appropriate titles to the revised versions of the articles and the order in which these could be placed in the book. He also advised to select KANISHKA for publication of the book in association with the IIPA. Shri Dutt was thus the driving force in bringing out this book and very well deserves my special thanks.

Last, but not the least, I am very thankful to Shri M.P. Gupta, Private Secretary, who took great pains in typing hundreds of pages of the articles on the computer. Many of these articles had to be typed and retyped several times to incorporate some changes and fresh developments during the time of writing. In spite of his other official responsibilities Shri Gupta cheerfully did all the typing work, at times for several hours on a day. In fact due to his dedication and sincere commitment in typing the articles he came to understand and know very well the substance and contents of each article. On a number of occasions when I had asked him about the article in which any particular point had been covered his reply used to be prompt and generally correct. Shri Gupta was thus a very valuable asset in bringing out the book and I express my sincere thanks to him.

U.C. Agarwal

CONTENTS

INTRODUCTION

For the last several years, after superannuation from the IAS (1985) and after demitting of post-retirement office of Central Vigilance Commissioner (CVC) in 1988, I have been writing articles on issues and concerns of current interest in the fields of public administration, financial management, socio-economic development, judicial delays, etc. Most of the articles were based on my public service experiences in several posts.

In the field of Public Administration several articles discussed the worrisome issues like deep-rooted and all-pervasive corruption in administration; reservation in government jobs and seats in educational institutions for the OBCs and judicial verdicts (like the Mandal Judgement) thereon; relevance and importance of All-India Services in a federal polity like India, the poor public image of the Police; declining norms, values and efficiency of the public services, etc.

After attending the World Ombudsman Conference in New York (1986) as India's representative while holding the post of CVC I wrote a comprehensive article on Ombudsman and its relevance for India. This article also covered the institutions of Lok Pal and Lokayukta for their perceived corruption prevention role at higher political and administrative levels.

On the financial management issues a number of articles were written on the ever growing fiscal-deficit problems of the Central and State Governments compelling them to resort to heavy market borrowings to make their both ends meet.

Some friends suggested that I might publish all these articles covering a wide range of subjects of public interest in a book. I was told that even though the issues and concerns pointed out in the articles were generally known, these still carried much weight, first, for giving a top level insider's view of some of the important issues and problems of governance and administration afflicting the country and secondly for suggesting practical remedial measures with illustrations and examples from real life.

On going through the large number of articles afresh, many of which were several years old, I found some difficulties in publishing them without carrying out substantial changes and modifications to make them meaningful now. For example, several of these articles were based on old incidents and events which were not of much significance now; several others relied on facts and figures which were no longer valid due to subsequent developments and changes. On subjects like "corruption" and "reservation" separate articles on different important aspects of these topics were written in the past. For example, there were quite a number of articles on the subject of reservation covering its different aspects like validity of reservation in promotion posts; exclusion of the "creamy layer" from reservation benefit; formulating an "exit policy" on reservation etc. All these issues it was felt could now be dealt with in one comprehensive article for better understanding of the subject. Such amalgamation of separate articles with extensive changes and modifications made it really a new article.

To keep the book within a reasonable size only a few selected topics covered by the several earlier articles with extensive changes and modifications which give them a new look and freshness have been included in it. These topics briefly deal with the slow and disappointing progress made so far by the country in achieving the socio-economic development goals laid down in the Constitution, particularly those that have been spelled out in the Directive Principles of State Policy (Chapter IV). The various road-blocks and hurdles to progress and ways to eliminate or minimise them have been discussed in different chapters of the book. For example, the first chapter with the heading "good governance: constitutional goals, achievements and disappointments" discusses how things were moving fairly well for the first few decades of Independence and how the country started going down from around the mid-seventies due to various faults and shortcomings in the functioning of our democratic polity.

Several instances and examples have been cited from personal administrative experiences of that time to support the points discussed in the chapter. The one most troubling problem coming in the way of India's progress and development is the rising tide of corruption in all spheres of public activities. Corruption has become widespread and deep rooted. This problem has been discussed in all its aspects in the chapter "Combating Corruption" giving a few most recent examples. An action plan for combating corruption suggested by the author as the then Secretary in the Union Ministry of Personnel & A.R. to Shri Rajiv Gandhi, the then Prime Minister of India (1985) has been included in this article. As CVC the author had dealt with several cases of corruption in administration. Earlier as Joint Secretary (Vigilance) (1971-73) in the Union Ministry of Personnel the author had dealt with cases of political corruption at the level of Ministers at the Centre and in the States.

Another serious blow to economic development has been the lack of sound financial management. Many populist schemes for short-term gains and huge wasteful expenditure of public funds in different ways have been driving the country towards financial bankruptcy. This problem has been discussed giving examples of wasteful expenditure of recent times in the chapter "Need for greater fiscal discipline and economy in expenditure".

From personal experience some examples of economy in public expenditure and adhering to strict norms of financial propriety observed by the top leaders during the early sixties have been cited. One such example quoted is that even a proposal from Prime Minister Jawaharlal Nehru's office to allow an additional special pay of Rs. 75 per month to Yash Pal Kapoor, his P.A., (who was already getting two special pays) was not agreed to by Shastriji, the then Home Minister of India, on the grounds of economy and propriety. On being informed of this the PM's Office also did not pursue the matter.

The problem of huge pendency of cases in the judicial courts has been discussed in the chapter: "more Judges, more delay: Parkinson's Law". The gist of this discussion is that appointment of more judges is not the real and long lasting remedy for reducing judicial pendency as more judges may lead to filing of more cases. The solution therefore lies in avoiding filing of millions of petty and unwarranted cases by the low level government officials mostly guided by corrupt motives. If more judges are appointed they will file more petty cases to make more money. Petty cases could be easily handled by mobile courts and decided on the spot rather than burdening the regular courts. Suitable cases have been cited from personal experience as examples of uncalled for litigations which clog the wheels of justice.

The many emerging faults of our democratic political system have been discussed in the chapter "Why and how to vote for democracy". Our democracy which ought to be "Government of the people, by the people and for the people" is gradually getting dominated by few powerful castes and at times by one single family within such castes. Some examples cited of such single family dominance in Government and major political parties are that of Punjab's Akali Government and Tamil Nadu, DMK Government, etc. If such a tendency is not checked there is the long-term danger of democracy getting degraded to "OLIGARCHY: or "Government of the few, by the few, for the few". "We the People" will be side-lined by few castes and families.

Quality of administration and the public services too are going down and have been discussed in the chapters: *(a)* Police-Public Perception; *(b)* Relevance of All-India Services in the Federal Polity of India; *(c)* Citizen and the Public Services; and *(d)* Role of Public Administration in national integration.

Importance of the independence of the Election Commission has been discussed in the chapter "Protecting the Independence of the Election Commission" to ensure "free and fair" polls in our democratic form of governance. Appointment of Shri M.S. Gill as a minister soon after his superannuation from the office of Chief Election Commissioner (CEC) has been observed to be an undesirable development as it may affect the credibility and impartiality of the Commission. There is the risk or the danger of some member of the Commission helping the ruling party out of temptation to get post-retirement benefit as quid pro-quo.

The importance of good citizenship values has been discussed in the chapter "The Constitution and Citizenship Values." Since ultimately people get a government they deserve much therefore depends on the vigilance and alertness of the citizens in safeguarding democracy. It has accordingly been highlighted as to why the people have to actively participate in the elections and vote for the best candidates irrespective of their castes or creed.

The two chapters on "Meaning and significance of Hinduism to make India a secular state" and on "Justice Sachar Committee Report on Muslim Backwardness" mainly deal with the importance of secularism in a pluralist country like India and what should be the rational approach to identify "Backwardness" and its removal. "Caste" or "religion" should not be the basis of identification of "backwardness."

The chapter "From the Official Secret Act (1923) to the Right to Information Act (2005)" gives the historical background and movement from *total secrecy to total transparency* or "Glasnost" in matters of governance and administration. The positive aspects of the RTI Act to promote transparency and accountability in Governance and Administration have been discussed in the chapter.

The chapter "India's Water Resources: some issues of concern" brings out the need and urgency to economise in the use of water and to augment its availability through all possible means like rain water harvesting, linking of interbasin rivers, construction of storage dams across major rivers to impound water during rainy season instead of allowing river flows to go waste into the seas, etc. The statistics given in the chapter bring out the importance and seriousness of the water scarcity problem that the world community and India may face in the near future unless timely remedial steps are taken. Instead of saying "do not waste money like water" we should now say "use water like money".

The chapter on "Caste-Census: not only folly but Disaster" questions the proposed idea of recording castes of individuals during the 2011 census. Undoubtedly this retrograde step will be a severe blow to the secular character of India's Constitution. Caste-Census was discontinued after the 1931 census. Some caste based parties and politicians now want to re-introduce caste census as they have vested interest in demanding higher reservation in jobs for the OBCs if census figures show their population to be higher. Dr. Ambedkar had feared the rise of "caste and creed" politics in free India and the likely appearance of political parties who will place their "caste and creed" interests above the need of unity and integrity of the country. Pt. Nehru had warned the State Chief Ministers in a letter he wrote to them (dated 27th June, 1961) that caste based reservation will be "not only folly but disaster." On seeing the rise of casteism in recent years the fears of our great leaders appear to be coming true rather too soon.

The chapter concludes with the hope that the present day leaders will follow the wise advice of Pt. Nehru in rejecting caste-census rather than follow the foot-steps of V.P. Singh who revitalized "caste" by accepting the caste-based reservation report of B.P. Mandal in 1989.

Different chapters in the book give an insider's view of some of the troubling problems of governance and administration which are slowing down the country's progress and development. With political will and determination these can be very much overcome or at least minimised.

1

GOOD GOVERNANCE: CONSTITUTIONAL GOALS, ACHIEVEMENTS AND DISAPPOINTMENTS

Assessment of the quality of governance to a large extent depends on a Government's ability to protect the life, liberty and property of the people as ensuring peace and tranquility through effective maintenance of law and order is the primary task of any good government. Promoting or facilitating socio-economic development programmes implemented by the government or the private sector may be taken as another important yardstick for measuring good governance. Poverty eradication, employment generation, improving educational and health care facilities of the people have accordingly been laid down as important objectives to be attained by the Indian state under the Directive Principles of the Constitution. Proper and responsive attitude of the administrative machinery towards the *aam admi* or the common man are also relevant for assessing good governance. Ultimately favourable opinion of the people towards a government is the real test of its quality of governance being good.

It is reasonable to expect "good governance" in a democracy described to be "government of the people, by the people and for the people". The rule of law and all that it implies have necessarily to prevail in a true democracy. However, in reality many of the so-called democracies, including India, are being viewed to be degenerating into "government of the few by the few and for the few". Such democracies are being termed as "oligarchies" where a few dominating castes or families or other small groups rule. Power in such degenerated democracies is monopolised by small privileged groups of people who manipulate the electoral processes through vote bank politics of caste, dynasty, language etc. Political parties based on caste, creed, language, region, or religion in India are presently trying to win elections by playing on their narrow identities. Their divisive electoral battles to grab power are proving to be serious road blocks to national unity and good governance. Since "power corrupts and absolute power corrupts absolutely", abuses of power by growing number of holders of public offices in India are becoming worrisome trends. Greater institutional control, transparency and accountability in the exercise of power are therefore of vital importance to prevent abuses of power by those occupying key public offices. Favourable conditions need to be created where all citizens must feel confident of their being equal before the law with equal opportunities for progress. No one should get the feeling of belonging to any privileged class for any special treatment.

The "Preamble" of the Indian Constitution embodies broadly the goals and ideals that the democratic and secular state of India should pursue for the happiness and well-being of all its people. The most important goal is to secure to all its citizens "justice – social, economic and political". This, in essence, summarises the very purpose of any good state and its governance. In a good or civilized state instead of might being right the rule of law and justice should prevail that is to say "right should be might." Some important aspects of this constitutional goal and the ways to achieve the same have been more explicitly spelt out in part IV of the Constitution containing the "Directive Principles of State Policy" (Article 37 to 51). Article 37 states that these Directive Principles "though not enforceable by any court are nevertheless fundamental in the governance of the country and it shall be the duty of the State to apply these principles in making laws."

Article 12 defines the "State" to include "the government and Parliament of India and the government and the Legislature of each of the states and all local or other authorities within the territory of India or under the control of the Government of India."

All these authorities comprising the State have to play their respective roles in implementing the Directive Principles of state policy. Some of these directives require the state, by way of good governance, to aim to achieve briefly the following goals:

- A social order for the promotion of welfare of all the people {Article 38 (1)};
- Minimization of inequalities in income and elimination of inequalities in status {Article 38(2)};

- The right to adequate means of livelihood to all men and women {Article 39(1)};
- Proper operation of the economic system so as to prevent concentration of wealth in few hands {Article 39(c)};
- Equal pay for equal work for men and women {Article 39(d)};
- Protection against abuse of health and strength of workers and the tender age of children {Article 39(f)};
- The right to work, to education and to public assistance in cases of unemployment, old age, sickness and disabilities {Article 41};
- To organize Panchayats as units of self-government {Article 40};
- Just and humane conditions of work and maternity relief {Article 42};
- Living wages for workers to ensure decent standard of life and adequate leisure {Article 43};
- Free and compulsory education for all children below 14 years of age {Article 45}; and
- Higher level of nutrition and public health {Article 47}.

While pursuing the above socio-economic objectives, several valuable fundamental rights guaranteed by the Constitution to all citizens have also to be protected. These rights include freedom of speech, expression, association, profession, belief and faith; [non-discrimination on grounds only of religion, race, caste, sex, or place of birth] equality of opportunity in matters of public employment, etc. An important aspect of good governance is also to treat every citizen with full measure of equality. The state should also respect the dignity of the individual and promote national unity and integrity. For this purpose Article 19(d) and (e) of the Constitution bestow on every citizen of India the right to freely move, reside and work in any part of the country. This fundamental right signifies that India belongs to all its citizens irrespective of their religion, caste, language or region. There is no scope for any narrow concept of Maharashtra for Marathis, Assam for Assamese, Tamil Nadu for Tamilians, and Rajasthan for Rajputs, etc. All Indians are "sons of the soil" in every part of India. An important task of good governance therefore is to ensure that this fundamental right is protected in letter and spirit in order to promote national unity and integrity. Maintaining national unity despite the immense diversity of the country and its people is an important part of good governance. To achieve "unity in diversity" is also an important constitutional goal. As stated in another chapter, after nearly six decades of independence we sadly find that many of the constitutional socio-economic development goals are still to a large extent unfulfilled. Nearly half of the Indian population numbering billion plus are still illiterate, more than one-third of them live in abject and dehumanizing poverty; several millions suffer from the same old diseases like malaria, filaria, TB, leprosy, blindness, and malnutrition. The infant mortality rate (IMR) continues to be very high.

The present low quality of human well-being does suggest the need for improving the quality of governance to a great extent to achieve the unfulfilled constitutional goals of socio-economic development. Presently life for bulk of our people continues to be "nasty, poor and short." No wonder that India ranks very low in Human Development in the world as reported in UNDP's Human Development Report of 2007. India holds a lowly position of 128 among 177 countries of the world surveyed by it. This survey is a composite index of the longevity, health, education and the general standard of living of the people. The HDI or Human Development Index published by the UN Agency annually has gained credibility and acceptability in the eyes of all member countries of the UN.

Why has India's political freedom even after more than six decades, yet to bring to the people freedom from hunger, unemployment, better health and educational facilities? The various causes and impediments in the way of faster socio-economic development need to be identified and examined for taking appropriate corrective measures. With its rich natural resources like extensive land area, vast and varied mineral deposits, plentiful of water availability and a massive billion plus population India has excellent potential to be among the few most advanced countries of the world—agriculturally, industrially and economically. With a well-planned and well-managed development strategy India could have become a prosperous super-power of the world by now. It needs, therefore, to be examined as to why the country is still counted as "underdeveloped" and what must be done to make India a "developed" country.

Speaking broadly, the quality of governance during the first three decades or so of Independence was quite satisfactory. This was primarily because the top political leaders of those years, who were at the helm of affairs of the nation, were the erstwhile followers of Mahatma Gandhi and were very much dedicated in their services for the progress of the country. They had the zeal, devotion and drive to speed up its industrial, economic and scientific development. A commendable beginning was accordingly made in taking up some important infrastructure projects, like power generation, steel production and building of all weather National Highways by constructing bridges over major rivers like Ganga, Yamuna, Brahmputra, Godavari, Krishna and Cauvery, involving huge costs. Agricultural research was also given due priority in order to achieve higher agricultural productivity and self-sufficiency in the production of foodgrains. The building of large multipurpose dams costing hundreds of crores of rupees across important rivers, e.g. at Bhakra, Hirakud, Damodar Valley, Nagarjuna Sagar, were not only well visualized but were rapidly executed without any cost or time overruns. On their timely completion vast areas of agricultural land were brought under irrigation and millions of units of electricity were also generated. Additionally, these projects were of immense help in controlling devastating floods which used to cause huge losses of property and human lives. Building of large-sized steel plants to produce millions of tons of steel at Rourkela, Bhilai, Durgapur, etc. and establishment of many new industrial units for the production of cement, fertilizer, paper aluminium, etc., contributed to rapid industrial and economic growth of the country. Several new medical, engineering and agricultural colleges and other technical institutions too were established for better human resource development. Thus services of thousands of well qualified doctors, engineers and other technical experts became available for implementing many developmental projects. Fundamental scientific research initiatives in areas like nuclear energy, telecommunication, ocean and space etc. were taken in hand to bring India at par with other advanced countries of the world in the new emerging scientific fields. The younger generation of large technical manpower helped the country in its rapid modernization and development of important sectors like telecommunication, railways, ports and airports etc. Many industrial activities like ship-building, manufacture of railway engines, wagons, coaches as also aeroplanes, were taken up to meet India's future demands for rapid economic growth. India thus gained a good foot hold on the new and advanced technologies and their applications. Knowledge and techniques for higher productivity in agriculture through production and sowing of High Yielding Varieties of seeds (HYVs) of wheat, paddy, etc. helped the country in gaining self-sufficiency in the production of foodgrains.

The many bold initiatives taken for the modernisation and economic development of the country in those years soon started bearing fruits. Some of the important mega development projects like the Bhakra and Hirakud Dams, several steel plants, ship building yards, aeronautical units etc. were with pride and justification described as the "temples of modern India" by the country's first Prime Minister, Pt. Jawaharlal Nehru. In the agricultural sector, because of the priority assigned to it, there was remarkable progress to bring about "Green Revolution". This made India more than self-sufficient in its massive foodgrain requirements. There was also "White Revolution" to make India the largest milk producing country of the world. As a result of these developments our leaders had no longer to go to the USA or other countries with begging bowls for import of foodgrains to feed the country's millions of hungry mouths. Progress in the agricultural sector, particularly in the food front was so commendable that for a few years India started exporting foodgrains to other needy countries after meeting its own huge requirements. This happy situation, however, did not last long as the higher foodgrains production could not keep pace with the country's growing population. Presently, there is again the need for another "Green Revolution" to meet our present higher requirements of foodgrains.

In the area of Human Resource Development (HRD) also, as mentioned earlier, India made tremendous progress. It could not only meet its own large technical manpower requirements but was in a position to lend services of thousands of its experts to several friendly countries of Asia, Africa and Latin America. For this purpose, on the suggestion of the author (being then in-charge of personnel management work in the Union Home Ministry), a special cell known as FAS (Foreign Assignment Section) was set up in 1961 to register the names of Indian experts willing to go abroad to work as and when required by any friendly country.

Services of thousand Indian technical experts (e.g. doctors, engineers, financial experts nurses and other paramedical staff) were made available to friendly countries like Iran, Iraq, Kuwait, Afghanistan, Mauritius etc. Some had been deputed under the Indian Techno-Economic Cooperation (ITEC) Programme of the Ministry of External Affairs and many others had been recruited directly by the friendly countries themselves on bilateral agreement basis with India. As the then ex-officio Chairman of the ITEC Programme, while holding the Post of Establishment Officer (EO) to the Government of India (1973-78) the author had occasions to visit several of these countries (in 1974 and 1975) where our experts were on deputation. Most of the Gulf countries preferred to have Indian experts in large numbers to meet their technical manpower requirements. During the author's discussions with the top officials of these countries the one request generally made by them was to extend the deputation period of our experts who were normally not to stay beyond five years. Indian experts had played a vital role in earning a good name for India in many Arab countries where they worked. This was specially so in Iran, Iraq and Afghanistan. In Afghanistan, a medical Centre known as Indira Gandhi Children Hospital was established under the ITEC Programme and it was immensely popular. The author had an opportunity of visiting this hospital and seeing the large number of patients being treated there and talking to some of them. I also visited some mini-hydro electricity projects in Afghanistan which had been completed by our engineers. These provided electricity to rural areas of Afghanistan. The farmers with whom I spoke were visibly appreciative of the good work of our experts.

Incidentally, during my week long tour of Afghanistan I had the good fortune to see the two huge and magnificent stone statues of Lord Buddha in the Bamiyan Valley. One was called the "Great Buddha" being 175 feet high and the other was called "Little Buddha" due to its slightly lower but still a great height of 150 feet. Unfortunately during the Taliban regime of later years these two great historical monuments, symbols of India's close political and cultural links with this land (now known as Afghanistan), were brutally destroyed.

A large number of well qualified Indian experts were also deputed to the UNO and its other allied bodies like the ILO, WHO, UNDP, World Bank, IMF and FAO. Many of the Indian officers on deputation occupied important senior and middle level posts in the UN organisations. In fact quite a few of them were considered to be the backbone of several UN bodies and they wanted to retain them beyond their normal deputation periods of five years. The author, as the then Establishment Officer (EO) to the Government of India, had in 1976 an opportunity to visit some of the above mentioned UN bodies to discuss their requests for longer retention/deputation of Indian officers. It was indeed very satisfying to know and report to the Central Government the high reputation of our officers on deputation to the UN bodies. Indian representation in the UNO at that time was considered to be higher than its normal entitlement. Entitlement for higher level posts in the UNO is largely based on a country's financial contribution to it. Even though India's financial contribution compared to several other major countries was on the lower side yet it had of much higher representation at the officers level than of those countries because of ready availability and higher expertise of our well qualified personnel. India in those years had acquired a good international image and was a reputed member of the UNO. Its democratic form of government, political stability and economic development based on the Five Year Plans had earned the praise of several important countries of the world. Large numbers of Indian experts serving in the UN bodies and other foreign countries also contributed to India's good image.

Many progressive legislations too were enacted during this period of good governance in pursuit of the constitutional goals to raise the socio-economic conditions of the weaker and disadvantaged sections of the people. To improve the lot of the farmers, the zamindari system introduced during the British rule was abolished; liberal tenancy laws were enacted to protect the interests of the actual tillers of the soil. Ceilings on land holding for individuals were lowered and surplus land was allotted to landless farmers.

In addition, a number of labour welfare laws were enacted to ensure fair wages, security of jobs, protection of health and safety of industrial workers. Special laws too were enacted to protect women and child labour. Because of its progressive labour legislations India became a leading member of the ILO. Socialistic approach and ideas of social justice as visualised in the constitution were the guiding principles of governance and development at that time.

An important factor that contributed to good governance in those early years was the trust bestowed by the political leaders on the civil services of the country, the main instruments of governance. The civil services were kept above party politics and there was no political interference in administration. The administration was expected and allowed to be non-political in dealing with administrative matters. Further, officers at senior levels particularly those serving in field posts were encouraged to take initiative and show dynamism in handling the problems of the people with due speed and urgency. They did not suffer from fear of adverse criticism or punitive action for *bona fide* mistakes if any in taking quick decisions when so required. This confidence building approach proved very useful, as immediately after the partition of the country its administration faced several challenging tasks for rehabilitating millions of penniless displaced persons driven out of Pakistan. Partition had also led to large-scale communal riots and killing of thousands of persons. All these were serious problems in the way of maintaining law and order. The public services of the Central and the State Governments as also the All-India Services, because of the confidence reposed in them, rose to the occasion and proved their worth by bringing about peace, harmony and normalcy in the country without much loss of time. Communal harmony was restored within a very short period. The 500 plus Indian native states too were merged into the Indian Union in less than two years–thanks to the strong political leadership of Sardar Patel, the then Home Minister and Deputy Prime Minister of India and the equally energetic drive shown by the senior civil servants like Shri V.P. Menon and others. The private property and privy purse amounts of these more than 500 Rajas and Maharajas were settled by the senior officers within a short time without many lengthy negotiations. The actions of the officers were later duly approved by the Central Government without raising a finger or doubt against any officer.

What was true of the Central Government was true of the State Governments as well in trusting their senior officers in the administrative fields. They were not supposed to act as paper pushers only, but were expected and encouraged to take decisions at their levels in anticipation of government approval where emergent situations so required. In this connection, from my personal experience, two cases during the early years of my service deserve to be quoted by way of illustrations. In one case, when posted as District Magistrate and Collector Puri (Orissa) in 1959, I noticed that there was undue delay in the construction of the chariots of the deities for the famous annual *"Rath Yatra"* of Lord Jagannath. The Raja of Puri being the head of the Temple administration was contacted by me to know the causes for the delay. He explained at some length the financial difficulties that were coming in his way and pleaded for some financial help from the government to speed up the work. Since any further delay in the construction of the chariots would have jeopardized the Rath Yatra festival and thus could have caused serious law and order problems, as the District Collector I decided to immediately sanction and pay to the Raja, the required amount out of the available funds at the Collector's disposal for some other works. In taking this decision there was full confidence that *post-facto* government approval would be forthcoming. As anticipated my action was duly approved when the matter was reported to government.

In another such case, as Secretary Power (Orissa) in 1970, I was once approached by the Chief Engineer Electricity to accord immediate government approval to purchase and airlift a few tons of some critical electrical parts and other costly items from the USA for the Talcher Thermal Power Plant. I was told by the Chief Engineer that the available stock of these items, earlier supplied by the US manufacturer of the power plant machinery, would last only for about 10 days. They were trying to use alternative domestic products of the required items but did not succeed. Hence, the need and urgency of imports. In the summer months at that time the state was solely dependent for power supply on the thermal power station at Talcher, as generation of hydro power from the only other Power Plant at Hirakud was very meager due to very low water level of the reservoir. The state at that time had only these two power plants (at Talcher and Hirakud). While expressing displeasure for giving so little time to the government for allowing import and airlifting of such high cost items– the required permission was however, immediately accorded at my level in anticipation of necessary government approval, later. To go through the normal procedures of getting financial approval, specially after answering queries, if any, raised by the Finance Department at officers and minister's levels would have taken at least a couple of days. Thereafter taking approval of the Power Minister of my own Department too would have taken some time. The normal procedure for obtaining financial sanctions in such cases is quite lengthy. Had the case been once referred to the Finance Department, I could not have taken any further action at my level without the financial clearance of the case. I had therefore, no option but to issue the sanction at my level first, before referring the case for *post facto* approval to FD so that the state does not suffer from lack of electricity due to closure of the Talcher Power Station. My decision, as expected, was duly approved later. In fact taking such decisions in anticipation of Government approval in urgent cases by higher officials at times, seldom raised any eyebrows. In today's changed environment and the risk of CBI probe at the slightest excuse, taking such decisions, however, *bona fide* and justified these may be, could invite trouble for oneself. The result is long delays due to the lengthy procedures, in taking decisions even in very urgent cases. How to restore the decision-making capacity of public servants at least in emergent situations and circumstances needs serious consideration. Officers at certain higher levels must be trusted to make them trustworthy and decisive. Unfortunately, the all-pervasive corruption has made every one untrustworthy and decisions taken without following the lengthy procedures even in emergent situations are likely to be viewed with suspicion. Accordingly, requirements of far too many consultations and clearances have now become unavoidable parts of the system. Files move from department to department and from seat to seat in each department for their comments and clearances before finalizing government decisions. This "red tapism" has thus been built into the system. Any one trying to do things more promptly by short circuiting the laid down procedures, when so required, is likely to become a suspect. India is thus globally viewed to have "the most bureaucratic bureaucracy". The good name it had earlier gained for good governance is now lost. Fighting corruption is undoubtedly very important and should have the highest priority. However, the strategy in tackling corruption should be such that *(a)* it does not harm prompt decision-making and *(b)* takes due care of honest public servants for their *bona fide* actions/decisions.

In this connection it is also important to realize that corruption prevention is not entirely a police, or CBI job. The Departmental heads have also to play a vital role. They are expected to know the efficiency, commitment and honesty of their colleagues and subordinates better. Accordingly, the normal practice specially in case of senior level officers (i.e. Jt. Secretary and above) was for the CBI to make prior consultations with their superior officers before registering any case of suspected corruption against any of them for investigation. On some occasions, particularly during the brief Janata regime of Morarji Desai (1977-80) cases against even some Secretaries to Government were *suo-motu* registered by the CBI without consulting the Cabinet Secretary for investigation. This had a great deal of demoralizing effect on the higher civil servants. They in fact started avoiding taking decisions at their levels even though they had the delegated powers to do so. Hence after Mrs. Indira Gandhi came back to power in 1980, to improve the quality and speed of the government machinery she decided that the CBI should be directed to follow the earlier practice of prior consultation before initiating any action against Jt. Secretary and other higher level officers. To formalize the practice which was earlier based on administrative convention the CBI was directed by written order to take prior approval of the competent authority before registering any corruption case against officers of the level of Jt. Secretary and above (i.e. decision-making level officers). This directive to the CBI subsequently came to be known as "single directive". It of course, did not prevent the CBI to register on its own corruption cases on *prima-facie* evidence of disproportionate assets or where an officer was caught red-handed while taking bribe in any trap case. The author was, at the relevant time, Secretary to Government, in the Union Ministry of Personnel and Administrative Reforms and had suggested to government to restore the authority of the higher officers and make them feel confident to take decisions at their levels where so empowered. They should also be enabled to play an effective role in prevention of corruption at lower levels in their organizations. Services of the CBI should of course be utilized where so required, but it should not be given a free hand in setting the law into motion against "decision-making" level officers i.e. Jt. Secretary and above. However, once a case is duly allowed to be registered there should be no further government interference in its investigation by the CBI.

Circumstantially, the author had over 15 years of service in the Union Ministries of Home and Personnel and Administrative Reforms dealing with Civil Service Management policies. This long association in dealing with civil service policy matters was in three separate tenures of central deputations i.e. in the years 1959-64; 1971-78 and 1981-85 in secretarial posts at all levels i.e. Under Secretary, Deputy Secretary, Jt. Secretary, Additional Secretary and Establishment Officer (EO) and finally Secretary to the Government of India. In some of the above posts as also in the post of Central Vigilance Commissioner (CVC) 1985-88, held after retirement, the author had close interactions with the CBI. In fact as Jt. Secretary (Vigilance) and later as Secretary Personnel, I had to deal with the administrative matters of the CBI. The CBI had generally been headed by competent police officers who also favoured sound administrative arrangements for prevention of corruption among public servants. They fully agreed that senior officers in all ministries and field organizations must play significant roles in controlling and preventing corruption in their respective organizations.

During my central deputation period of 1971-78 Morarji Desai's Janata Government was in power for a short span, as mentioned earlier.

I have separately mentioned about the role of the CBI during that period and what changes in that role were required. Services under two different political regimes, i.e. Congress and Janata, which were not friendly to each other, helped me to understand the importance of civil service neutrality and the role of the All-India Services for good governance. For this purpose it is essential to ensure a sense of security among the higher decision-making level officers of the rank of Jt. Secretary and above to enable them to function without fear or favour. They in fact provide continuity of administration and in taking decisions, when so required, at times of political transitions. It would be unfortunate if they remain as helpless onlookers out of CBI fear in taking important decisions on such occasions. That would defeat the very purpose of "permanent" civil services.

Incidentally, after the advent of the Janata regime in 1977 (March) even though I was not disturbed from my assignment at that time of Additional Secretary and Establishment Officer (EO) dealing with the postings and transfers of senior officers, by virtue of that post I came across some cases of harassment and transfer of senior officers by the government on flimsy grounds or on grounds of political vendetta. Two secretaries to government were even arrested by the CBI without the knowledge of the Cabinet Secretary, with whom I had checked the matter. Political vendetta was presumably the cause. Some high level officers were also prematurely reverted to their state IAS cadres even though they had only a few months left to retire from service. As a matter of long standing practice, All-India Service officers on central deputation are not reverted to their states at the fag end of their service or after they have been promoted as secretaries to government. A couple of officers unable to bear the shock of sudden and untimely reversion even succumbed to untimely death. The change of political regime during this time proved to be quite disturbing and injurious to good governance. Corrective steps needed to be taken to restore the confidence and the political neutrality of the civil services in the interest of sound and clean administration. That was the reason to restrain the CBI from registering corruption cases against senior officers without prior government approval.

In a subsequent writ petition (*Vineet Narain and another* vs. *Union of India*) the Apex Court however, held that the statutory powers of the CBI cannot be circumvented or compromised by any executive order (i.e. the "single directive") of the government. That really implied that the statutory powers of the CBI, if required to be amended had to be done through a statutory provision of law. Government accordingly decided to make such a legal provision under Section 27(6A) of the Central Vigilance Commission Act 2003 which reads as below:

"The Delhi Special Police Establishment (i.e. the CBI) shall not conduct any inquiry or investigation into any offence alleged to have been committed under the Prevention of Corruption Act, 1988 except with the previous approval of the Central Government where such allegations relate to:

(*a*) the employees of the Central Government of the level of Joint Secretary and above; and

(*b*) such officers as are appointed by the Central Government in corporations established by or under any Central Act, Government companies, societies and local authorities owned or controlled by the government."

The author having superannuated in the meanwhile (i.e. 1988) was however invited as a former CVC to express his views before the Joint Parliamentary Committee, headed by Hon'ble Shri Sharad Pawar, M.P., which was examining the relevant Vigilance Commission Bill before it became an Act in 2003.

The author strongly supported the above mentioned provision which gave the required statutory power to implement the earlier "single directive" of Government, to the CBI. The main idea behind this legal provision (which was in fact on my suggestion) was to make the senior officers more confident in taking *bona fide* decisions at their levels when so empowered.

An article written by me on this subject at the relevant time and published by the *Hindustan Times* has been included as Annexure 1 for further clarity on this important issue. Incidentally, the CBI at present, without any statutory provisions as such, has to take the prior permission of the Chief Justice of India before registering any corruption case against any judge of a High Court or of the Supreme Court. This is because of an order to this effect passed by the Apex Court in one of its judgements. The "single directive" issued to the CBI by government for taking their prior approval before registering any corruption case against any senior officer of the rank of Jt. Secretary and above was thus in tune with the order of the Apex Court relating to members of the higher judiciary. However, since this executive order of government was not upheld by the Apex Court in the Vineet

Narain case it had to be incorporated as a statutory provision in the Vigilance Commission Act 2003.

The quality of governance due to several factors and causes started to decline from around the 80s onwards. From then on, the higher norms and values observed in the governance of the country started gradually to be ignored. No means were considered unfair by politicians and political parties to grab and retain power in order to exercise authority over the State Administrations in serving their own political and personal ends. Their election promises and rhetoric to serve the people after coming to power were seen to be hollow and not given much weight by the people. Institutions like the judiciary and the civil services, which were meant to be above party politics gradually started to face political pulls and pressures of the unscrupulous politicians in power. High level corruption, particularly among the holders of top political offices began to become rampant and open, without any fear, shame or stigma. The 80s and 90s also saw the revival of some of India's age old vices like casteism, communalism, nepotism and regionalism. These evils had been kept under tight control by the earlier leaders with their nationalistic and Gandhian backgrounds. Those leaders had strong commitments to national unity and integrity and did not allow any divisive tendencies to arise nor encouraged allegiance to narrow identities of caste and creed. They were generally "One India" and "our India" minded leaders. The whole of India was one for them. As time passed, the lofty constitutional provisions of equality before law and non-discrimination between citizens, on grounds only of caste, creed, race, etc., began to be violated on one pretext or the other. One such pretext was found to justify special treatment in the matter of Government jobs and seats in educational institutions for certain politically powerful castes and groups of people, by classifying them as "Other Backward Classes" (OBCs) under Article 16(4) of the Constitution. If this special treatment had been restricted to a small number of truly "backward" and weaker sections of the people, as was intended by the Constitution makers, there could not have been any breach of the "equality provisions" of the Constitution. But for the purpose of electoral gains the "backward class" net was cast far too wide so as to include many undeserving castes and classes of people within its fold. Even the comparatively advanced sections of the "backward classes" occupying high political and administrative offices, appropriately termed as the "creamy layer", were given reservation benefits. In fact those constituting the "creamy layer" became the main beneficiaries of the backward class reservation. Being comparatively better educated and economically comfortable they were able to corner most of the reserved jobs in Government services and seats in higher educational institutions. The poor and genuinely weaker sections of the backward classes derived little benefit from reservation and continued to be as backward as before. There was hardly any "social justice" in this kind of reservation policy. It only amounted to rewarding the politically powerful groups of so-called backward people. This serious departure from the constitutional ideal of "equality" opened the doors for similar acts of special treatment to several other groups of people. This policy has also been socially divisive. (This subject has been dealt with more elaborately in another chapter dealing with OBC reservation.)

The quality of administration and governance came down further in the eighties onwards, firstly due to the spread of massive and rampant corruption and secondly, due to the lack of seriousness in mitigating the sufferings of the people by the democratically elected governments and their machinery of governance. At the grassroots or at the cutting edge levels, where administration comes in direct contact with the common man *or aam aadmi,* the lower level officials were found to be callous, unresponsive and unsympathetic in solving the day-to-day problems of the people. Their attitude towards them was generally found to be negative and unhelpful. The common complaints of the people related to harassment and rude behaviour by the lower officials, and also unabashed corruption among them. People in general felt that the colonial British rule was comparatively much better than the so-called democratic rule of the elected political leaders of free India. During this period, decried by some as the period of "pseudo-democracy", people felt that while the size of the administrative machinery had phenomenally increased, the quality of public services had phenomenally declined. It is said with anguish that "there are more public servants but little of public service". In the name of public welfare schemes and huge expenditure on them, only corruption seems to have flourished and enriched the so-called "public servants" in charge of implementation of the various developmental schemes. Many of these "public servants" take little interest in the welfare of the people but allegedly misappropriate a good part of the development funds placed at their disposal.

As stated in another chapter hardly 15 per cent of the money for development is said to be fruitfully utilized and the rest goes to the pockets of greedy contractors, politicians and officials. Many of them are said to have become millionaires or even billionaires while the people for whom the development works were to be done continue to be the same poor "slum dogs". No wonder that the value of the individual assets declared by many politicians, who stood as candidates for the 15th Lok Sabha elections in 2009, ran into hundreds of crores of rupees. Reportedly 300 MPs of 2009 vintage are crorepaties while in 2004 they numbered 154. There has undoubtedly been eradication of poverty of some such political class of our people. The popular perception is that there will be few politicians, who after having become MLAs/MPs even once, are not millionaires. Some of them who held ministerial posts have even allegedly become billionaires. Unfortunately, the elected members of municipalities and municipal corporations too are allegedly not lagging behind the MPs/MLAs in amassing huge illegal wealth. Therefore, how can they be expected to provide good civic services for the benefit of the urban inhabitants? Accordingly, people suffer from lack of good roads, sewerage, electricity and clean drinking water etc., in every town and city of the country. Millions of urban poor also live in nasty and dehumanizing slums. The Urban Renewal Mission Plan undertaken by government for some years for urban development has under the prevailing climate of corruption, yet to show the desired results.

To move papers in most government offices, "speed money" by way of bribery has to be paid by the applicants to the concerned public servants. They have no choice but to comply with the illegitimate demands of the dealing hands in various government/local body offices in matters like getting ration cards, telephone connections, passports, birth and death certificates, sales tax and income tax clearance certificates, motor driving licenses and their renewals, registration of vehicles, approval of building plans, conversion of plots from lease-holds into free-holds, registration of various legal documents, etc. Thus for transaction of work in Government offices people have to pay legal taxes to the public exchequer and illegal levies or bribes to the dealing officials or babus. The total of such bribe amounts paid to the public servants is said to be much higher than the total amount of legal taxes paid to the government. Corruption among public servants has now become a generally accepted and unavoidable phenomenon. In fact it is said that this "extra income" or "upri" through corruption, in addition to the normal salary also counts in the social standing of public servants.

Though there is a feeling of helplessness and pessimism in the prevention of corruption, things can still be improved if there is genuine desire and determination to do so. For in the present circumstances and times of widespread corruption also, there are still a good number of honest public servants at all levels who have not deviated from the path of honesty and integrity in the performance of their public duties for public good. It is not uncommon or unusual for some individuals to have an inborn or natural instinct to follow the right path and to do the right things. Public servants of such high moral character have accordingly remained honest and incorruptible under the prevailing circumstances as well. These individuals of high integrity and honesty are indeed the valued gifts of God and should be well utilized to curb corruption in different areas of government work. The top political leadership has also to show the will and good leadership qualities to fight corruption with the help of such honest public service-oriented officials. It is well said that "where there is a will there is a way". Corruption can of course be checked and very much reduced, if not eliminated altogether if there is genuine desire and determination to do so. The first essential and good step to be taken to minimize corruption would be to considerably curtail the economic and commercial activities of Government. To be in business should no longer be the business of Government. The policy that the "commanding heights" of the economy should be in public hands appears no longer to be valid under the changed global economic environment. Economically, the world is no longer divided by "narrow domestic walls". It has truly become a global village and India has rightly and wisely chosen the path of economic liberalization by opening its economic doors to the private sector–domestic as well as foreign. Past experiences also show that the policy of state monopoly and rigid control of the economy reduced production of goods and service on the one hand and fueled corruption on the other. The government at long last, after its bitter experiences realized the wisdom of privatization and liberalization of the economy for speedier development and growth and prevention of corruption. Accordingly, several industries reserved for the public sector have by now been thrown open to the private sector. Disinvestment of government shares in the PSUs too has been accepted as a policy to be followed in a measured manner. Reportedly 10 per cent shares of all the listed and also of the profit making PSUs will be disinvested and their receipts utilized for the funding of important social sector schemes.

To move forward in the course of liberalistion several regulatory functions of government too need to be reviewed and minimized to bring down the role of government in trade and industry. Over regulation, according to some experts, by interfering with the normal market forces of demand and supply adversely affects economic growth. Some essential regulatory controls are no doubt necessary to prevent undesirable private sector players to manipulate market forces for their illegitimate gains at the cost of public good. The massive Satyam Computers scam of recent times (2006-08) is an example of this. There have been several multi-billion dollar financial scams in the USA and UK also in the recent past, in the private sector, which prove that the capitalist free market economy too is vulnerable to corruption and other abuses. Therefore some necessary government regulations for the smooth operation of the economic forces and to check frauds are necessary and desirable.

To bring about improvements in the functioning of the Administrative machinery particularly at the grassroots, several Administrative Reform Committees and Commissions were set up in the past. They had enquired into the working of government agencies in areas, like Agriculture, Rural Development, Health Care, Education, Banking, Postal System, Railway Services, Telecommunications, Police and Judicial Courts, etc. Some important administrative reforms and improvement measures were recommended in the reports of the following committees/commissions:

1. Paul Appleby's report on "Public Administration in India" (1951)
2. V.T. Krishnamachari's report on "District Administration" (1952)
3. J.B. Kriplani's report on "Corruption in the Railways" (1955)
4. K. Santhanam Committee's report on "Prevention of Corruption" (1964), and
5. The Administrative Reforms Commission headed by Morarji Desai (1968-70).

The last named Commission, headed by Morarji Desai, had made comprehensive studies of administration in several important spheres and submitted as many as 19 reports. Some of these were concerning *(i)* the machinery of Government, *(ii)* Personnel Administration, *(iii)* Centre-State Relations, *(iv)* Redressal of Citizen's Grievances, etc. The author had examined these reports in 1971 as Joint Secretary in the Central Ministry of Personnel & Administrative Reforms. These reports had generally emphasized the desirability of greater decentralization of power and functions of Government to expedite decision-making and for speedier implementation of developmental programmes and projects. Emphasis was laid on bringing administration closer to the people, and on making it more transparent, and accountable in the exercise of its powers. Openness of administration was considered to be essential to ensure justice, to reduce corruption and to prevent harassment of the people. All stakeholders as a matter of right should be informed if they so desired as to why and for what reasons a particular decision was taken by any public authority. In fact this long standing demand led to the enactment of the Right to Information Act 2005 (RTI). Transparency or openness was expected to prevent decision makers from wrongly obliging influential persons at the cost of deserving individuals. The RTI Act could indeed serve as an effective instrument to improve the working of the government machinery.

To improve the performance and supervisory roles of higher officers, longer tenures in their postings had been recommended by all Administrative Reform Commissions in the past. It was seen that officers in some states got transferred too often with every change of government. In states like Uttar Pradesh the average tenure of DMs and SPs was found to be no more than six months. This was too short a period to make them capable and effective in understanding and dealing with their local problems or to curb malpractices, if any, of their subordinates. Many recommendations had also been made by most of the Administrative Reform Commissions and committees to keep members of the civil services above party politics, so as to inspire public confidence in their impartiality and fairness. They were not to be shifted from their posts with every change of government. Such transfers had the risk of making civil servants political minded and try to be in the good books of one group of politicians or the other for their service security and career advancements. In our democracy, political heads may change on the basis of popular votes but not the "permanent" civil servants. Under the existing administrative system they continue to hold their civil posts and provide continuity of government functioning irrespective of political changes after elections.

Civil servants themselves are required, under their conduct rules, to be above politics and not to involve themselves in party politics in any manner. (An article written by me in April 1991 and published in the *Tribune* is enclosed as Annexure 2).

Making changes and improvements in administrative procedures and practices, rules and regulations, forms and techniques alone may not be sufficient for good governance. The human elements in charge of running the administrative machinery have to show greater sense of fairness, impartiality, devotion and dedication to their duties and the policies and programmes of the government for the well-being of the people. Here also, unless the top leadership is found to be serious in improving the quality of life of the people, the lower layers of administration are unlikely to show any greater will or enthusiasm. The common sense view is that the lower level officials generally follow the footsteps of their higher bosses. Accordingly, if there is corruption at the top levels there may be more of it at the lower levels. The top leadership has accordingly to be clean and above suspicion and set good examples of being role models for their subordinates.

To put the Indian democracy and its governance on the right track again, it is essential that more honest and public spirited citizens participate in the political processes of our democracy, specially in the exercise of their right to vote at the time of elections. They must take active and abiding interest in the governance of the country. (This has been dealt with more elaborately in chapter 20)

The grassroot level administration has to be more people friendly through better and wider empowerment of elected Panchayat Raj Institutions (PRIs) at the district, block and village levels in dealing with local issues. These institutions need also to be placed on sound financial footing. Being closer to the people, they ought to be empowered to decide through panchayat adalats minor civil and criminal cases, which would give relief to the people from running to judicial courts in distant towns and cities. This would also relieve the regular judicial courts of their ever mounting load of cases. There should, of course, be proper guidance and supervision of the village adalats at the initial stages to ensure legality, impartiality and fairness in their decision-making. For this purpose retired Judicial Magistrates could be made honorary advisers to these adalats. Most of the local development works could also be entrusted to the PRIs. In fact reportedly, a good beginning has already been made in a few states to hand over all local development works in the districts to the PRIs. They could also be empowered, as an experimental measure, to give some of the legal certificates, like birth, death, marriage, caste, character etc. to their local residents. As mentioned earlier administration in many respects, at the grassroots, should be run by the local people themselves. That would bring about true local self-government to achieve the Gandhian ideal of "Gram Swaraj."

Initially, there may be understandable reluctance in expanding the scope of work of the Panchayats as many of them may not be free from caste, creed, or other social prejudices. Some of them have also been found to be of the old conservative mindset and outlook, resisting all social changes, however good and enlightened these may be. The goal should however be, to make as much use of these democratic institutions as possible through proper training and guidance in the service of the people, and to minimize the role of the bureaucracy. By and large the PRIs are expected to be less rigid and less formal in handling the day-to-day problems of their local residents whose individual backgrounds and antecedents would be better known to them. The bureaucracy, being rule bound, generally tends to be rigid and negative in its approach and less inclined (except through corruption) to make relaxations or exceptions, even where justified due to any special circumstances. The democratic PRIs on the other hand are expected (hopefully without corruption) to show deserved sympathy and understanding to concerned individuals in special situations. In a vast country like India, there is no escape but to decentralize governmental functions and powers to the maximum possible extent to avoid delays and corruption. The constitutionally recognized PRIs (after the 73rd and 74th Constitutional Amendments) are now the appropriate bodies to be entrusted with sufficient powers and functions for good governance. In due course these bodies may have younger leadership to guide them and manage their affairs in accordance with requirements of the changed times and social environments. No society can always remain static in its thinking and living. Healthy changes have to be accepted and younger leadership, from time to time, through democratic elections is the real answer to this.

To sum up, the socio-economic goals broadly outlined in the Directive Principles of State Policy of the Constitution have yet to be realized to a large extent, even after several decades of independence and development planning. It is disappointing to see that the quality of governance instead of improving is going down, as corruption is going up from year to year. Far too many laws, rules, regulations, forms and formalities, many of which are redundant, have been enacted and enforced by the Government over the years. These have suffocated the life of the people and unduly increased the importance of the lower bureaucracy by providing them enormous scope and opportunities for corruption. The elected representatives of the people, barring some exceptions, too have not proved to be of much help to the people. They are by and large professional politicians and are believed to be hand in glove with the petty officials to serve their own political ends. They themselves are reportedly indulging in all kinds of corrupt activities, including taking illegal money from government servants to become their God fathers and help them in matters like transfers, promotions and postings. Some of them instead of fighting corruption are said to be patronizing corrupt officials and sharing their corruption incomes. They seem to be the face of a new kind of zamindari system. As a result, though a democracy, India can hardly boast of having good governance for its billion plus population. The Five Year Plans of development, for employment generation and poverty eradication, however well visualized, have not yielded the desired results due to rampant corruption, inefficiency and lack of dedication of the public servants in their implementation. Accordingly, nearly one-third of our billion plus people belong to the BPL (Blow Poverty Line) category and nearly 50 per cent of them are illiterate. India thus has the largest percentage of poor and uneducated people in the world and ranks almost at the bottom of the Human Development Index (HDI) prepared by the reputed international agencies. Our democratic leadership also appears, by and large, to be more interested in grabbing and retaining power for their own narrow political ends rather than for the good of the country and the people. In the prevailing circumstances "good governance" appears, to be a far cry. Electoral promises to bring about "Ram Rajya" are of course made by all political parties on the eve of every general elections, but they know, and the people as well know that these are hollow promises or are "election lies" and do not deserve to be taken seriously for compliance.

For the present even though "untruth" rather than "truth" seems to be prevailing, hopefully, ultimately "truth shall prevail". It however, depends on the citizens themselves as to how soon they would defeat the wrong doers and ensure the victory of the honest and selfless leaders in the political arena through proper use of their right to vote at the time of elections. In the end it may be worthwhile to quote the wise political truth that "people get a government they deserve". Democracy by itself cannot ensure good governance unless the citizens make proper and effective use of their democratic rights to achieve the desired goals. There is much truth and wisdom in the sayings *"Suptsya Singhsya Mukhe na Pravasanti Mrigaha"* and "eternal vigilance in the price of liberty".

ANNEXURE–I (Pl. See Page 14)

CBI

AUTONOMOUS FROM WHOM?

(The Rationale behind the "Single Directive")

A wide ranging judgement was delivered by a three judge bench of the Supreme Court in December 1997 in the writ petition *"Vineet Narain and others* vs. *Union of India"* headed by the Chief Justice J.S. Verma, and comprising of justice S.P. Barucha and Justice S.P. Sen. The judgement dealt with some aspects of the functioning of the CBI, the Enforcement Directorate and the Central Vigilance Commission.

The only matter discussed here is the court's ruling that the CBI' power to register and investigate cases of corruption against some categories of officers cannot be restricted by any executive instructions and conditions. The court accordingly struck down the "Single Directive" ...the gist of which was that the CBI has to take prior consent in the case of a Joint Secretary level officer, of the Secretary of the concerned ministry, of the Cabinet Secretary in case of a Secretary level officer and of the Prime Minister in case of the Cabinet Secretary before registering a corruption case against any of them. The intentions behind this was to provide some safeguard to the above category of senior "decision-making level" officers who exercise higher responsibilities and are expected at times to promptly decide and respond to emergent situations. They are expected to take even risk involving decisions at times. Their senior and superior officers with knowledge of the ministry/organizations, its goals and tasks, its working procedures and practices, as also the character and record of service of their junior officers, were better placed to decide on the merits or otherwise of CBI's suspicion of corruption against them and registering cases for investigations.

Under the law, the CBI has the power to investigate an "offence" which is defined by the Criminal Procedure Code as "any act of omission or omission made punishable by any law." The purpose of the "Single Directive" was to let the senior and superiors of a suspect officer decide whether any suspected action or decision of the officer amounted to an "offence" to justify investigation by the CBI after registering a case. Thus the CBI was not left free to be the sole judge in deciding what decision of a senior officer constituted a punishable "offence" foı investigation by it. The CBI also did not possess adequate knowledge and experience required to evaluate correctly, complex economic or commercial decisions based on any policy compulsions even if any of these may go wrong at times. Another consideration was that once the CBI took up investigation after registering a case, the suspect officer would undergo harassment, humiliation and mental agony even if he was later let-off by the CBI itself on finding the suspicision to be untrue.

I have some knowledge about the background and the rationale behind the issue of the Single Directive having had a fairly long tenure in the Union Ministry of Personnel and Administrative Reforms and holding various senior posts.

To appreciate the background and rationale of the Single Directive, attention needs to be drawn to the eventful years of the Emergency (1975-77) the years of Janata Rule (1977-80) and the period of Indira Gandhi's return to power (1980-84). Some of the senior civil servants during those years had watched the dramatic political and administrative events from close quarters. By virtue of the post (i.e. Establishment Office or EO to the Government of India) I then held I had several occasions to hear tales of woe arising out of probes on actions and decisions of some officers in various ministries and the PSUs. They had come under the scrutiny of one enquiry committee or the other set up by the Janata Government. Some officers deservedly and some without much fault had to suffer humiliation. In some cases, political prejudices and vendetta also played a part. At least a couple of officers could not recover from the shocks of those times and died prematurely. Two senior Secretaries of the Union Government were arrested by the CBI in 1977 in their offices on mere suspicion of some wrong doing without the knowledge, let alone permission of the Cabinet Secretary. The accusations were later found to be flimsy and both the officers were let-off honourably. They had in the meanwhile suffered intense mental agony. Such unfortunate happenings did impair the morale and confidence of the civil services generally and particularly of the higher decision-making level officers. Seeing some of their colleagues taking *bona fide* decisions having run into trouble, they avoided taking important or controversial decisions.

As a result the usual slow pace of decisions-making in Government became notoriously more slow during the Janata regime. The public accordingly ridiculed it as "a Government that does not work". Its inaction and inability to govern after having demoralised the higher civil services, and due to other factors led to its premature collapse and Indira Gandhi was voted back to power. Her apt election slogan to provide "a Government that works" paid rich electoral dividends.

A number of administrative studies recommended that credible safeguards be provided to top level officers against hasty CBI investigations and enquiries based merely on their own suspicions, without consulting and taking the views and opinions of their superior officers into account. These administrative developments and corrective measures as advised by the experts led to the issue of the "Single Directive". In fact, even before this Directive was formally issued, a healthy administrative convention existed under which the CBI Director discussed with the Secretary concerned and the Cabinet Secretary vigilance cases if any against senior officers before formally initiating investigations after registering cases against them. Due to breaches of this convention at times, its formalization in the form of a Directive for compliance by the CBI became necessary. By the way, the "Single Directive" restrictions on the CBI do not apply where direct and clear evidence of corruption is available to it in a trap case where someone is caught red-handed accepting bribe. The application of the Directive is limited to cases of inference of corruption drawn by the CBI due to any suspicious nature or peculiarities of any decision or action of any officer. In such cases only the application of higher minds of the seniors and superiors was considered essential to provide protection to innocent officers before initiating any legal action.

When in the banking sector a situation developed where banks overflowing with funds avoided lending to the credit-starved industry out of fear of CBI investigations lest any of their *bona fide* loan decisions went wrong, the Finance Ministry had to think of a way out in the interest of economic and industrial growth. It accordingly decided to set up a High Powered Board of experts in finance to examine the CBI proposals of investigations against high level bank officials before cases were registered. This was in line with the "Single Directive". On similar considerations, the Ministry of Industry was also contemplating on setting up a pre-investigation Board to provide an insurance to higher executives of the PSUs in taking *bona fide* commercial decisions without fear. After the striking down of the Single Directive by the Apex Court these protective arrangements too will become inoperative being restrictive of CBI jurisdiction.

In deciding that the CBI enjoys unhindered legal powers to register and investigate cases, the apex court has referred to Section 3 of the Delhi Special Police Establishment Act 1947. The reliance of the Attorney General, in support of the "Single Directive", on the apex court's judgement in *K. Veeraswami* vs. *Union of India and others* 1991, was also ruled out as inapplicable. In that cases, the apex court had held that the Prevention of Corruption Act is applicable to the High Court and Supreme Court Judges. A condition was, however, laid down by the court in that judgement that "no criminal case shall be registered under Section 154 Cr.PC against a Judge of the High Court or of the Supreme Court unless the Chief Justice of India is consulted and his assents to such an action being taken.

After the judgement of the apex court the "Single Directive" and the safeguards it provided to the "decision-making" level officers in Government has become inoperative. Similarly, the functions of the High Powered Board of the Finance Ministry would no longer be valid so far as the CBI investigations are concerned.

The Government of the day would now have to decide if these arrangements need to be continued by suitably amending the SPE Act and the Criminal Procedure Code. The ruling of the apex court is that the restrictions imposed by the above arrangements on the CBI, are invalid not being part of any law.

In my view despite many scams and scandals involving many holders of political offices and high level public officials, it may not be wise to assume that there are no more honest officials left who need to be provided any safeguards and insurance against malicious accusations and investigations. That kind of assumptions may not be in the interest of good governance. It cannot also be assumed that the CBI alone is incorruptible, the CBI under wrong leadership, desirous of cheap popularity and media publicity, could also become an instrument of harassment. The CBI should not, therefore, have the final say with regard to registering of cases against senior officials.

The opinions of their superiors should be obtained in the interest of not only protecting the morale of the officials but also for the sake of organizational efficiency and justice. The association of the CVC in this process would be of benefit he being an independence authority. For this legal provisions could be made so that cases of differences between the departmental authorities and the CBI are placed before the Central Vigilance Commissioner (CVC) and his decision on the matter to be final and binding on all concerned.

The judgement of the Supreme Court has already directed the Government to make the CVC a statutory body. In another directive the court has laid down that "the CVC shall be responsible for the efficient functioning of the CBI." The association of the CVC in these matters would, therefore, be in keeping with the judgement of the apex court.

The Tribune dated 19.4.1991

ANNEXURE-II (Pl. See Page 21)

KEEP BUREAUCRACY ABOVE POLITICS

The large-scale reshuffle of IAS and IPS officers holding the posts of District Magistrate and Superintendents of Police in a number of states, including U.P., Bihar and Haryana, on the eve of general election to the Lok Sabha has understandably been viewed adversely for more than one reason.

Firstly, these changes made just a day prior to the application of the general ban imposed by the Election Commission on transfer of all officials connected with election work violated the spirit behind the order–the intention to ensure public creditability of a "free and fair" poll. Had the changes been few, these could have been defended on administrative grounds of placing the right persons at the right places. However, considering their large number, suspicion of possible impure motives have been aroused–for there could not haves been too many wrong officials at the wrong places.

Secondly, these untimely movements have made the position of the officials concerned also vulnerable. Some sections of the press have already reported that the changes were made on caste and communal considerations to derive undue electoral advantages. Against this background, even correct actions and fair decisions of the concerned officials may smell of partisan conduct. Some honest and upright officers may also be accused of having ignored or facilitated electoral malpractices and communal or caste violence. Thus they have been placed in an unenviable position. The Election Commission has done well to have disapproved the transfers and advised five states for the present to restore status quo ante. Whether its action will bear fruits remains to be seen.

Thirdly, the undesirable consequences of these transfers may be felt after the elections. Depending on the electoral outcome, there may be another wave of transfer of officials. That could justifiably give rise to feelings that certain officers of proven "loyalty" have been rewarded and some honest black sheeps among them pushed to unimportant administrative corners.

Fourthly, the election-eve changes of key officials on alleged considerations of caste and political loyalty could be viewed as attempts to politicize the bureaucracy. In recent years, reshuffles made at the higher levels of the bureaucracy with every change of government in many states is indicative of some degree of politicalisation of the civil services.

Feelings are gaining ground even within the civil services that political closeness and personal loyalty to powerful political superiors has become more rewarding than mere seniority or merit. Politically neutral but otherwise honest and efficient officials are getting overshadowed in ever-increasing numbers by their politically acceptable juniors. While such juniors on considerations other than merit, seniority or competence are made to occupy the centre-stage of administration, their more deserving seniors are accommodated in posts of lesser importance with little or no work. These posts, where necessary are upgraded only to protect the pay etc. of the sidelined seniors or to overcome legal hurdles.

I recall a scandalous instance in a southern state (i.e. Tamil Nadu) where to promote an acceptable junior to the post of the Chief Secretary 10 of his seniors were each given the pay of a Chief Secretary by upgrading for pay purposes an equal number of non-descript posts. One such post was that of the Resident Commissioner of the State in Delhi. Incidentally, most State Governments have utilized the posts of Resident Commissioner in Delhi to post officers of the level of no more than an Under Secretary to that of a Chief Secretary as and when so required.

Several such flexible status posts with little work have cropped up in most states for adjusting very senior officers whose political stars have declined. Pay of the posts are upgraded or down graded as required. Another device usually adopted is to post unwanted officers, even of the level of a Chief Secretary to minor public sector undertakings as Chairman or Managing Director. Dethroned police chiefs are also accommodated in a similar manner. The posts of Home Guards or Heads of Fire Brigades or Police Housing Boards serve as resting places for them.

Generally, higher level appointments are becoming co-terminus with a political party or persons in power who make such appointments. Nearly every change of political guards lead to large reshuffle of top officials in most states. In fact, the political identification of officials is becoming so marked that even the bureaucracy itself is able to predict as to who among the officials in different services will occupy which top posts if 'X', 'Y' or 'Z' political party or individuals come to power.

Although in the states most such reshuffles concern senior IAS and IPS officers, some time even technical officers heading the PWD or Electricity Boards or organizations like Irrigation, Forest, Excise and Mining are also not spared. Generally, the more honest, straightforward and rule-abiding officers figure in the hit lists unless any of them is able to muster political support for survival.

Unfortunately, the pernicious trend of rewarding "loyal" and committed officers ignoring merit or seniority is no longer confined to the states. During the last couple of years, successive governments at the Centre have also been accused of having made certain higher level appointments of officers on considerations of personal closeness and loyalty to the political bosses disregarding merit and seniority. As in the states, the less fortunate seniors at the Central level too were adjusted in minor posts with necessary pay protection. Many IAS or IPS officers were reverted to their state cadres even on the verge of their retirement.

Where higher level appointments were made on political considerations by one government, there could hardly be any justifiable objection if such appointments were reversed by the successor government. In fact, often the aspirants within the bureaucracy had prompted or persuaded the successor governments to make undesirable changes after elections by pleading their own loyalties and services rendered in the past.

It would, indeed, be a great pity if the civil services are weakened, demoralized and used as personal tools by the ruling politicians. The country will be deprived of one of its strongest pillars of government structure if the bureaucracy is divided on caste, communal or on political lines. The knowledge, skill and competence of the permanent civil services helped the country a good deal in tiding over the difficult times during the early post-partition years, when maintenance of law and order and political consolidation of the country were the main tasks. In the subsequent stage of economic planning and development also, the bureaucracy has proved no less equal to its new role.

Even during the current phase of political disarray and uncertainty in many states and at the Centre, the permanent civil services in spite of many failings and damaged morale have provided the much-needed administrative order and continuity. Prevailing conditions indicate that in the years to come in many states and even at the Centre, political changes may be a more recurring feature at shorter intervals. It would, therefore, be in the larger interest of the country to keep the permanent civil services above political, caste or communal bias, so that they continue to be a source of strength in providing administrative unity and stability to the country.

The Prime Minister, Mr. Chandra Shekhar, was perhaps correct when in his broadcast to the nation on March 7 1991, expressed his views about the bureaucracy in the following words: "We have a bureaucracy upon which we can depend .... Without exaggeration I may say that they are among the most patriotic sections of the population." Mr. Chandra Shekhar has been at the centre-stage of Indian politics for long. Until recently, he was outside the government. His views could therefore be taken as unbiased and objective.

To keep the civil services fit and reliable instruments of good governance its management ought to be kept free from politics. They could be expected to give their best if postings and promotions are linked only to seniority and merit. The management of the Civil Services should be largely entrusted to Civil Service Boards headed by the Chief Sectaries in the states and the Cabinet Secretary at the Centre with least political interference.

In fact, two Civil Services Boards have been in existence for many years at the Central level. One of these Boards, chaired by the Secretary, Ministry of Personnel, dealt with service matters like placement and promotion of officers below Joint Secrtary. The other Board, chaired by the Cabinet Secretary, dealt with similar matters of officers of the level of Joint Secretary. The Cabinet Secretary himself dealt with the cases of higher level appointments. I had close association with both the Boards for nearly a decade and headed one as the Secretary of the Union Ministry of Personnel and was Secretary of the Board headed by the Cabinet Secretary in my official position of Establishment Officer (EO) in the Ministry of Personnel. Barring a few occasions the advice and recommendations of these Boards were generally accepted by the Cabinet Committee on Appointments, headed by the Prime Minister. Actually, on several occasions the State Governments were advised to set up similar Civil Services Boards to check the frequency and arbitrariness in the transfer and postings of State Government officers. Unfortunately, very few State Governments showed much interest in such arrangements.

In the final analysis, the State Governments could be persuaded to observe some discipline in the matter of Civil Services Management only if the Central Government cures itself of the growing malady of caste, communal and political bias in making appointments to senior level posts. Arbitrariness in postings, promotions and transfers of government officials at the Centre is now becoming as common as in the states. This trend needs to be curbed by making the Civil Services Boards more effective.

2

COMBATING CORRUPTION: PREVENTIVE, DETECTIVE AND PUNITIVE MEASURES

Of the many social, economic, and political ills like poverty, unemployment, illiteracy and ill-health, that confront India, the most damaging and challenging of them all is the problem of widespread administrative and political corruption. In fact, the menace of political and administrative corruption has hindered the fight against other problems. Deep rooted corruption has lowered the efficiency and credibility of all important institutions of governance and public services. As a result government no longer inspires public confidence or trust for providing any worthwhile public services. The public perception is that large amounts of money allotted for economic development and public welfare schemes are misappropriated, misused or wasted by the ruling politicians, contractors and public servants. It is also believed that for making illegitimate gains for themselves the government tax collectors in connivance with tax-payers allow a good part of the government dues from various taxes and duties to be evaded. This benefits the tax-payers and the tax-collectors at the cost of legitimate government revenues. Therefore even though heavy taxes and other kinds of levies are imposed each year, no surplus funds are available after meeting the normal day to day consumptive expenditure of the government for any productive investments or for social welfare activities. In fact, practically all the State Governments, local bodies and the Central Government as well have become financially bankrupt during the last three decades or so. Their treasuries are generally empty most of the time. They, therefore, depend on bank or market borrowings to a large extent to make their both ends meet. This is leading to heavy debt burdens and unbearable interest payment liabilities thereon. (This has been elaborated in another chapter dealing with the problem of fiscal deficit).

Widespread corruption, reckless expenditure on several populist schemes and other types of callous wastage of public funds for years together, irrespective of the political party in power have severely damaged the financial and administrative health of the country. The result is the continuing social and economic backwardness of India compared to several developed countries of the world. As an example, India now (in 2009) has more illiterate people, (i.e., over 450 millions) than the total population of the country (of around 334 millions) at the time of Independence in 1947. Thus in this respect India may be said to have moved backwards from its pre-independence status. Due to rising population growth and lack of matching expenditure on social and human resource development the country continues to be quite backward. In addition, corruption among top political leaders and higher officials has vitiated the general climate of honesty and integrity in the country. Accordingly financial outlays do not result in matching outcomes. Top-level corruption in government has also adversely affected the ethical norms of the civil society. This is in keeping with the saying—*Yatha raja, tatha praja*. When the moral level of the higher ruling class (or say the "Raja") goes down, the moral character of the common people (or say the "Praja") also goes down. It is acknowledged that persons in power ("Mahajanas") generally set the ethical norms and standards in any society for others to follow. Hence the saying: *"Mahajanaha Jena gatah sa patha"*

The fall in the moral values of our society in general could be seen from the regrettable conduct of some of our well known professionals like doctors, engineers, lawyers and financial experts, etc. Many doctors are allegedly known to be more money minded than persons engaged in trade and business because of their excessive monetary demands from the patients. Several engineers too have been found executing public works with poor quality materials. They do so allegedly with the malafide motive of making money disregarding the possibility that these works may collapse and cause loss of human lives and property. People also often hesitate to go to hospitals as these are regarded to have become not only casual in patient care but also commercial minded and greedy and allegedly prolong the hospitalization of their patients. Similarly financial experts like auditors often allegedly do not hesitate to hide financial frauds during their auditing work to earn illegal money. A good many private businessmen and traders too allegedly suffer from no sense of guilt to sell life-endangering adulterated foodstuffs like oil, ghee, etc. and fake medicines. Greed and lust for money have become so overpowering that these appear to have deprived large sections of our people in government or outside from any sense of guilt in wrong-doings. This is because the "mahajanas" or our top social and political leaders have failed to set good examples. We have long discarded the Gandhian values of adopting good means for good ends. The general climate of honesty, integrity and ethical norms in our social and political conduct have suffered a great deal due to the evil of all pervasive corruption. After such a big downfall any attempt to bring back the country on the right path would indeed be a great and formidable task. It would require the leadership and inspiration of great leaders like those illustrious men and women who led the freedom movement of India.

Shri I.K. Gujaral, a former Prime Minister while in power, had once observed that, "Corruption has seeped into the veins of our nation." He, however, pleaded helplessness to tackle it as it had become deep-rooted and a way of life. He helplessly stated, "I have no magic wand" for its cure. The important question now is, has corruption indeed become incurable and uncontrollable and that any fight against it is futile without a 'magic wand'? To deal with this agonizing problem it may be worthwhile to examine how and when corruption became so serious a matter in India and what measures had been devised and implemented in the past to curb it and why these have not given the desired results. The solution may lie first in finding the root causes of corruption and thereafter devising suitable means and ways to remove them. The fight against corruption may not be fruitless if genuine and determined efforts are made to control, contain and curb it after knowing the real causes of the malady. No 'magic wand' but right and whole hearted efforts and strong political will are required to control and prevent corruption. A multi-pronged strategy of preventive, detective, and punitive measures to combat corruption have to be devised.

To give a brief historical background, corruption became quite visible when it started showing its ugly head in India during the Second World War period i.e. in the early forties. Dr. Radhakrishnan, in his speech, following the famous "Tryst with destiny" speech of

Pandit Jawaharlal Nehru on the midnight hour of 14-15 August 1947 warned the Government and the nation about the emerging problem of high level corruption. He said "Unless we destroy corruption in high places, the love of power, profiteering and black marketing which have spoiled the good name of this great country in recent times, we will not be able to raise the standards of efficiency in administration as well as in the production and distribution of the necessary goods of life."

Corruption, meaning "abuse of public authority for private gains" or simply speaking illegal money making by persons in power has been acknowledged to be as old as the birth of the "state" or "government." It is also by and large accepted to be a global phenomenon though the extent, nature and ways of corruption may vary from country to country and from time to time. In this connection the observations of Chanakya or Kautilya, the great advisor to king Chandra Gupta Maurya recorded in his famous book "Arthasastra" in the 3rd Century B.C. are worth noting. He had stated: "Just as it is impossible not to taste honey—that one may find at the tip of one's tongue so it is impossible for one dealing with government funds not to taste at least a little bit of the king's wealth." However, the worrisome aspect of corruption in India at present is that it is no longer "a little bit" but a very large portion of public funds allotted for development and public welfare purposes that are eaten up or misappropriated by the concerned public servants. It is widely believed that only about 15 per cent of the public funds, or even less are used for public benefit and the rest are unscrupulously grabbed by the public officials in charge. Corruption has thus become the biggest hurdle to India's progress and socio-economic developments. Corruption came to light initially in departments like the Civil Supplies, PWD, Forest, Excise and Police, etc. during the Second World War period (1939-45) due to shortages of essential goods for civilian use after meeting the defence requirements. This led to the introduction of controls and rationing of food items like, wheat, rice, sugar, oil and other essential commodities like cement and steel etc. for supply and use of public at large. Government officials in charge of civil supplies began to make illegal money by obliging those who were in urgent or larger need of such rationed items and were prepared to pay some gratification. Corruption also reached higher levels when huge amounts of public money began to be spent on war related activities and construction works. The taste of corruption "honey" during the Second World War years by some government servants of few departments mentioned earlier tempted many of their colleagues in several other departments to make illegal money wherever possible. To earn "Upari" or, income through corruption became such a habit or addiction among large sections of government employees that corruption ceased to be a matter of shame or stigma. After independence large number of development projects were taken up under the Five Year Plans by the Central and State Governments. Many PSUs for diverse economic activities too were set up. The role of government thus gradually got enlarged from mere maintenance of law and order to developmental and economic activities as well on a big scale. These provided large scope and wider opportunities to taste corruption "honey" to larger number of public servants. After the commanding heights of the economy came into public hands or the public sector the tentacles of corruption also reached higher political and administrative levels. Soon the ministers realized their importance and the opportunities available to them to become rich by illegal money making. They did not, barring some exceptions, fail to succumb to the temptations of making huge amounts of money through abuses of power. They also did not hesitate to indulge in acts of nepotism and favouritism to help their near and dear ones. It is well said that when things start to go wrong they go wrong all the way. It also proved that "power corrupts and absolute power corrupts absolutely." The Santhanam Committee Report of 1964 on corruption prevention accordingly stated, "we heard from all sides that corruption had in recent years spread even to those levels of administration from which it was conspicuously absent in the past." The report further observed, "there is a widespread impression...that some ministers, who have held office during the past 16 years have enriched themselves illegitimately, obtained good jobs for their sons and relations through nepotism, and have reaped other advantages inconsistent with any notion of purity in public life."

In the early forties when corruption started affecting government servants of some departments it was considered necessary to have legal powers to counter it. This led to the enactment of the Prevention of Corruption Act, 1947. Earlier an anti-corruption police organisation known as the Delhi Special Police Establishment (DPSE) had also been set up under a Parliamentary Act of 1946. This anti-corruption body later became a part of the CBI (Central Bureau of Investigation) in 1963. A number of other legal and administrative measures too were formulated and notified to ensure integrity among public officials. These included amendment of the anti-corruption law to place the burden of proof of honesty on an accused officer found in possession of assets disproportionate to his known and legitimate sources of income. While under our normal laws, an accused is presumed to be innocent until proved guilty by the prosecutor, under the new anti-corruption legal provision a public servant accused of having disproportionate assets has to himself prove his assets to be legitimate and his being innocent. All government servants were also required to submit annual property returns to make sure that all their financial transactions were above board and legitimate. The fundamental civil service rules were also amended to provide for premature retirement of government servants of doubtful integrity on reaching the ages of 50 and 55 since charges of corruption could not always be proved in a court of law.

Unfortunately in spite of such necessary legal powers, and the establishment of an anti-corruption police agency (CBI), corruption continued to grow unabated and reached such heights that even the Santhanam Committee could not have visualized it in the early sixties when it had studied the problem of corruption in government. The many scams and scandals of the eighties and thereafter revealed most glaringly that persons accused of graft and other wrong doings were no less than some former Prime Ministers, Chief Ministers, high-profile Cabinet Ministers, some Governors as also some top officials of the PSUs and government. As time passed even some Secretaries to the Central Government, including two Cabinet Secretaries, some High Court judges and even one Supreme Court judge too were accused of corruption. Chairmen and some members of the State Public Service Commissions too were found to be selling jobs for money. The chairmen of State Public Service Commissions as also their members are appointed by the State Governors with security of tenure to safeguard their independence and to give them high status and prestige. But the arrest sometime back of the chairman of Punjab Public Service Commission, Ravinder Pal Singh Sidhu on charges of taking huge amounts of bribe for recruiting candidates to various State Public Services came as a shocking news. The televised pictures showing huge bundles of currency notes stuffed in his various bank lockers left one speechless. It was unbelievable that corruption had reached such areas and such high levels. Selling jobs for money by constitutional appointees cannot but be a matter of great shame. Similar accusations against some persons connected with the Maharashtra Public Service Commission too were made. The former chairman of the Maharashtra State Public Service Commission, Shashi Kant Karnik was also arrested on chargers of corruption. Previously allegations of bribery were made only in the recruitment of lower category employees like police constables, primary school teachers, low level railway personnel by the Departmental Boards or Agencies set up by the government. But by now the virus of corruption has affected even the constitutional bodies like the State Public Service Commissions.

In recent months a few other shocking high level cases of corruption were reported. Among these were the cases of the chairman of the Central Board of Excise and Customs, the Chief Commissioner of Customs and Excise and that of a former chairman of the Unit Trust of India. According to media reports, the corruption charged Chairman of the Customs and Excise Board in league with various undesirable individuals engaged in smuggling and illegal imports, amassed huge unaccounted wealth for himself. He must have deprived the state of its legitimate revenue by doing this and by his shameful example prompted several of his lower subordinates to indulge in similar malpractices. This amounts to betrayal of trust and power vested in him as a high level public servant. The case of a former UTI Chairman suspected of corruption also stood on a similar footing. Millions of small investors lost their hard earned savings as the UTI betrayed their trust by investing in shares of semi-bankrupt or otherwise sick companies due to the corrupt motives of its chairman. No less shocking was the recent media reports on the front pages of important newspapers that Dr. Ketan Desai, President of the Medical Council of India (MCI) was arrested by the CBI (on 23rd April 2010) for allegedly taking a bribe of Rs. 2 crores to allow new courses in the private Gian Sagar Medical College of Patiala. The MCI is responsible for maintaining uniform standards of medical education and recommends the recognition or de-recognition of medical qualifications obtained from institutions in India and abroad. The MCI President is thus usually an eminent professional and plays a significant role in the field of medical education. For such a high level professional to be charged of corruption should be a matter of serious worry and concern. The alleged bribery amount of Rs. 2 crore contained in two card-board boxes was also seized by the CBI in support of their charges of bribery against Dr. Ketan Desai while arresting him.

Sometime back, the Tehelka exposures had given a few video pictures of the magic of corruption in gaining easy access to higher level defence officials and obtaining vital information as to how defence weapons purchase deals could be struck with suitable palm-greasing of the concerned officials. In the *hawala* related cases, some papers i.e. the Jain diaries seized in 1991 revealed names of several high level politicians to whom money had been paid either for 'services' already rendered or for making future 'use' of them. Those who had accepted these large sums of money being politicians were undoubtedly persons of great worldly wisdom and would have been well aware that no one doles out such large sums of money without any ulterior motives. They knew that it was meant to be a kind of *quid pro quo.*

The long delays in the investigation of high level corruption cases also show the indifference and casualness to its prevalence. But for the intervention and prodding of the judiciary, the *hawala* cases mentioned above may not have been uncovered. Even so all the accused got away scotfree as apart from the mention of their names in the Jain diaries no other worthwhile evidence was collected against them during investigation by the CBI. No undue pains were taken by it to find out the end uses of such corruption money or if any of the suspects had assets disproportionate to their legitimate incomes. Further even though the *hawala* cases were detected in 1991 these were finally decided after much prodding and monitoring by the apex court in 1998, i.e, after seven long years. All this shows the lack of seriousness in curbing high level corruption.

Similarly, even though huge cash of over Rs. 3 crore was found in the residence of the Central Minister, Sukh Ram in 1996, while investigating charges of corruption against him, the judicial verdict was still awaited at the time of writing in this case. In another case of corruption though he was convicted by the lower court to three years of rigorous imprisonment he was granted bail to go on appeal to the Delhi High Court. There can be little dent on corruption unless at least the high level cases of corruption are speedily decided and those found guilty are punished severely within, say, six months of detection of their offences. Again according to the present judicial practice a person is presumed to be innocent unless proved guilty 'beyond all reasonable doubt'. No one can find fault with this healthy judicial norm of a civilised society in punishing any accused. However, considering the all-pervasive nature of corruption there is perhaps need to suitably change the existing judicial norms in corruption related cases. In the departmental vigilance enquiry cases 'preponderance of probability' criteria is applied in finding the guilt of the accused. For example, in the case of accused persons where CBI found huge sums of cash in their bank lockers or in their residential premises—the 'preponderance of probability' would be that the money was illegitimate and corruption tainted. Unless valid evidence of legitimacy of the money is given by the accused in his defence the departmental enquiry verdict would go against him. A similar criterion for trial in courts could also be adopted in corruption cases.

The low rate of convictions in corruption cases (about 5% to 7%) is largely because of faulty investigations, long judicial delays and death or hostile attitude of witnesses. However, considering the alarming rise of corruption, specially among the top-most officials and political persons, detection and trial of such cases require far greater concern and prompt action. Anti-corruption rhetoric and well-coined slogans alone will not be adequate response to prevent the rising tide of corruption. Concrete and practical measures have to be taken in fighting corruption.

To effectively deal with corruption, a three-pronged action plan as mentioned earlier comprising of suitable preventive, detective and punitive measures may be devised and implemented. Even though the problem of widespread corruption is being repeatedly highlighted and also decried no effective remedial measures appear to have been taken. Efforts made so far have been sporadic, unsystematic and lukewarm. In tackling corruption presently emphasis is more on dealing with individual cases of corruption and that too involving more of petty officials. Even though this may be a necessary part of the fight against corruption, the real cure lies in locating the breeding grounds or the root causes of corruption and removing them. As malaria cannot be eradicated by merely destroying some malaria mosquitoes here and there but by cleaning their breeding grounds, so also corruption prevention requires identifying its main causes and taking appropriate remedial measures to remove them. Merely catching and punishing a few corrupt individuals here and there may not mitigate or end corruption. While the few corrupt individuals when spoted and caught need to be quickly punished, the basic causes of corruption have to be removed in the fight against it. For this purpose it may be desirable first to identify the most corruption-prone areas and individuals for priority of attention rather than spreading anti-corruption efforts too thinly everywhere. A very systematic and planned approach may be more fruitful in the war against corruption.

Secondly since corruption became widespread after Independence due to involvement of Government in a big way in socio-economic developmental activities it may be worthwhile to review the role of government in this sphere. To prevent corruption in government apart from taking other steps one commonly accepted view is that the role of Government in economic and commercial activities should be considerably reduced. While admittedly Government has still an important role to play in the vital infrastructure sector like power, transport and communications, etc. the other areas of economic activities should be left to the private sector. The Indian private sector has by now acquired sufficient managerial skills and financial resources to undertake such of the economic activities which were earlier reserved for the public sector. The role of government should now be confined to that of a facilitator, coordinator and a regulator and not that of an actual economic actor.

Thirdly, in the regulatory field also Government should have a minimum possible role. Overregulation has the danger of slowing down economic activities. Too many laws to regulate the day-to-day life and activities of the citizens and to impose all kinds of economic, political and administrative restrictions on them are neither desirable nor healthy. These provide excuses, scope and opportunities for corruption to the enforcement agencies at lower levels in charge of enforcing the regulations. While some laws and regulations are essential for maintaining law and order, discipline and harmony in society, overregulations of the type we have in India have been seen to cause avoidable harassment to the common citizens and to those engaged in trade and business. For example, the requirement of all kinds of certificates like birth, death, marriage, family planning, caste, and place of residence, etc., are proving to be fertile grounds for corruption among the concerned public officials. While the undeserving and dishonest applicants always manage to get such certificates with the help of touts and middlemen using corrupt means the thousands of honest applicants are often made to run from pillar to post to get any certificate. They are harassed and turned away until the appetite for corruption of the offici·ls concerned is satisfied. It is time to review the need for many of these certificates. Should not a solemn statement of facts being true by the applicant with suitable warning of penal action if these are found to be false suffice? The warning may also include the risk of withdrawal of any benefit secured by a false statement at any future date. This would be a convenient and safe course to adopt at least in the case of persons with known identities.

The need for the production of ration cards for getting passport, for registration of vehicles, for the issue and renewal of driving licenses or for opening of bank accounts etc. should also be reviewed at least for such class of citizens whose identities need no proof e.g., of public servants of the central, state and local bodies and PSUs. The list of such exempt categories could also include staff and officials of reputed private companies. The bureaucracy at present has spread its tentacles too far and wide which is facilitating illegitimate money-making by dishonest officials. Unfortunately, the elected representatives of the people too have developed vested interests in these regulatory matters. They have as is generally believed started to share parts of the corruption booty of the corrupt public officials. It is, therefore, time to reduce the powers and functions of the administrative machinery as much as possible. A leaner and thinner administrative machinery may be more worthwhile for corruption prevention. Technological advances too should be made use of as much as possible so that the citizens can get their official transactions like payment of various taxes and service charges etc. done through the inter-net. That would thus avoid human contact with corrupt officials.

The license-permit quota raj is said to have ended but even the remnant government clearances that are still required in the industrial sector, in export-import areas, in the inspection of factories, etc., provide ample scope and opportunities for corruption among large sections of lower officials. There are even now far too many categories of inspectors meant to enforce laws like the Weights and Measures Act, the Prevention of Cruelty to Animals Act, the Shops and Establishments Act, the Food Adulteration Act and the Factories Act, etc., etc. This problem leading to millions of pending cases in the courts has been discussed in another chapter. Some of these numerous regulatory functions could be combined for enforcement purposes in one authority. Some of these could also be entrusted to various associations of commerce, industry, trade unions, associations of consumers and shopkeepers etc. by way of Public Private Partnership (PPP). Private bodies need to be associated in regulatory work as much as possible to prevent delays and corruption among the lower government officials. Hordes of inspectors only vitiate the climate of integrity. Overregulation has unduly increased the workload of judicial magistrates and of the higher courts also. Large scale law-making is only leading to large-scale law breaking and corruption. Simply speaking too many unnecessary laws are putting too many unnecessary restrictions on the people and are becoming fertile grounds for corruption. The "rule of law" because of its excessiveness has degenerated into the "rule of petty officials." Excess in everything leads to negative results. Hence the saying "Ati Sarvtre Barjeyet" (avoid excess in everyting).

Sometime ago, a study by the author of the case workload of the magisterial courts of Delhi to consider their request for several additional magistrates disclosed that nearly 95 per cent of the case-work related to various miscellaneous laws and only 5 per cent related to serious criminal offences like theft, robbery, dacoity, and murder etc. under the IPC. Most of the other offences were of a technical nature involving minor breaches of laws. These could have been best handled by mobile courts on the spot in a summary manner instead of being made cases for trial in regular courts. That involved long-drawn procedures and provided scope for corruption to the lower court staff like the Peskars, as also the police and the process servers etc. For example in a large city like Delhi, cases of public nuisance for obstructing free movement on roads and pavements, minor traffic offences and other offences like late closure of shops and establishments, using unauthorised loudspeakers could run into several thousands on any single day. These cases ought to be handled by mobile courts rather than by the regular courts for the sake of economy, speedy justice and corruption prevention. The author's study accordingly concluded by saying that the existing number of magistrates were more than sufficient to handle the case workload provided the law enforcement work was done in a more selective and rational manner and the mobile court system was introduced to deal with minor offences. Unfortunately, in many areas of our administration the emphasis is more on the quantitative aspect of work and much less on its qualitative aspect. The administration has accordingly spread out rather too much. It has become numerically too large, financially too costly and quality-wise too inefficient, (slow moving) and corrupt.

No wonder that more than 97 per cent of the Central Government employees are of D and C categories dealing with routine types of work. Therefore, one cannot but conclude that the smaller the administrative machinery the better it may be in quality, in efficiency, and in integrity.

It is also very important to bring about greater openness and transparency in administration. Since undue secrecy breeds and hides malpractices and corruption, government transactions should be sufficiently open for public scrutiny. Fortunately, a well-thought-out Right to Information Act (RTI) has since been enacted in 2005 (*please see another chapter nineteen dealing with RTI Act*) to enable people to obtain copies of all Government records that they may wish to see. For example, people have the right to know if all sales and purchase transactions of public authorities were bona fide, financially sound and served the intended public purposes. In some cases it was found during audit and scrutiny of accounts that large unwanted stocks of certain high priced items were purchased in some government organizations. This was done allegedly at the behest of some favoured sales agents. There were instances of purchase of electric cables by DESU in a year to last for several years. Similarly, there were instances of purchase of paints in one year to last for over 12 years by some PWD officials. Some cases also came to the notice of the author (while holding the post of Secretary Health in Orissa) during his inspection of the government medical stores that while medicines and other medical items not required much or frequently were purchased and stocked in large quantities but medicines required frequently and in larger quantities were stocked in meagre quantities. Obviously all was not above board in making such purchases. Cases are also reported at times in some PSUs where machines in working order are sold as scrap at low prices and their replacements purchased at high prices. Greater openness in such government transactions is therefore necessary to check corruption or other malafide actions.

Some important electoral reforms too are called for to prevent the increasing infiltration of criminal elements into politics. Reportedly a large number of criminals are at present holding high political offices. They have damaged the climate of integrity in administration to a great extent. According to the figures made public by one of the Election Commissioners of India in 1997 as many as 700 of the 4,000 or so MLAs in the country at that time were 'history-sheeters' and 40

MPs were of similar unsavoury characters. It was also revealed that in the 1996 General Election 1,500 of the 13,952 contestants in nine states were 'persons with criminal records' which included cases of murder, dacoity, rape, theft and extortion etc. The number of such criminals winning elections has by now increased much more. The general belief is that while initially political parties used criminals to capture election booths and win the electoral battles now the tables have turned. The criminals now use different political parties to get elected themselves by infiltrating into them and standing as their election candidates. After winning elections they manage to get important ministerial posts and amass wealth by abusing their powers. As a result one finds that some serving as also some former chief ministers are currently facing CBI or Enforcement Directorate (ED) investigations for corruption charges. For example, one ex-chief minister (Shri Madhu Koda) of Jharkhand as reported had allegedly through corruption amassed over Rs. 4000 crores, which is almost one-fifth of the annual budget of the state he once ruled. The Enforcement Directorate (ED) has reportedly during its investigation of this case found Shri Koda having illegitimate assets abroad too. Democracy is thus getting subverted by criminal elements through money and muscle powers. Corrupt political elements reportedly provide support and patronage to corrupt administrative officials also. Curbing administrative corruption, therefore, first requires the curbing of political corruption. If the political environment gets criminalized and corrupted, the administrative environment is bound to get polluted too. Corrupt ministers generally dislike upright and honest officers but prefer to have pliable officers as their aids and advisors. Honesty obviously cannot survive in an environment where dishonesty has an upper hand. It is accordingly very necessary for protecting honest and meritorious officials that the civil service management functions should be made the sole responsibility of statutory Civil Service Boards comprising of senior civil servants. The political heads of any department/ministry should have, if at all, minimum possible role in the postings, transfers and promotion of officers. Any kind of politicalisation of the permanent civil services would undermine their efficiency and integrity. That may also block or delay penal action against corrupt officers enjoying political support or protection. The traditional internal control and management system of the civil services has in course of time been eroded. This has to a great extent undermined the morale, discipline and integrity of the civil servants.

Good and honest officers feel insecure and unsure of getting their due on the basis of their merit and performances alone. Many accordingly perforce cultivate influential politicians to be their godfathers. Often senior and superior officers are seen to be afraid of their own juniors and subordinates having influential politicians as their godfathers. They feel diffident to control or prevent any wrong doings of such politically influential juniors and subordinates. This situation ought to be corrected by minimizing the role of the politicians in the management of the civil services. (In this connection article written by me and published by INFA on 4.10.1988 is annexed.)

Another important cause of corruption in administration may be due to certain discretionary powers vested in the ministers in matters like allotment of plots of land, houses, shops; agencies of various PSUs like petrol pumps, telephone booths, etc. Such discretionary powers ought to be withdrawn or drastically reduced and subjected to proper guidelines. Names of all beneficiaries of discretionary favours ought to be compulsorily published to detect cases of abuses of power, if any. The erring individuals should also be suitably penalized.

To deal with high level administrative corruption at the Central level, the Santhanam Committee had recommended the setting up of an independent Central Vigilance Commission (CVC), keeping ministers out of its purview, but bringing all public servants of the Central Governments and its PSUs within its jurisdiction. This Commission was to be headed by a high level CVC with the same measure of autonomy, independence and status as that of the Comptroller and Auditor General of India or the Chief Election Commissioner. The Commission was to be given a statutory basis through a parliamentary law and was to be legally empowered "to initiate, conduct and complete such action as may be considered appropriate, including prosecution against a public servant found guilty" after preliminary investigation of the complaints by the Commission. Power to decide to initiate disciplinary action or prosecution was to be vested in the Vigilance Commission itself by withdrawing these powers from the Government.

Unfortunately, the CVC scheme finally accepted and notified by the government by a Resolution of 1964 fell far short of the Santhanam Committee's recommendations. The basic weakness of this scheme was that the Central Vigilance Commission had no statutory basis but was the creation of a Government Resolution which was liable to frequent changes at the Government's sweet will. This had, in fact, been happening, affecting adversely (as noticed by the author while holding the office of the CVC in 1985-88) both the independence and the jurisdiction of the Commission.[1]

The Commission had also not been given the ultimate power as was recommended, to decide on the initiation of disciplinary action or prosecution of any corruption-accused public servant. This power continued to lie with the Government but with the condition that it be exercised with the "advice" of the CVC. Cases of disagreement with the Commission on its advisory functions could only be included in the Commission's Annual Report to Parliament. Such annual reports were, however, not to be sent directly to Parliament by the Commission but through the Ministry of Personnel and Training–the designated administrative ministry. The Commission's reports were often placed before Parliament, by the ministry after much delay to serve any purpose and were also rarely discussed. Thus, cases of non-acceptance of the Commission's advice by the Government even in important matters hardly caused any worry or embarrassment to the Government. For investigation of any complaints made to the Commission, it had no investigating agency of its own but had to depend on the Government-controlled CBI or the departmental vigilance units of different ministries. The CVC with its limited powers thus proved to be rather ineffective in preventing corruption in administration to any visible degree. He was made to be a crusader without a sword.

Fortunately the CVC after the enactment of the CVC Act of 2003 has become a multi-member statutory body with some control over the CBI in corruption related cases. This upgradation in status and powers of the Central Vigilance Commission may help the Commission to a good extent in the prevention and detection of corruption in administration.

The primary responsibility to detect and check administrative corruption of their subordinates should, however, lie with the Secretaries to Governments, the Heads of Departments and the Director-Generals of concerned field organizations. For this purpose, they have to be given adequate legal powers not only to initiate actions against the guilty but also to protect the honest. Under the present arrangements and practices, however, the CBI has by and large overshadowed the secretaries to Governments and all other senior level functionaries mentioned above in matters of corruption prevention. They have as a result become somewhat lukewarm and indifferent in their anti-corruption role. This has resulted in the spread of corruption at lower levels as the officers at higher levels are seen to be somewhat powerless onlookers. They themselves suffer from the fear of CBI probe against them at the slightest excuse. Even the honest officials among them have little hope to get higher level official protection against any unwarranted CBI probe. Ascendency of the CBI in corruption prevention has thus lowered administrative efficiency as even senior officers are seen to avoid taking speedy decision for fear of making any mistakes, however, *bona fide* these may be. There is, therefore, need to have proper checks and control over the CBI. It needs to be realized that the CBI a police body by itself cannot be the proper and competent judge in deciding whether any *bona fide* decision of a senior officer if found to be mistaken at a later date *was* malafide and corruption motivated. One has to admit that at times even good decisions taken with good intentions may go wrong. CBI a police organization should not be the final authority in deciding such mistaken decisions to be *abinitio malafide*. The senior official colleagues of the individuals concerned who took the decision should be allowed to express their views and these views should play an important role in arriving at the final decision regarding the true intention of the official concerned. Unfortunately, the police in India, validly or otherwise, does not enjoy the reputation of being objective and fair minded in deciding to initiate criminal action against any public servant holding high level posts. There are allegations and fears that policemen do often foist false cases, extract false confessions, and fabricate false evidence against innocent victims on malafide considerations. In addition the CBI seldom admits its mistakes. It would accordingly be unwise and unsafe to allow the police to initiate vigilance action at least against senior officials (of the level of Joint Secretary and above) on their own and without prior approval of the prescribed authority. All senior level officers have to realize that it is their duty to control and prevent corruption in their organizations. They cannot leave this task to the CBI alone. Services of the CBI have of course to be utilized for investigating cases of corruption and for maintaining discreet surveillance over persons of doubtful integrity. CBI's power of prosecution on corruption charges should have proper checks and balances specially with regard to senior officers of the "decision-making levels" so that innocent individuals are not victimized. (This subject has been discussed more elaborately in the first chapter.)

To be able to tackle corruption among officials, the Santhanam Committee had stated that absolute "integrity on the part of the ministers at the Centre and in the States is an indispensable condition for establishment of a tradition of purity in public services." It thus gave priority to prevention of political corruption among ministers for prevention of administrative corruption. To tackle the problem of rising corruption among ministers, the Santhanam Committee had also recommended that specific allegations against any of them should be promptly investigated by "an agency whose finding would command respect." The Committee for this purpose suggested the constitution of a 'National Panel' of eminent persons by the President of India. Allegations of wrong-doings and corruption against any minister could then be referred to an ad-hoc committee of three persons out of the above mentioned larger national panel. This Committee should thereafter inquire if there was any *prima facie* truth in the allegations to justify the initiation of further legal action under the Prevention of Corruption Act. The suspect minister, as a matter of convention, was also expected to resign after a prima facie case was established against him and a deeper probe was considered necessary. No action was, however, taken on the above recommendation as the ruling political class did not like to be subjected to any independent probe by an outside body. Even the later recommendation of the Administrative Reforms Commission (ARC) of 1966 to set up the institution of Lokpal to investigate alleged cases of political corruption against ministers at the Centre has yet to be implemented. Many a times in the past (i.e., in 1968, 1977, 1989, 1995 and 1996), some kind of Lokpal Bills were religiously introduced in every session of Parliament but these were, to the best of my knowledge, intentionally allowed to lapse on the ground of lack of Parliamentary time for their discussion. The author had for some time dealt with the Lok Pal Legislation matter as Jt. Secretary (Vigilance) and Secretary in the Union Ministry of Personnel and Administrative Reforms, the nodal ministry dealing with corruption prevention policy in government. The last Lokpal Bill of 1998 of the BJP Government has not yet been placed before the Parliament. It would be desirable to pass the Lokpal legislation to deal more effectively with political corruption. To curb administrative corruption without controlling political corruption as opined by the Santhanam Committee would indeed be very difficult. It needs no emphasis to say that one cannot clean the bottom without cleaning the top. The top layer in our administration comprises of the elected political leaders in their capacity as ministers. They have to set examples of honesty and integrity to bring about honesty and integrity at lower levels of administration.

Since political and administrative corruption are very much interlinked, it is essential to curb political corruption first in order to curb administrative corruption. To deal with political corruption not only the long-delayed Lokpal institution should be installed at the Centre but also the existing Lokayukta institutions in the States should be further strengthened by empowering them to investigate corruption cases by their own investigating agencies. These institutions should also be headed by eminent persons of judicial and non-political backgrounds. Further politics should be freed from the clutches of criminals through appropriate electoral reforms. These reform measures have been ignored far too long. Like verification of the character and antecedents of Government servants before their appointments, the character and antecedents of candidates wishing to stand for elections should also be subjected to public scrutiny. The media and the voters should scrutinize the antecedents of electoral candidates so that persons with criminal records do not get elected. For this purpose they ought to be given adequate time and sufficient information about the background of the potential candidates by their respective political parties. To facilitate this it may be made obligatory to publish the names of all their potential candidates by the political parties at least three months in advance of any election. This advance list of likely candidates may include names of twice the number of actual candidates to be proposed for any seat by any party so as to allow them sufficient scope to choose any of them finally i.e. in keeping with election schedule of the Election Commission. No one outside the published lists should however be allowed to stand on any party ticket. That should enable the media and the Opposition parties to probe and comment on the character and merits of such potential candidates. Voters too would get more time to decide for whom to vote at the time of actual elections. Thus the parties may become more selective in finally choosing the right candidates.

To sum up, the following preventive, detective and punitive measures are essential for curbing corruption. Incidentally, a good part of this action plan was suggested by the author in 1985 as the then Secretary in the Union Ministry of Personnel & A.R. to the then Prime Minister Shri Rajiv Gandhi and who had also approved it.

Some additions to the earlier action plan have now been made keeping in mind the subsequent developments like the enactment of the Vigilance Commission Act, 2003 and the RTI Act, 2005.

Action Plan for Combating Corruption

A. Preventive Measures

1. Simplification of rules and procedures,
2. Reducing the areas of discretion and patronage of ministries,
3. Need for greater deregulation to reduce areas of corruption and harassment of the public,
4. Introduction of public information and assistance counters in public dealing offices,
5. Establishment of public grievances redressal machinery in each ministry/department,
6. Systematic and at times surprise inspections by senior officers,
7. Monitoring disposal of cases with a view to check delays, and
8. Curbing outside interference in the administrative and personnel management areas.

B. Surveillance and Detective Measures

1. Need for greater surveillance in known corruption-prone areas, particularly at the public contact points;
2. Closer watch on officials of doubtful integrity by the vigilance agencies;
3. On a selective basis periodically, the declared movable/ immovable assets of persons of doubtful integrity to be actually verified; and
4. As a follow up action of (3) above traps and raids to be organized, where so required.

C. Deterrent Punitive Measures

1. Lokpal legislation to be passed to deal with political corruption;
2. Investigation of cases to be speeded up according to a time bound schedule;
3. Procedure for disciplinary action to be improved for speedier finalization of corruption cases and deterrent punishment awarded;
4. Provision for summary trial of corruption cases by courts;
5. Legal powers to be acquired for confiscation of ill-gotten wealth;
6. Power of premature retirement of persons of doubtful integrity to be enforced more effectively;

7. Close monitoring of all anti-corruption measures; and
8. Wide publicity of punishment awarded to guilty persons.

D. Other Reform Measures

1. Political and electoral reforms to be introduced to curb the entry of criminals into politics; and
2. Right to Information Act (RTI) to be effectively used as a weapon by the citizens, the media, and the NGOs in exposing cases of corruption.

Corruption prevention has to be a continuous endeavour. Its success would greatly depend on the will and resolve of the political and administrative leadership. The media, the NGOs and the citizens would also have to play the pivotal roles in exposing corruption and educating the people in the fight against corruption.

Since corruption has become widespread and all-pervasive, an effective vigilance strategy for better results should be as suggested earlier to give priority of attention to the most corruption-prone areas and individuals instead of wasting time and efforts in running after too many petty officials in too many spheres of government activities. Corruption at higher levels and in key public interest areas need to be combated on greater priority basis since anti-corruption resources available to the government are limited. The high level corruption cases involving top politicians or top officials should also be tried in special courts as speedily as possible and severe punishments inflicted on those found guilty. Such few but important cases would have greater impact on corruption prevention. Attempts should be to keep the top clean and corruption free so that they could become role models for persons at lower levels of administration. The fact that while corruption in the early forties was limited to a few lower level employees of a few departments (like the civil supplies, PWD, and the Police) but has by now engulfed all other departments of government and has also reached the highest levels of administration shows that corruption prevention has lacked good strategy and resolute action. Sadly corruption has now not left even the higher judiciary beyond its grip. The media another strong pillar of democracy also appears to have become a victim of corruption. A kind of unhealthy trend of wrong reporting or manipulating "news" and "views" by some sections of the Press at the behest of interested parties on payment of money by way of corruption is said to be emerging. Similarly, some TV channels at times tend to distort the truth in their coverage of criminal incidents to malign some individuals allegedly at the behest of their opponents for wrongful monetary gains. A truly honest, truthful and independent media would be the most effective tool to fight corruption. It is accordingly important that to be a crusader for truth and justice and to inspire public confidence the media should remain above any suspicion of corruption. Money power at times is also allegedly used to influence the voting of MPs/MLAs in the legislatures. For example, on one occasion a few MPs of the Lok Sabha displayed in the House bundles of currency notes allegedly paid to them by some pro-government individuals to seek their votes in favour of government in a "no confidence motion" to be tabled in the House shortly. This type of corruption to buy vote is now known as "note for vote" or "cash for vote."

At times, when some "Questions" are asked for reply during the "Question Hour" by some MPs at the behest of interested parties there are allegations of corruption in seeking some specific and authentic information through such questions.

All these sad and shocking developments show how strong and all devouring the demon of corruption has become. To combat this monster is no easy task. It can be fought only with the combined and sustained efforts of the government, the media and the citizens. In an age of declining ethical, moral and spiritual values on the one hand and rising consumptive and materialistic culture on the other, fighting corruption requires strong political will and major political, legal and administrative reforms. One does not see much ray of hope for these to happen in the near future. An example is worth citing for this cause of pessimism. Recently (March 2010) the UP Chief Minister Ms Mayawati was shown on TV channels with a huge garland, reportedly of 65 kg—weight around her body. It was said to have been presented to her by lakhs of her down-trodden followers. If the garland would have been made of flowers as is normally the practice in honouring any great and noble person, there would have been all praise and admiration from every one for Mayawati for the love and respect shown to her by her followers. The elephant size garland (perhaps in keeping with BSP's political symbol) was however made of bundles of brand new 1000—rupee currency notes estimated to be several crores of rupees in value. Doubts accordingly arose as to how and where from the poor masses of Maywati's followers could get so much of money so quickly. How could Mayawati a "Dalit ki Beti" became "Daulat ki Beti" so soon? Suspicions of corruption of some kind or the other began to be widely talked about. The Income-tax authorities also reportedly began to investigate the matter. The fear however is that such investigations are generally never ending. In such cases the law comes to a dead end on political grounds. The public feeling is that cases of political corruption even when found to be true usually get honourably settled on political *quid-pro-quo* basis. Therefore to check high level political corruption, the Corruption Prevention Law need to be so amended that within the shortest possible time investigation and trial of such corruption cases are completed.

ANNEXURE (CORRUPTION)

Published by INEA on 4.10.1988 **(Pl. See page 47)**

Press Freedom Vital to Fight Graft

Once again in the strife between truth and falsehood, truth has prevailed. Whether out of its own belated good senses or due to the universal condemnation by the public and the Press, the Government finally decided not to proceed further with the Defamation Bill, 1988. It is to be hoped that this kind of ill-conceived legislation will not see the light of day ever again in this country. Not only this Government but future Government too should not interfere with the freedom of speech and expression of the People and the Press, guaranteed under Article 19 of the Constitution. Without liberty of thought and expression, there can be no real democracy or government of the people, by the people and for the people. The political rulers in a democracy are the people's representatives who exercise the sovereign power of the people on their behalf. The people have, therefore, a right to know and the Press is their most valuable aid in keeping them informed as to how the rulers are exercising their delegated power at the State and Central levels.

Unfortunately, for our rulers during the last few years and, more particularly, during the last few months, the Press has been reporting adversely on them. Many acts of misdemeanour, misconduct and maladministration on their part have been widely reported in great details. There have been reports in highly responsible papers about high-level corruption involving huge amounts by way of kickbacks and commissions in important defence and oil deals. Many State level politicians have also been reportedly involved in grabbing land and other valuable properties for themselves or for their near and dear ones at throw-away prices. Palatial houses have been built with ill-gotten money. There have been reports of influence peddling, nepotism and favouritism in important project contracts, grant of licenses and appointments of judges and civil servants. Profitable agencies of the public sector undertakings have been secured through pulls and pressures of political high-ups by their close friends and relatives.

There have been press reports of discriminatory enforcement of state laws like the Income Tax Act, Foreign Exchange Regulation Act and other economic laws. The favoured ones are spared and the opponents harassed and oppressed. Numerous cases of intimidation, police excesses, arrests and prosecution on fabricated evidence of mediamen, honest public servants and political opponents have appeared in the Press in various parts of the country. Cases of administrative inefficiency, gross negligence, delay and harassment of the citizens at the hands of the ever-expanding, callous and insensitive municipal, State and Central level bureaucracies fill the pages of local, regional and national newspapers. But the people's representatives at all levels, including the highest, have little time to read these reports let alone investigate and punish the guilty or evolve preventive mechanisms. The general complaint is that they have virtually shut the doors of their residences and offices and posted uniformed guards outside to bar those aggrieved from approaching them. They have become even more secluded than the kings and monarchs of olden days.

Regrettably, the present day rulers appear quite content with turning deaf ears and blind eyes to all the complaints and exposures. They responded recently to these reports with the contemptuous Defamation Bill, essentially designed to gag the Press. Truly, the rulers get the advisers they deserve. Good and honest men will not do certain things with the result that others with pliable conscience hang around the easy-going rulers to advise and oblige them. The formal democratic institutions like the political party, Parliament and the Cabinet are kept in the dark most of the time and also spared the trouble of debate and discussion. They are approached at the last moment only for obtaining their formal stamp of approval without any questioning. When things go wrong, as they often do, no one is there to assume responsibility. This is, indeed, a strange type of Government with "collective responsibility."

In such a prevailing state of affairs, the Press in India has done a commendable job in keeping the people duly informed about the acts of omission and commission of their elected representatives at all levels of Government. In fact, this fear of detection and exposure by the Press has been of vital importance in the fight against mounting corruption. There may be some sections of the Press which may blow up small things and indulge in yellow journalism. But generally the reputed local and national papers have acted with maturity and a high sense of responsibility in reporting the cases of corruption. The Press has also been of great help in bringing to the notice of the public cases of financial irregularities, maladministration and malpractices spotlighted in the annual reports of the Vigilance Commission and the Comptroller and Auditor General of India. Allegations of corruption appearing in the Press also gave valuable information time and again to the Vigilance Commission and enabled it to pursue these further in the best national interest. In fact, the fight against corruption would be very difficult without the active help of a free and responsible Press which, often enough, provided information earlier than official sources set up for the purpose. To muzzle the Press would be to give a free hand to corruption and pave the way for the collapse of democracy.

Already, two other important pillars of democracy, Parliament and the Judiciary have been rendered virtually powerless to exercise any curb on the political executives. Brute majority of the ruling party has ensured parliamentary approval of any legislation or other Government business be it good, bad or indifferent. No fault-finding of any kind is liked or allowed. The meagre voice of the Opposition members is easily silenced leaving them no option but to "walk out" in protests. The judicial forum, too, is not of much help against myriad acts of discrimination, arbitrariness and denial of justice to the citizens. Heavy workload and large number of vacancies at any given time of judges in the courts continue to frustrate speedy justice. Moreover, when acts of injustice run into million, no judiciary can help. The administrative machinery itself has to be set right to prevent injustice. No less than the Chief Justice of India, Mr. Justice P.N. Bhagwati, himself stated while addressing the Supreme Court Bar Association in November 1987 that the "judicial system in the country is almost on the verge of collapse...".

Instead of finding fault with the Press for exposing the political leaders, the powers that would do a great service to the country and its democratic system by, first, laying down a code of conduct for themselves and, second, by devising a suitable machinery to look into the allegations of corruption, made against them by responsible individuals and the Press. True, the malady of political corruption is not new to this country. What is however new, shocking and shameful is the great height it has reached and the large dimension it has acquired. Corruption among the lower level of politicians raised its ugly head in the first decade of independence. The Santhanam Committee looked into the problem and observed in its report in 1964 that "the people of India rightly expected that when the Government of the country passed into the hands of disciples of the Father of the Nation who were in their own individual capacities known for higher character and ability, Governments in India, at the Centre and the States, would set up and achieve a standard of integrity second to none in the world, both in the political and administrative aspects. It has to be frankly admitted that this hope has not been realized in full measures."

It is also true that no country under any system of Government, be it a democracy, military dictatorship or monarchy, is altogether free from corruption. Even socialist countries have not been able to eliminate corruption. There are occasional reports of corruption in the Soviet Union and China. Newspapers reported sometime back about the trial in Moscow of Yuri Chirbanov, Brezhnev's son-in-law, on charges of bribery. The Japanese Prime Minister, Mr. Tanaka, had to quit office and go to prison sometime back following proof of bribery on purchase deal from the Lockheed Corporation. In America, Mr. Nixon had to quit the office of President due to the Watergate scandal. Many other top people have suffered similar fate in other countries due to indulgence in corruption or malpractices. Most civilized countries have, however, devised effective means of detecting and punishing high level corruption speedily. In those countries, the disease of corruption is kept within tolerable limits and is rarely indulged as boldly, openly and on such a wide scale as in our country. Hardly any politician has gone to jail in India for indulging in corruption.

The need of the hour, therefore, is not the Defamation Bill but the enactment of the long-pending Lok Pal Bill. This legislation has been before Parliament in one form or the other since 1971. Several times it had lapsed and was reintroduced with promises of early enactment. However, following assumption of power, people tend to give low priority to ethics or public morality and do not like any check on them. If high level corruption and abuse of power go unchecked, the lower level bureaucracy will become more corrupt, oppressive and tyrannical towards the common people. They will have no one to look for relief and justice. The result will be a great social upheaval, disorder, violence and ultimately break-down of our democratic system. The trends are already visible for any one to see. The Prime Minister has invited a national debate on the issue of "defamation." But there is a greater need first to debate and lay down a proper code of conduct for all those who hold public offices. The agreed code of conduct must be legally enforceable. The authority to enforce this code could well be the Lok Pal (one or more), independent of the executive, the legislature and also the judiciary.

An independent authority of the Ombudsman type would also be set up after public debate to look into public grievances other than those involving corruption. Even after effective steps are taken to tackle public grievances and high-level corruption, it will be dangerous, indeed suicidal, to gag the Press, which has been valiantly engaged in exposing and fighting corruption and maladministration. In fact, the Press has, in a limited way, been playing dual role of a Lok Pal and Ombudsman. The need of the hour is not the Defamation Bill, which has been wisely though belatedly dropped, but an enforceable code of conduct for public men and the enactment without further delay of the long promised legislation on the institution of Lok Pal.

NOTE

1. The Vigilance Commission has since been made a Statutory Body under a Paliamentary Act of 2003.

3

RELEVANCE OF ALL-INDIA SERVICES IN THE FEDERAL POLITY OF INDIA

The federal polity of India has been viewed by some constitutional experts as "neither purely federal nor purely unitary." Dr. Ambedkar, one of the main architects of the Indian Constitution, had observed that "it can be both unitary and federal according to the requirements of time and circumstances."

The various constitutional provisions dealing with distribution of legislative, judicial, financial and administrative powers between the Centre and the States leave little doubt that the polity, though federal in form, is unitary in substance. Formally, the subjects which fall within the State and the Central spheres as also in their concurrent jurisdictions have been enumerated in the Seventh Schedule of the Constitution making the polity federal in form. However, in several important spheres of governance, the Centre has been bestowed with more decisive and even overriding powers. By way of illustrations, the Centre has larger sources of revenue and controls major portion of the nation's purse strings; Parliamentary laws override State laws to the extent the latter are repugnant to the Central laws and the higher judiciary though common between the Centre and the States, the power of appointment of High Court and Supreme Court judges is vested in the President. Similarly, State Governors are Presidential appointees and hold their offices during his pleasure. President's rule which really means Central rule under Article 356 can be imposed by the President in any State if in his view there is a breakdown of the Constitutional machinery. Parliament has also the power to alter the area, boundary and name of any state; it can reorganize any of the existing states and can create new states by merging one or more or by splitting any state (Article 3). Thus, the Centre has far superior and pivotal role in the federal polity. In many respects, it also functions as the friend, philosopher and guide of the states. For socio-economic development of all the states, the Central Planning Commission plays the lead role and is also the main coordinating body.

There were well considered reasons to give primacy to the Centre in the Constitutional framework. The founding fathers of the Constitution, many of whom were great leaders and illustrious sons of India, had deep knowledge and understanding of India's long history. The one basic lesson of Indian history that they were painfully aware of was that the country had time and again got fragmented whenever the Central authority became weak and lost control over the ambitious provincial satraps or chieftains. On such occasions, many of them had declared their independence from the Central power. Thus when the British Crown took over the governance of India in 1857, nearly one-third of the country was ruled by over 500 princely states of varying sizes. The other two-thirds of India was brought directly under the British rule. During this period, the entire country including all the native states, for the first time became politically one and came under British sovereignty. To safeguard the political unity and integrity of independent India, the framers of the Constitution deliberately decided to make appropriate constitutional provisions for a strong centre to enable it to exercise its authority to curb any fissiparous tendencies or separatist movements if any in any state or region. At the initial stages of Constitution making, to prevent the partition of the country on the basis of Jinnah's "two-nation" theory, greater provincial autonomy and a very limited role for the Centre was envisaged. However, once partition became unavoidable and was formally announced in June 1947, the Constituent Assembly's Union Powers Committee unanimously recommended that "it would be injurious to the interests of the country to provide for a weak Central authority which would be incapable of ensuring peace, of coordinating vital matters of common concern ... and that the soundest framework of our Constitution is a federation with a strong Centre".

The relevance and role of some of the well-conceived national level institutions and instruments of governance, e.g. common higher judiciary, common Election Commission and the common All-India Services (AIS) provided in the Constitution have to be viewed in the above historical backdrop.

Two All-India Services, i.e. the Indian Civil Services (ICS) and the Indian Police (IP) were already in existence for many decades prior to independence. The ICS in fact had come to be known as the "Steel frame" of the British administration in India.

Sardar Patel, the then Home Minister and Deputy Prime Minister of India made the following observations in the Constituent Assembly to support the continuance of these two existing services with their changed names of IAS and IPS.

"In consultation with, and with the unanimous support of Provincial Governments, we have evolved two new services to take the place of the Indian Civil Services (IGS) and the Indian Police, viz., the Indian Administrative Services (IAS) and the Indian Police Service (IPS). We have made recruitment, have issued rules of recruitment, discipline, control, etc. and haves entered into agreements with candidates for these services."

"It needs hardly to be emphasized that an efficient, disciplined and contented service assured of its prospects as a result of diligent and honest work, is a *sine quo non* of sound administration under a democratic regime even more than under an authoritarian rule. The service must be above party and we should ensure that political considerations, either in its recruitment or in its discipline and control, are reduced to the minimum, if not eliminated altogether."

He also stated that in an All-India Service, it is obvious that recruitment, discipline and control, etc. have to be handled on the basis of uniformity and under the direction of the Central Government as the recruiting agency. He further mentioned that "all these matters have been settled at a conference of Prime Ministers (as the Chief Ministers were then known) convened in 1946 and the details have been settled by correspondence with Provincial Governments. No criticism, therefore, can be made that either in the formation of these services or in the preparation of necessary rules and regulations, provincial susceptibilities and views found no place. Indeed, at this historic time there was a remarkable unanimity between the views of the Provincial Governments and those of the Central Government throughout on these questions."

It may be noted that even before the framing of the new Constitution, after independence the Central Government had in 1946 consulted the Provincial Governments regarding the future of the existing two All-India Services. As stated in the Constituent Assembly by Sardar Patel, there was "a remarkable unanimity" between the provincial leaders to continue the existing All-India Services in the new federal set-up of the country also. The Constituent Assembly, however, only wished to empower Parliament under Article 312 in a general way to create "one or more All-India Services, common to the Union and the State" by law and leave it at that. It had not considered it necessary to specifically give any constitutional status or recognition to the two existing All-India Services, i.e. the IAS and the IPS. Sardar Patel did not agree to this and wanted that such important matters could not be left to the future uncertainties. Accordingly, clause (2) was added to Article 312 which reads:

> "The services known at the commencement of this Constitution as the Indian Administrative Service and the Indian Police Service shall be deemed to be services created by Parliament under this article."

This constitutionally ensured the continuance of the two existing All-India Services. Sardar Patel it appears had appre-hensions about the future shape of things to come with regard to Centre-State relations and the possible power struggles between the two on various issues. His fears did prove to be correct as shown by subsequent events, for, despite several attempts made by the Central Government, no new All-India Services, in other functional areas except the Indian Forest Service, could be created thereafter. The states had become averse to part with their powers for appointment to various services by creating more All-India Services where the Central Government will have the power of making apppointments. Any national approach in solving problems or disputes with the help of the Central Government has now become rather difficult and time-consuming. The states have become more assertive of their powers. They wish to have greater autonomy in areas of governance falling within their spheres.

During the British rule, to ensure higher standards of governance and uniformity of administration throughout the country, several All-India Services had been created in addition to the better known ICS and IP. The other All-India Services were in the fields of Education, Medical and Health, Engineering (Roads, Buildings, Irrigation) and Forests, etc. Between 1919 and 1935 with the commencement of gradual devolution of powers and functions to the provinces, barring the ICS and the IP, all other then existing All-India Services were provincialised and each state was free to make its own recruitments. Since this had led to noticeable fall in the standards of administration, the need for the revival of the earlier other All-India Services had been felt. Keeping this in mind, the All-India Services Act of 1951 dealing with the creation of the IAS and IPS was amended by Parliament in 1963. The amended version of the Act empowered the central government to create and notify All-India Services in the fields of Education, Health, Engineering and Forests in consultation with the states. But as mentioned earlier, this power has remained only on paper except for the creation in 1966 of the Indian Forest Service. Unfortunately, with the march of time, leaders of All-India stature and vision are becoming scarce. "Narrow domestic walls" are getting erected to divide the country. The Central authority, due to a variety of reasons, is fast losing its hold over the states. Fortunately, at the dawn of India's independence, the galaxy of great leaders who had framed free India's Constitution had duly recognized the importance of the existing All-India Services and had given them constitutional status. They had realized that to maintain close administrative links and understanding between the Centre and the states in a vast country like India, continuance of the All-India Services would be of immense importance and advantage. These common services had in the past greatly helped in the smooth maintenance of law and order throughout the country. It was realised that these services would also be equally useful for coordinated socio-economic development of the country visualized in the Constitution. The Directive Principles of the State Policy in Chapter IV of the Constitution had enumerated several areas of socio-economic development requiring coordinated economic policies and planning.

Some basic features of the All-India Services considered useful for Centre-State cooperation are as below:

1. Recruitment is on an All-India basis by the Union Public Service Commission without any state quota.
2. Allocation of the selected candidates to different State cadres are made by the Central Government.
3. Common training is organized by the Central Government at the National Academy of Administration for all the officers allotted to different states.
4. Important senior posts in the state administrations are included in IAS/IPS cadres for being manned by the IAS/IPS officers

of the states concerned. Postings to individual posts in the states will be done by the states.

5. Each State cadre includes 40 per cent of its strength as "Central Deputation Reserve" for manning senior posts under the Government of India on tenure deputation basis—for the IAS in the Central Secretariat and for the IPS in the various Central Police Organisations like the IB, CBI, CRPF, BSF, ITBP, etc.

This arrangement visualized that there will be no separate Central Cadre of IAS or IPS officers for higher Central Posts but officers from every state cadre will be drawn upon to man such posts under the Central Government on deputation basis. Central Government will post officers to posts under them. This unique system thus gave a sense of participation to every state at higher levels of Central Administration i.e., general and police. It thus made the federal polity a truly 'cooperative federation'. Since 'tenure deputation system' ensured rotation of officers at intervals of 3 to 5 years, the Central Government was able to know more closely the administrative practices and developments in every state at regular intervals. Similarly the state governments came to know of the way of the functioning of the Central Government in different spheres from their own officers reverting from Central deputation on completion of their tenures. This system also helped to develop a feeling of camaraderie among holders of senior level posts under the State and Central Governments. This is of vital importance for the smooth conduct of the day-to-day government business at the centre and at the state levels. Many issues thus usually get amicably settled at the level of senior officers belonging to the same service without assuming political dimension or becoming unduly controversial. The system of common recruitment, common training and the feeling of belonging to the same service among IAS/IPS officers do enhance their mutual trust and cooperation while holding key senior posts at the Centre and in the states.

Realising the importance of the 'tenure deputation system', considerable care has always been taken on the management of the All-India Services so that IAS officers from the states revert to their respective state cadres on completion of Central deputation of 3 years at Under Secretary level, 4 years at Deputy Secretary level and 5 years at other higher levels. As long as there is no slackness in strictly adhering to this time-bound arrangement of fixed Central deputation periods, the IAS would continue to be of mutual benefits to the Central and

State Governments. Any serious violation of this arrangement may prove fatal to the whole concept of the All-India Services. In fact, some wrong thinking at one time had led to the creation of a Central "pool" of officers of the IAS from among the state deputationists who were not to revert to their state cadres on completion of Central tenures. This was done ostensibly on the ground that some IAS officers had acquired specialized knowledge in the economic and commercial sectors in the Government of India and had become more useful to some Central Ministries. In course of time, as was bound to happen, this "pool" degenerated into a "cess pool" as many officers could manage to get into the "pool" allegedly more through favouritism and nepotism and less due to any specialized knowledge as such. Soon Government realized the harmful effects of this "pool" which prevented regular rotation of officers between the Centre and the States and it was finally wound up. One hopes that such "pools" will not be set up in future. At the Central Government level the Establishment Officer to the Government of India, better known as the "EO" is required to enforce the tenure deputation system for the IAS officers. He is to ensure that an IAS officer on Central deputation reverts to his state on completion of his tenure. The author held the post of EO and Additional Secretary in the Ministry of Personnel for a long duration of 5 years (1973-78) and had the satisfaction of managing the system smoothly with full cooperation of the states.

One important feature of the All-India Services which helps in national integration is that each state cadre comprises of not less than 50 per cent "outsiders" i.e. officers belonging to other than the home state. At senior levels it becomes necessary at times to post "outsiders" to sensitive places and posts in a state to withstand local pulls and pressures. W.H. Morris Jones, an eminent foreign scholar of Indian Administration was of the view that "the stable, effective and democratic government in India during the post-Independence period rested to a large extent on the institutional inheritance of the All-India Services from the British rules." This has also been the view of a number of commissions and committees appointed to study administrative reforms. The Sarkaria Commission on Centre-State Relations had also gone into the role and relevance of the All-India Services in great depth. On the issue of "need for All-India Services" the Commission stated in para 8.7.01 of its Report (1988) as below:

> "Considering the totality of the views presented to us on the subject of All-India Services, we observe that there is a near

unanimity in regard to the vital need for these services. It is significant that most of the State Governments have expressed in positive terms that the services, by and large, fulfilled the expectations of the Constitution framers."

Surprisingly, but happily even though diverse political parties have come to power in different states after 1967, there has been little opposition to the existing All-India Services from any of them at any time. They have generally been in favour of continuing the existing services even though they were reluctant to the creation of any more AIS in fields like education, health and engineering. Presently the judiciary is, however, considering to have an All-India Judicial Service.

The Sarkaria Commission's own views about the All-India Services were as below:

> "We too are of the view that the existing system of All-India Services is unique as well as the most appropriate method of securing the best available talent from universities and other centres of learning, and shaping such talent into cadres of intelligent, highly skilled and dedicated officers, with national outlook and experience in a variety of challenging administrative and management tasks. More importantly, the All-India Services provide a valuable link between the Union and the State Governments, enabling the numerous day-to-day problems in Union-State relations to be sorted out with comparatives ease. Another important feature of the system is the ready availability at the senior levels in the Union and the State Governments of officers of proven ability and experiences at both levels of government. But for the systems, the smaller or the less developed States would not have been able to attract such persons to their individual Civil Services."

These views very well reflect the role of the AIS in our federal polity.

After examining other viewpoints and the basic features of the All-India Services, the Sarkaria Commission came to the following conclusion (para 8.7.07 of Report):

> "We are convinced that these services are as much necessary today as they were when the Constitution was framed and continue to be one of the premier institutions of maintaining

the unity of the country. Undoubtedly, the members of the All-India Services have shown themselves capable of discharging the roles that the framers of the Constitution envisaged for them."

Unfortunately, of late, particularly after the nineties there has been a perceptible fall in the sound management of the All-India Services. Neither the top political leaders nor the senior civil service administrators barring some exceptions, have displayed genuine all-India vision and outlook to make proper and effective use of these services. Since every aspect of governance is now being viewed from narrow regional, race, caste, political and communal angles, the role of the All-India Services is getting eroded. Such well conceived constitutional institutions and administrative arrangements appear to be losing importance and may fall apart. Since the persons holding top managerial offices at political and administrative levels are being guided more by self-interest than public interest, institutions and instruments of governance are fast losing their original purpose and relevance. The All-India Services which were visualized by Sardar Patel to be kept 'above party' and free from 'political considerations' are now increasingly getting politicized. As a result, whenever there are changes of governments in the states, there are large-scale transfers of IAS and IPS officers. This obviously lowers their morale and confidence. Many of these officers are, rightly or wrongly, getting identified as loyalists of one or the other political party or of one political leader or the other. Political neutrality of these services is no longer taken for granted. The political and administrative upheavals in some states, in recent times, more particularly in Tamil Nadu (in June 2001) badly damaged the purpose behind the creation of the All-India Services. The severity of political warfare in Tamil Nadu did not leave officers of the All-India Service officers unhurt or unaffected adversely. A few Chief Secretary level officers in the state were arrested on the alleged ground of corruption but according to the views of the members of the service these arrests were made on account of political vendetta against the concerned officers. Whatever the truth may be in this case, the general trend is to transfer or to initiate cases against a number of senior IAS/IPS officers on every change for government on their alleged closeness or loyalty to the previous party in power. One cannot also say with any certainty that the suspected officers were free of any political role. The way some undeserving officers are appointed after their retirements from service to various offices particularly those with political weight show their pre-retirement closeness to the political party in power. The attitude and response of the Central Government, unfortunately, appear to have become somewhat lukewarm in the proper management of the All-India Services. It appears to have left matters entirely to the State Governments and consequently, officers have started cultivating state level politicians to safeguard their service interests. Their All-India outlook is getting lost for survival in the state administrations. Even for Central postings, on tenure deputation, officers allegedly have to lobby with various politicians and "arrange" their own postings. The Central Establishment Board, it is alleged, only formalize such "arranged" postings. The Board, it is believed, is no longer as effective as it was in the past to uphold the concept of All-India Services and oversee justice being done to every IAS officer. The officers seem to have been left to fend for themselves. The general view among the officers is that this is leading to demoralization and also to politicalisation of the service. The AIS scheme may not be as fruitful as it was intended to be by the Founding Fathers of the Constitution if the services are not kept above party politics.

In the present changed environment, the role of the All-India Services, therefore, does need to be reviewed. To make the services effective links between the Centre and the states, the legitimate service interests of the AIS officers ought to be protected. Cases of injustice and individual harassments at the state or the central levels need to be speedily looked into and set right by the Central Government, which is their appointing authority. Central Government should similarly exercise greater disciplinary control over the erring members of these services and ensure their being non-political. Another unfortunate development is that far too many members of the All-India Services presently face charges of corruption. Some of them allegedly have amassed huge illegitimate wealth. This has greatly tainted the earlier good image of honesty and integrity of the IAS officers. Undoubtedly, there are still good many talented officers who are wholly honest and painstaking in the performance of their duties. They are also above political alignments. Many of them, however, at times get overshadowed by some of the "smarter" officers who enjoy political support and patronage and are unduly rewarded not only while in service but also after retirement. This is leading to the politicalization of the AIS. It is, therefore, time to objectively review the situation and restore the morale, efficiency, honesty and effectiveness of the All-India Services if these are to prove their worth and need to be continued. In my view their continuance is still very vital for the administrative unity of our vast country and for maintaining closer administrative links between the Centre and the states. In this connection extracts of an article written by me earlier and published by the Hindustan Times highlighting the need for AIS Officers to rise above local politics are reproduced below.

Article Published in the Hindustan Times

Centre's Power of Bringing AIS Officers on Central Deputation

"The controversy regarding the transfer to the Centre of three Indian Police Service (IPS) officers of Tamil Nadu Cadre by the Central Government has created intense friction between the Centre and the State.

The Central Government's order transferring to the Centre the three Tamil Nadu Cadre IPS officers has been questioned by J. Jayalalitha Chief Minister of the State. She has viewed it as "politically motivated" and a violation of the practice of taking prior concurrence of the state concerned before selecting any of its All-India Service officers for central postings.

A background of the All-India Services (AIS) scheme (mainly for the IAS and IPS) may be relevant to understand the roles of the Central and State Governments in the management of these services, which, under Article 312(1) of the Constitution, are "common between the Union and the States." This is a unique feature of our federal polity as officers of the AIS (i.e. the IAS, the IPS, and the IFS) recruited by the Centre through the UPSC hold key assignments, both under the Central and State Governments.

After recruitment, the Centre allots AIS officers to different state cadres. The Centre has no separate cadre of its own but brings officers of the levels of Deputy Secretary and above from all the state cadres on deputation for three to five years for posts at the Centre. For this purpose each state cadres in addition to their own requirements have been allowed a 40 per cent additional strength called "Central Deputation Reserve" (CDR) to meet the Centre's requirements of AIS officers for Central Government posts. This arrangement provides uniform standards of administration throughout the country and facilitates greater Centre-State cooperation in administrative matters.

The need for the AIS was discussed by Sardar Patel the then Central Home Minister with the provincial premiers (as they were then called) after the country's independence. He stated in the

Constituent Assembly that there was a remarkable unanimity between the views of the provincial governments and the Central Government for the continuance of the AIS in the new federal set up of the country for its governance and administration.

While providing for the AIS in the Constitution, Sardar Patel had cautioned that the services "must be above party and we should ensure that political considerations, either in its recruitment or in its discipline and control, are reduced to the minimum, if not eliminated altogether."

The Sarkaria Commission, appointed to look into Centre-State relations, reported in 1988 that "the AIS provide valuable link between the Union and the State Governments, enabling the numerous day-to-day problems in the Union-State relations to be sorted out with comparative ease."

The management of the AIS has been free from friction as the Centre always allowed a free hand to the states in the matter of postings and transfers of their officers in the state posts. Similarly, the States cooperated with the Centre in making available officers for central deputations against its 40 per cent CDRs for central posts. To spare officers for central postings also gave them a sense of participation in the central administrative spheres.

Normally, the states annually send names and lists of their officers who can be spared for central deputation during the year. The Centre selects any of these officers for central posts as and when required. Usually, no officer is selected from outside the state list for central deputation except rarely when services of any particular officer are required for any specific post, considering his special background.

A spirit of mutual understanding and cooperation helped in smooth cadre-management of the AIS even when different political parties ruled at the Centre and in the States. Some problems did arise in 1984 because of the then prevailing serious law and order problems in Punjab, Jammu and Kashmir and Assam. Since Punjab was under president's rule at that time there was no difficulty for the Centre in making administrative changes, involving transfer and postings of some AIS officers of Punjab, Assam also did not present any problem. In J&K, however, the state was reluctant to allow one of its officers to be posted at the Centre due to certain political consideration. It, therefore, became necessary to amend the AIS (Cadre) Rule, 1954, to empower the Centre to take any state cadre AIS Officer on central deputation even against the wishes of the concerned state. Majority of the States did not object to this proposed amendment to empower the Centre to post officers from the states to the Centre if so required under special circumstances.

The present order requisitioning the services of the three Tamil Nadu cadre IPS officers need to be looked into keeping in mind the AIS scheme, and the rules and practices relating to the cadre management. Is the central order "politically motivated", as alleged by the State Chief Minister, or did the three IPS officers transferred by the Centre allowed themselves to be used as "political tools" in arresting M. Karunanidhi the former Chief Minister, Tamil Nadu and two Union Ministers belonging to DMK?

Under the AIS scheme, the Centre has an important role to play if it finds that any officer is getting involved in local politics. It also has 40 per cent share in the services of these officers. They need to remain above party politics and their statutory powers are not to be misused for settling political scores or for satisfying political vendetta of any ruling party.

The Centre, as the appointing authority, has the ultimate disciplinary control over them. There have been cases where in the exercise of its powers under Article 309(2)(b) of the Constitution, the President had dismissed a few AIS officers while serving in the states for their acts of grave misconduct.

The special powers vested in the Central Government through the 1954 Amendment mentioned earlier are however to be exercised rarely and only under special circumstances. These powers are not meant for routine transfers. Any *mala fide* or arbitrary use of the special legal powers could make them questionable and also adversely affect the AIS scheme."

Shri Rajiv Gandhi on assuming the office of the Prime Minister of India somewhat suddenly in 1984 after the assassination of Smt. Indira Gandhi was understandably not quite conversant with various policy and institutional arrangements relating to the civil services including the All-India Services scheme. He once seriously wanted that the postings of Chief Secretaries and Director-Generals of Police of the states be made by the Central Government since these officers were too frequently changed by the states on the change of governments.

He thought that since the President of India is the appointing authority of the AIS Officers the Central Government had the power of making their postings and transfers in the states. It was explained to him by the author (who was the then Secretary, Ministry of Personnel & A.R. dealing with the subject) that the AIS scheme providing a "common" pool of officers was agreed upon by the states on the clear understanding that postings of these officers to posts within the states will be done by the States and for posts under the Centre by the Central Government. Constitutionally the President only appoints the officers to the AIS services but is not empowered to make their postings to any post within the states. That power vests in the State Governments. Shri Rajiv Gandhi though not quite happy with this restriction on the centre's power had to accept it. His idea of course was to ensure that top officers are not changed too often.

On an earlier occasion Home Minister Chaudhary Charan Singh in the Janata regime of Morarji Desai (1977-80) had desired that only Hindi speaking officers of the IAS be posted in the Home Ministry to promote the use of Hindi. As the then Establishment Officer (EO) to the Government of India who suggested names of suitable IAS officers for the vacancies in the central ministries the author met Chaudhary Charan Singh to explain to him the idea behind AIS scheme. It was politely stated that the AIS scheme visualized by his historic predecessor Sardar Patel was to maintain and strengthen the administrative unity of India by having a "common" pool of IAS/IPS officers for holding key central and state posts. In selecting them for posting to various posts at the Centre, their professional suitability and merit were the main criteria. There was no intention to discriminate on grounds of ones mother tongue. Their All-India outlook and mind set should not suffer by giving preferential treatment to Hindi speaking officers among them for posts in the Home Ministry which prominently represent the unity of India. It was also emphasized that he being the present successor of Sardar Patel might like to further strengthen the policy of uniting India in all possible ways. To take Hindi speaking officers alone to the Home Ministry may also be resented by the non-Hindi states. Chaudhary Charan Singh after giving due thought to all aspects agreed to the existing practice in the placement of IAS officers in the central ministries including the Home Ministry.

4

POLICE–PUBLIC PERCEPTION: A CASE OF DELHI POLICE

Delhi police due to its various faults, failures and shortcoming has been coming under adverse criticism in the media rather too frequently. For example, once a police SHO reportedly arrested and beat up a young boy presumably for his audacity to object to the wrong parking of the SHO's vehicle near a marketplace and blocking the passage of other vehicles. The SHO's sense of ego was perhaps hurt as he considered himself to be above the law and above any criticism within his jurisdiction. To drive home his unquestionable authority he not only slapped the boy but also arrested him and took to the police station. It so happened that the boy was the son of a Secretary to the Government of India. In another such case a few days earlier there were media reports that a retired professor of Delhi University had been roughed up and slapped by another police SHO for no apparent reason. In both these cases because of high level complaints the concerned SHO's were suspended pending investigation of allegations of highhandedness against them.

Sometime later (in February 2008) in the course of a PIL hearing the Delhi High Court took the police to task for its abuse of power and highhandedness. In this case two innocent individuals were wrongfully arrested under Sections 107/151 of the Cr.PC on the false excuse of preventive detention for maintaining peace and tranquility in the area.The real facts of the case as found during the court hearing were however that the two persons had raised their voices against extortion of money by the concerned police personnel. In deciding the PIL the Delhi High Court accordingly held the police to be guilty of abuse of power and directed the state government to pay Rs. 25,000 as compensation to each of the two innocent victims of police high handedness. In another PIL hearing by the court it was found that the police in connivance with a local politician, arrested a person who objected to his land being encroached upon by the politician. The court in this case observed that the "Police cannot act as an agent of those who do unauthorized construction and cannot be an accomplice of those who swallow their neighbour's rights." The innocent victim was ordered by the court to be set free and the state government was directed to pay him Rs. 75,000 as compensation. In these two cases the Asst. Commissioner of Police (ACP) acting as SEMs (Special Executive Magistrate) had wrongfully rejected the bail applications of the arrested persons. The Delhi High Court found fault with the ACP for rejecting the bail plea and his failure to render justice against the high handedness of his subordinates. In a more recent case of March 2010 as reported in the media, the Delhi High Court ordered the Delhi Police Commissioner to pay a compensation of Rs. 5.32 lakh to a 55 year old resident of Sangam Vihar in a false rape case and 17 other false cases launched against him for his audacity to have made complaints against the police.

In another case the High Court directed the Police Commissioner to send a written apology to the accused Prem Pal and each of his family members (wife and four children) for launching a false case against him. Justice S. Murlidhar had also observed (according to media reports) "If confidence has to be restored among the citizenry that the police is meant to protect their rights then such expression of contrition by those at the helm is imperative."

Several such recurring instances of abuse of power and high handedness by the Delhi Police have tarnished its image in the eyes of the public who consider it to be unhelpful and prone to resort to all kinds of harassment. Accordingly, as far as possible, people in Delhi distance themselves from the police. To improve its public image Police as the law enforcement agency has to be more law abiding and less arbitrary or authoritarian. Its attitude towards the people should be more positive and helpful.

Even the Supreme Court, as reported in the Press sometime back, had observed about the police that "the Court will show to this country what type of police force they are paying taxes for." The Court had also observed that: "if these police officers serve a sentence then only they will learn lessons." The observation was made by the court, while hearing a matter relating to non-tracing of a kidnapped girl by the Delhi police for an unduly long time.

It should be a matter of serious concern that the popular image of the police, which was never too good, is getting worse with each passing day. This only means that the police is not quite bothered about the frequent criticisms levied against it. Far too many lower and middle level policemen are found by the people to be not only rude, casual, and lethargic in performance of their public duties but are also highly corrupt. They, it is believed, do not lift even their little finger unless some money is slipped into their palms. They act only after suitable palm greasing. Police and corruption are viewed by the people to be inseparable. The general impression is also that the police often arrives at the places of crime long after the worst is over. The police is also rightly or wrongly believed to have some kind of understanding or MOU with known criminals to get a share of their illegal income from theft or robbery. A judge of the Allahabad High Court had even reportedly observed once that the police was "the most organized group of criminals." Even though such a harsh and sweeping observation is unfair, yet unfortunately this reflects the commonly held views of the public about the police in India. Hardly any one has a good word for it. Delhi Police being in charge of maintenance of law and order in the National Capital enjoys a higher status in the police force of the country. But even so it has no better public image or reputation than the police elsewhere.

It must however be accepted that there are very many honest and upright policemen who are impartial, considerate and fair minded in performance of their duties. They do not suffer from any arrogance of power. Such reputed and dedicated policemen had often been found to handle many serious law and order problems, calmly, carefully, competently and even at the risk of their lives at times. Unfortunately the good work of such capable and honest policemen get obliterated on account of the questionable conduct and deeds of many other ill-reputed policemen. Remedial measures need therefore to be devised to improve the poor public image of the police and to make it more people friendly. The police reform measures should, however, be such that in making the police more responsible and accountable it is not unduly deprived of necessary legal powers to effectively tackle law and order problems. Police should be neither too harsh nor too soft but conduct itself according to the needs of any given situation. There has to be a rational balance in the empowerment of the police and maintaining adequate supervision and control over it. For this purpose an appropriate and effective system of checks and balances in the exercise of police powers has to be devised. In fact no institution of governance should have such unchecked powers as may make it unaccountable, irresponsible and insensitive to the hardships of the people. Transparency and accountability need to be in-built into the organizational set up of all governmental bodies more so of the police in view of its vast powers over the life, liberty and property of the people. The more powerful is a public body the more should be the supervision control over it so that there is no abuse of power by any of its members.

In judging the police one should also take into account the unpleasant nature of its duties. These at times lead to rough and violent confrontations by the police with hard core criminal elements. One cannot also overlook the fact that the police these days specially in the national capital Delhi is very much overworked. A large percentage of them are engaged in the security duty of various categories of VIPs, and VVIPs. According to recent (2009) media reports while on an average 34 policemen are earmarked for security duty for each of the above nearly 14200 VIPs in Delhi, only one policeman is available for 600 *aam aadmi*. These figures may somewhat keep changing but there is no doubt that a very large percentage of the available police manpower in Delhi is engaged on VIP security thus leaving the aam aadmi to his own devices and luck for his safety and security. This to some extent explains the pressure under which police in Delhi operates. Often the policemen are required to remain on duty continuously for many hours in hot summer and cold winter.

At times, being pressurized by various vested interests including powerful politicians, the police also finds itself handicapped to function freely and according to its own best judgement. When powerful anti-social elements enjoying political support and patronage indulge in criminal acts, police becomes somewhat slow and un-decisive in taking timely action against them. Powerful politicians reportedly, at times with police connivance, harass their opponents in different ways e.g. by initiating false criminal cases against them or by getting their houses raided and searched on one false ground or the other. Honest and upright police officers also admit that some police officers willingly oblige their political bosses in performing such illegal acts at their behest with selfish motives of gaining immediate or future career advancements as a *quid pro quo*. Unfortunately this trend of politicization of public services is to be seen not only in the case of police but in other categories of public officials as well. Of late quite a few civil servants feel comfortable to be at the beck and call of influential politicians in power in order to derive unmerited service benefits with their help and support. Many such ambitious public servants seeking malafide personal gains are damaging the quality and impartiality of public administration. Police with its immense powers like the power of search, seizure, arrest and the power to initiate criminal action against any one by treating him as a "suspect" if allowed to abuse these powers would be of great danger to the life, liberty and safety of the people and to the rule of law. Hence it is of vital importance that there is effective supervision and control over the day to day work of the police by a non-police authority as discussed later. It has to be ensured that police functions in an impartial manner and well within its legal limits.

During the short-lived Janata Party rule of 1977-80 the Delhi Police managed to acquire more powers by introducing the Police Commissioner System in Delhi through the Delhi Police Act, 1978. The purpose of this Act, as it says, was to "amend and consolidate the law relating to the regulation of the Police in the Union Territory of Delhi." The Police Commissioner system was already in vogue in a few other metropolitan cities like Calcutta, Bombay and Madras. Broadly, under this system, the magisterial powers of the District Magistrate (DM) relating to law and order are vested in the Police Commissioner. In Delhi this has been done under Section 70 of the Delhi Police Act, 1978. Exercise of magisterial and police powers by a single authority i.e., the Police Commissioner of Delhi was considered useful and necessary to speedily deal with any serious law and order situation. Under this system, the police no longer has to take prior approval of the DM or any other civil magistrate so empowered under the law in matters like imposing curfew (Section 144 Cr.PC) or for making preventive arrests (under Section 107/151 Cr.PC) or for resorting to firing when required for crowd control or to prevent rioting etc.

Under the new system all such magisterial powers have been vested in the Police Commissioner himself and his subordinate Police

Officers like Deputy Commissioner of Police (DCP) and Asst. Commissioner of Police (ACP). Delhi has thus ceased to have a separate non-police civilian officer as its District Magistrate (or DM– usually an IAS officer). Under Section 4 of the Police Act, 1861, applicable in the non-Police Commissioner areas of the country the District Collector of a district, in his capacity as District Magistrate (DM), has the power of "general control and direction" over the District SP. The relevant provision of this section reads:

> "The administration of the police throughout the local jurisdiction of *the magistrate of the district shall under the general control and direction of such magistrate* be vested in a District Superintendent...."

The District Magistrate in Delhi accordingly had the power of "general control and direction" over the District Police prior to the introduction of the Police Commissioner system in 1978. No police officer had any magisterial powers at that time. The main intention behind magisterial control over the police was to check and prevent the risks of arbitrary exercise of power by the police. The police had the fear of accountability to the DM on a day to day basis due to the general power of supervision and control over it vested in him.

That power of "general control and direction" under the Police Act of 1861 enabled the DM to inspect police stations, hear public complaints against the police and generally keep himself informed of the crime situation in his district. To make him more effective he had the power to record remarks on the work and merit of the Superintendent of Police (SP) and other senior district police officials in their ACRs (Annual Confidential Reports). He was consulted with regard to the postings and transfers of the SHOs in his District. This system of magisterial control over the police enabled the general public to approach the DM or the SDM in cases of any police harassment or misconduct. The police thus had greater accountability and magisterial control over it.

After the police related powers of the DM were vested in the Police Commissioner under the Police Act of 1978 the police is no longer answerable to any other non-police district level magisterial authority. The Delhi Police of course is answerable to the LG Delhi who is the "Administrator" of Delhi, (the erstwhile UT) under Article 239 of the Constitution. Even though Delhi "UT" has by now become a "State" the Delhi Police continues to be under the Centre. The L.G. appointed by the President is also the "Administrator" of Delhi with regard to subjects not transferred to the Delhi State. In that capacity the LG Delhi exercises general control over the Delhi Police. The common man at the grassroots may not, however, find it easy to have access to the LG. Thus for the people the police in Delhi has become the single all powerful authority in matters of criminal law and its administration.

This cannot at all be called a sound arrangement from the people's angle. They must not feel to be living in a "Police Raj". If "Inspector Raj" was bad "Police Raj" would be worst.

At present there are no other non-police civil officers below the LG who can hear complaints of the people against the police on a day to day basis as no one has been so empowered. There can be little dispute that the "Police" in Delhi should come within the domain of the Union Government as Delhi is the seat of the Central Government. A government without police powers would be toothless and weak. The Centre has to discharge the special responsibilities of providing security to the President, Vice-President, Parliament and the diplomatic missions. No doubt as the Commander-in-Chief of the armed forces the President has the security chain of the armed forces in the Rashtrapati Bhawan. But still the Delhi Police has a major role to play in the President's security cover. The Union Government has also to ensure the security of foreign dignitaries visiting the Capital of the country. The peaceful functioning of the Central Council of Ministers and the Central Secretariat also greatly depend on ensuring law and order in the city by the Delhi Police. There are therefore bound to be problems of peace and security if police in Delhi is made a State Subject and the Delhi Police is placed under the Delhi State Government. For there have been and there would be times when the Central Government and the State Government of Delhi are headed by two different political parties. At times their political differences and disputes may lead to serious law and order situations in Delhi due to organization of popular dharnas and demonstrations with political angles. The Central Government therefore must not find itself at the mercy of the Delhi State Government wielding police powers. The Police in Delhi should therefore undoubtedly remain under the control of the Central Government for its smooth functioning.

The introduction of the Police Commissioner system in Delhi too has advantages in taking speedy action at times of breakdown of law and order. Such situations in the national capital are bound to be many as aggrieved people from all over the country often come to Delhi to express their grievances before the national Parliament or the Central Government. They organize massive processions and dharnas which disturb the peace of the city. The Delhi Police has to deal with all such situations being responsible and accountable for maintaining law and order in the national capital. There should not therefore be any dilution or division of its authorities in managing crisis situations in the capital.

Keeping the above background in mind and the powers vested in the Delhi Police it is very necessary that the Delhi Police has to have greater supervision and control over it of a non-police civilian authority like a Police Ombudsman. This Body will not interfere with the actual functioning of the police but would oversee its work to prevent abuses of power if any. It would also look into the complaints if any of the people against the police. It may also inspect police stations, jails, etc.

It is seen that people generally hesitate to lodge complaints before the higher police officers regarding any abuse of power by their lower subordinates. They fear that such complaints may harm the complainants by way of revengeful actions by the aggrieved subordinate police officers. There have been cases of this nature as mentioned earlier. This may be an important reason as to why there are very few corruption cases in the courts against the police even though corruption is known to be rampant and widespread among the police personnel in Delhi as elsewhere.

There are frequent media reports of cases involving police torture, rape and custodial deaths in Delhi. The report of the Amnesty International (for 1992) gave details of many such cases in Delhi. This report says, “Some of those who have died in police custody appear to have been innocent of any crime. Often they were detained illegally with no case or charge registered against them. Once a prisoner’s death has occurred, it appears to be common for police to implicate the victim in a crime or else deny that they had been detained at all” (p. 41 of the Report). This is a very serious charge and deserves remedial action by way of greater accountability and supervision over the police. The Ombudsman type Supervisory Authority mentioned earlier may comprise of three high level persons with judicial, administrative and police service experiences. One member from the police service may be useful to scrutinize complaints from the police angle. The role of the Authority may however be confined to matters relating to registration, investigation and prosecution of criminal cases and public complaints of police corruption, highhandedness or any other wrongful action by them. "Police" not being under the Delhi State, the State Assembly can hardly discuss shortcomings of Delhi Police. The Central Government and the Parliament in spite of their best intentions and efforts may not find sufficient time to deal with day to day police matters of Delhi. The situation therefore has to be tackled as suggested by setting up an Ombudsman type body. The position of the Police Commissioner system of Calcutta, Mumbai, Chennai etc. stand on a different footing as police being a state subject in those states, the state legislatures are in a position to voice public grievances against the police, if any. They have also separate D.G. Police over the Police Commissioner. Delhi, however, has no other D.G. over the Delhi Police Commissioner. Hence to make up for these shortcomings in the special circumstances of Delhi a non-police supervisory body would be a necessary and desirable arrangement. It would without curtailing the law and order related powers of the Delhi Police provide a suitable mechanism to deal with the legitimate grievances, if any, of the people against the police. In this connection it is worth mentioning that in 2006 the Supreme Court of India in its judgement in *Prakash Singh and others* vs. *The Union of India* had issued some landmark directions relating to Police Reforms. One of which mandated the establishment of independent Police Complaints Authorities to adjudicate public complaints of police misconduct. The Human Rights Watch in its Report (August 2009) on Police brutality in India had also observed that:

> "the Prakash Singh directives, with their focus on political interference, may fail to significantly reduce arbitrary arrest and detention, torture and other mistreatment, and deaths in police custody. These abuses cannot be ascribed solely to illegitimate political influence, although the problems are linked because of *de facto* impunity provided by political patrons. It further mentioned that "activists and lawyers have repeatedly pointed out the danger of reform agenda that seeks to free police from political control without making them more accountable to the public."

It therefore advised that—

> "while changing laws to prevent political figures from exercising undue influence over police is critical, it is equally necessary to ensure that political control is replaced with accountability of the police to the community. Accordingly, police reform efforts should include steps to hold police accountable for human rights violations."

Obviously the "human rights" aspect have to be viewed differently when the armed police (like the CRPF) deal with Naxals or the Maoists insurgents. Ordinary unarmed citizens should not be treated on the same footings while giving more powers to the police. Unfortunately the police clamours for more powers by citing the cases of terrorists, Maoists and Naxals etc. The role of the civil police dealing with the ordinary citizens or *aam admi* should not at all be linked with the role of the *armed police* dealing with militants, terrorists or other armed insurgents. Two separate police organizations should deal with these two entirely different law and order police roles. Their powers, equipments and training must necessarily be different. The police role dealt with here relates to the civilian police and the *aam admi.* Human rights of these common citizens need to be protected from any police excesses or high-handedness. This calls for as mentioned earlier of a non-Police, Ombudsman type complaints handling authority with legal powers to investigate public complaints against the police.

To improve the quality of policing it is also necessary that the police personnel, particularly at the middle and lower operational levels are provided necessary facilities like housing, health care and time to rest properly while on long hours of duty. Equally important is to ensure regular physical exercise and training for the police personnel. They must be physically fit and also look to be so. A policeman with bulging belly gives a poor impression of his fitness. Policemen and officers should also have stability of tenure of at least 2-3 years at any one place and post. Frequency of transfers and postings at short intervals as at present in some states has a demoralizing effect on the police personnel. Even in Delhi there is need to take care of this aspect. To boost police morale and efficiency Police Establishment Boards comprising of police officers should be constituted to look after all service matters like placements, promotions and security of tenure, etc. of policemen at different levels. A well managed and well trained police force, free from any political interference is expected to be more impartial, fair and humane in performance of its duties and its conduct towards the people. A non-police Vigilance Authority will make it more responsible and law abiding and help to improve its public image.

5

MORE JUDGES MORE DELAYS: PARKINSON'S LAW

On Government of India's decision to appoint some additional judges to the Supreme Court, the then Lok Sabha Speaker Somnath Chatterjee reportedly opined (2009) that "more the number of judges more would be the delay." This recalls to mind the famous Parkinson's Law according to which "work expands so as to fill the time available for its completion." Would it accordingly imply that more the judges more will be the cases filed before them to fill the additional judicial time available? Would more judges therefore have little or no impact on clearing the huge arrears of court cases even if the situation is not worsened. In this connection a brief examination of the causes of judicial delays and large pendency of cases would be relevant.

In a seminar on Judicial Reforms the President Pratibha Patil had expressed serious concern on the long judicial delays and the emerging "culture of the lynch mob" (2009). Frustrated with the poor functioning of the police and long judicial delays aggrieved persons at times are being driven to take the law into their own hands. They even beat some accused persons to death for their criminal acts. This is happening as the course of justice has become too slow.

Chief Justice of India Hon'ble K.G. Balakrishnan equally concerned with the problem of judicial delays was of the view that lack of "proper and good governance" was one of the important causes in driving the litigants in larger numbers to the Judiciary for relief. This is resulting in huge number of court cases and consequent delays in their disposal. According to the Chief Justice of India the present size of the Judiciary and number of judges in the courts being unable to cope with the rising tide of cases has to be suitably raised. The figure of pending cases was reported to be (as on 30th June 2007) 37.1 lakh in the High Courts and 2.5 crore in the lower courts.[1]

As against the present sanctioned strength of 792 judges in the High Courts and 15,399 judges in the lower courts the additional requirements as put forward was 1539 more judges for the High Courts and 18,479 more judges for the lower courts. This would mean that the size of the judiciary has to be raised nearly three times of what it is now.

To increase the present strength of the judiciary by nearly three times would obviously mean huge financial costs. It has to be kept in mind that additional judges would require additional PAs/peons/ process servers, police personnel, land and additional buildings, for housing several new courts. It is extremely doubtful if our present financial situation can bear such massive additional expenditure on additional courts. It is therefore necessary to examine what could be some other reasonable way out. May be that it would be more advisable and desirable to file lesser number of court cases in regular courts by following some rational system of scrutiny of complaints and petitions seeking legal relief. Presently there appears to be far too many petty cases involving minor or technical breaches of law clogging the wheels of Justice. Hon'ble Justice Anand former CJI had once in this connection cited the case of a poor boy arrested for stealing three cigarette packets and languishing in jail as an under-trial as there was none to bail him out. Another such unfortunate case cited by him was of an under-trial prisoner arrested for alleged crime of gambling from whom the total cash recovered was only one rupee and ten paise.

My own study (while posted in the Union Ministry of Home Affairs in the mid-60s) of the judicial workload of the Delhi Courts to consider their demand for large number of additional magistrates also found that there were far too many minor cases pending in the courts which could have been very well dealt with on the spot by mobile courts. It was found that of the several lakhs of pending cases

1. The latest pending figures of cases (as on 30th June 2009) given at the conference of Chief Ministers of States and Chief Justices of the High Courts on 16th August 2009 by the Chief Justice of India are:

Supreme Court:	52,592
High Courts:	40,17,956
Subordinate Courts:	2,71,19,092

at that time only around 5 per cent or so related to criminal offences under the Indian Penal Code (IPC) and the balance nearly 95 per cent were for breaches of the provisions of scores of other miscellaneous laws, like the Motor Vehicles Act, The Closure of Shops and Establishments Act, Public Nuisance Offences under the Delhi Police Act, Weights and Measures Act, Prevention of Cruelty to Animals Act, etc., etc. Bulk of the cases booked under these Acts hardly merited regular court trials but could have been disposed of by mobile courts on the spot. Regular courts need not have been flooded with such cases as most of these hardly served the real intention behind the relevant legislations. For example, thousands of cases had been filed against horse cart owners under the Prevention of Cruelty to Animals Act. Their "offences" were for causing "cruelty" to the horses by alleged overloading by a few KGs than the legally permissible load limits. During a visit to the Tis Hazari Courts these accused persons told me that they are being summoned to attend the courts for months together as on each hearing date their cases got adjourned for one reason or the other. Being daily workers they lost their earnings on every such court hearing days and had to starve. They legitimately asked if this was not greater cruelty to the horses as the animals too starved on those dates along with their masters. They further argued that they knew the actual load carrying capacity of their horses and could ill-afford to be cruel to them as their own livelihood depended on the good health of their horses.

Similarly, under the Motor Vehicles Act, lakhs of cases had been booked and a simple disposal method had been devised. On every hearing date a clerk or a peon of the court stamped the court verdict on the order sheet of each case file with the words *"accused appears, pleads guilty, fined rupees X."* Similarly thousands of Food Adulteration Act cases pending for months related to only adulteration of milk with water. These cases got adjourned time and again due to the non-appearance of the accused persons. Summons could not be served as the addresses given by the accused were generally false. Any attempt to trace them turned out to be a wild goose chase. Thus considerable court time was wasted in the disposal of these cases.

The problem of large volume of court cases under these numerous laws had arisen as the law enforcement Inspectors were required to file a certain minimum number of cases every week/fortnight. The emphasis, as a proof of good performance of duty, by them was on the quantitative and not on the quality aspects of law enforcement. The Inspectors concerned, accordingly tried to prove their merit by flooding the regular courts with thousands of cases involving only minor or technical violations of the laws. To protect themselves from harassments by the Inspectors the shopkeepers in some markets told me while discussing the prosecution cases against them that they regularly pay fixed amounts or "haftas" to different categories of Inspectors. Some kind of MOU had been devised to limit prosecutions only to the minimum number of cases required to be filed by each inspector for their career advancements. The shopkeepers told that this was the only practical way they could find to limit corruption and court cases under the given circumstances of "Inspector Raj."

After conclusion of the study, no additional magistrates were found to be necessary. The Delhi Administration on the other hand was advised to take recourse to mobile court system for better enforcement of the minor laws and other petty offences. That system was accordingly introduced on the basis of my report but does not seem to be in vogue any longer.

Once, more judges and magistrates are appointed and thus more judicial time is available for deciding cases, there is every possibility of the courts being flooded with larger number of petty and minor cases. The MOU between the law enforcement Inspectors and the shopkeepers or other professional offenders mentioned earlier would be suitably revised upwards for filing many more cases to keep the expanded judiciary also submerged with petty cases. Hopefully apart from the Inspectors there are no other vested interest (e.g. lawyers, court staff etc.) in flooding the judiciary with huge number of cases. It needs to be emphasized that the judiciary is hardly at fault for the huge number of cases and long delays in their disposal. Since bulk of the litigation is initiated by the law enforcement agencies of the central and state governments they have to take care to avoid overloading the judiciary with petty cases. The emphasis should shift from mere quantitative to the qualitive aspects of cases for proper law enforcement. Further to prevent court cases the quality of governance has also to improve. Once people have more faith and confidence in the government of the day they may not unnecessarily knock the doors of the judiciary. Presently the judiciary enjoys greater faith of the people in getting justice and hence the problem of mounting case workload of the judicial courts. However, increasing the number of judges may be only a very costly and temporary remedy to reduce pendency of cases. In the long run the number of court cases may again increase leading to more delays. The real and long-term remedy may be to take care of the other important aspects mentioned earlier i.e. prevention of uncalled for litigation through good governance and rational ways of law enforcement. Mobile court system should be reintroduced to reduce the number of regular court cases. All state agencies, including the police, should be discouraged from filing too many petty cases and thus burdening the judiciary. Law enforcement has to be more efficient and cost effective. Preventive aspects of it should receive greater attention. In this connection it may be useful to make a study of the huge number of pending cases to know the nature of offences and the specific laws violated in these cases. On the basis of such a study suitable ways and mechanism could be devised to reduce litigation and court cases. Obviously it may not be financially possible to keep appointing more and more judges together with the other categories of supporting staff for any unchecked large volume of cases. The number of regular court cases ought to be kept within a reasonable upper limit keeping in view financially affordable size of the judiciary. In the Conference of the State Chief Ministers and the Chief Justices of the High Courts held in New Delhi on 16th August 2009 Hon'ble K.G. Balakrishnan, Chief Justice of India in his speech drew attention to the large pendency of cases in the courts and the ways to effectively deal with this problem. He said:

> "While expanding the size of the judicial system is an important objective, I must also highlight the importance of pursuing several other strategies to streamline the administration of justice. All of you are conversant with the benefits of resorting to Alternative Dispute Resolution (ADR) methods, especially since civil judges are now empowered to refer disputes for resolution through Permanent Lok Adalats, Mediation and Negotiated settlements. Most of the High Courts and numerous District Courts have established 'Mediation' centres for the twin purpose of resolving disputes as well as training judicial officers and lawyers in these methods. For many categories of cases filed before the courts–such as those relating to traffic offences and petty property disputes, methods such as conciliation and negotiation are far more appropriate than the traditional model of adversarial litigation. While

the Legal Services Authorities have been increasingly organizing Lok Adalats for many categories of disputes, it is also important to inform the general public about the utility of these methods. On account of incomplete information about the various options, an aggrieved party often chooses to proceed with lengthy-adversarial litigation instead of choosing more conciliatory methods. Even the Code of Criminal Procedure was amended in 2006 to include provisions for 'plea-bargaining' but public awareness about the same is quite limited."

It goes without saying that all of us need to think about and promote solutions that need not always be "Court-Centric."

The number and size of judicial courts for rendering justice should be such that it is financially affordable. Presently there is need for greater focus and priority on larger expenditure on developmental activities for promoting economic justice to the vast masses of poor (BPL) people of the country. Poverty eradication and employment generation should accordingly be allotted more funds. That would also help in reducing crimes, court cases and judicial workload. There is need to monitor and reduce uncalled for litigation to prevent long and large pendency of court cases. Alternative ways of handling disputes as suggested by the Chief Justice of India which are not "court-centric" have to be made use of. Appointment of more judges should therefore be avoided as far as possible.

6

CITIZENS AND THE PUBLIC SERVICES

Shri A.S. Kulkarni was a distinguished member of the Rajya Sabha. On his demise in 1992, Members of the Upper House irrespective of party affiliations paid him glowing tributes. His candid expression of views, particularly on matters relating to public morality and cleanliness in public life were appreciated by all. As Central Vigilance Commissioner (CVC 1985-88) the author had occasions to talk to Shri Kulkarni a number of times as his was a powerful voice and support in the fight against corruption. I remember one of his speech in the Rajya Sabha in August 1988 when the House was discussing the Prevention of Corruption Bill. He had then stated in a forthright manner that "previously we used to come here by rickshaws and then by taxi...now I find many members of Parliament–People's representatives–have got posh cars to come to Parliament. Similar is the case with the Members of the Lok Sabha. Where does the money come from? Where is the nexus?" Had Shri Kulkarni lived a little longer (say up to 2009) he would have been more astonished and anguished to find the "people's representatives" having become millionaires and some even billionaires while millions of people continue to be poverty stricken and the same old "slum dogs." Shri Kulkarani's question now understandably would have been where from the people's representatives could get hold of Alladdin's magic lamp to have become millionaires and billionaires overnight? If so why did not they think of the people being their representatives to remove their poverty too. Shri Kulkarni's passing away was indeed a great loss. The number of such persons who practised and advocated ethical values and standards in life is diminishing fast.

I was rather pained and surprised to read in the papers, that soon after the House had paid tributes to Shri Kulkarni on his sad demise, a notice too was issued on the same day to his widow that she would have to vacate the residential house allotted to Shri Kulkarni before 28th June 1992 i.e. within a short time after his demise. This was indeed a shocking and most impolite way of informing Mrs. Kulkarni about the need for her to vacate the house by the specified date. It amounted to a very heartless and insensitive way of enforcing the house allotment rules. Fortunately, soon after the notice came to the knowledge of the Members of the House and the Deputy Chairman, corrective steps were taken. An inquiry was also ordered, as to why a notice was issued in such uncalled for haste. But for these corrective steps much of the sympathy and sadness expressed on Shri Kulkarni's death by the Members in the House would have been meaningless.

The unfortunate incident took place presumably because the relevant house allotment rules lay down that a Member's entitlement to residential facilities expires within a few weeks after he ceases to be a Member or on his demise. However, if some responsible officer in the Rajya Sabha Secretariat had applied his mind a notice in pursuance of the rules could have been issued after a decent interval. More appropriately, in such a case some senior officer of the Rajya Sabha Secretariat could have personally called on Mrs. Kulkarni and politely explained to her the rule position regarding the duration of entitlement of houses to the family of the demised Member. There are certainly decent ways of performing even unpleasant duties. However, ethos and culture of our public services presently appear to be anything but decent and polite. This case is a typical example of the general lack of good, helpful and dignified behaviour in most of our public services in performing their duties. Such faulty behaviour is seen, more or less, in all categories of public servants no matter whether they belong to the Legislature, the Judiciary or the Executive organs of the state. The acts of omissions and commissions of the public servants of the executive branch are however more visible since they have wider and more frequent public contacts and dealings. There are undoubtedly several considerate, helpful and more humane officials as well, who try to implement even unpleasant rules or orders in a manner which would cause least amount of mental agony or harm to the persons concerned. But overwhelming number of public servants in India are viewed to be negative and unhelpful in their work and outlook. They find excuse after excuse for not being sympathetic and helpful.

Another widely held public view is that government officials act with greater speed in discharging negative or unpleasant duties than in performing helpful and beneficial work. The unfortunate notice issued to Mrs. Kulkarni so promptly is only an example of the speed in which a harmful or negative work is done by public officials (barring exceptions) in the name of enforcement of laws and rules. The common citizens face such acts of unsympathetic behaviour and bureaucratic responses almost daily from the lower level officials of the local bodies, State or Central Government authorities. For example, often telephone and electricity bills (of the Public Sector Units) are received after months of delay and with accumulated large payment liabilities. Even though there may be complaints of wrong billing and other inaccuracies, no heed is generally given to these but extreme speed is shown to disconnect telephone or stop supply of electricity if there is slight delay in making payments. Hardly any consideration is shown to requests to delay such disconnections on account of some one being critically ill in the family or that the family is in the midst of performing some important social or religious function with guests around. The general excuse given is that rules do not permit any exception being made. The experience of most aggrieved citizens is that all such rules vanish in thin air when suitable illegal payments are made to the persons concerned. The disconnections thereafter could be delayed as long as desired. For a law abiding citizen however it is generally a frustrating experience to get the disconnected connection restored after the bill amount has been paid. The official machinery in such cases moves grudgingly and very slowly. It has its own ethics of "work to rule" which are invariably to the disadvantage of the public. They abuse their powers in all possible ways to extort illegal money with no sense of guilt. This kind of unsympathetic behavioiur and corrupt motives on the part of public officials have unfortunately become widespread being common in practically every sphere of their public dealings. The malady is getting worse with every passing day. The display of authoritarianism, arbitrariness and arrogance in public dealings of the colonial era have not shown any perceptible change for the better. In fact these faults are said to be on the rise. There is also politicalisation of officials at the lower levels to some extent. Due to this, officers at higher levels feel somewhat marginalised and ineffective in their supervisory roles. The lower level officials in some cases have become pawns of unscrupulous politicians. Public complaints can do no harm to these indifferent or ill-behaving officials so long as they look after the interests of their political masters and enjoy their protection. Application of the laws, rules, orders etc. under which unpleasant things are said to be done due to lack of discretion is not always valid. For, generally all laws and rules do provide a general clause of exception which permits suitable relaxations being made in their application where "undue hardship" is likely to be caused. Any such relaxation, of course, requires approval of a senior level competent authority. This kind of legal provision for making exception is based on the law of natural justice. Time, place and circumstances in which an individual is placed are normally to be taken into consideration in applying to him the laws and rules where required. Unfortunately, our trumpeted "rule of law" is fast degenerating into "rule of the petty officials." They have practically a free hand to set any law into motion at their sweet will for its slightest breach even of a technical nature only. "Justice tempered with mercy" is a concept virtually unknown to the bulk of our official machinery. For most of them payment of illegal money alone can temper justice. They have also little to do with compassion or "human face." This has made a mockery of the promise to ensure the dignity of the individual by the state as enshrined in our Constitution. It is unfortunate that due to all such conduct and behaviour of the public servants in India, specially the "Police", the administrative machinery is viewed with contempt by the public at large. The administration is generally taken to be more harmful than helpful to the people. Accordingly any communication from a department of Government received by post by a citizen raises apprehensions in his mind even before he reads the same. The reason usually given for this is that only harmful and negative communications are sent by the public authorities by normal post. To get any beneficial order or decision of government one has not only to make several trips to the concerned office but also incur some corruption expenditure for the same.

To improve the standing and esteem of public services among the citizens it is necessary to change the negative and unhelpful attitudes of the public servants. For this they have to be visibly pro-people and genuinely concerned with their problems. Much can be done to improve the attitude and behaviour of public servants through proper training, guidance, supervision and good examples. The training of public functionaries should cover not only vocational knowledge and skills but also behavioural aspects. Laws and rules have no doubt to be enforced however pleasant or unpleasant these may be but in doing so there should be no lack of good manners and politeness. Dignity of the individual concerned has to be kept in mind. Under the prevailing culture and ethos, greater emphasis is laid on observing the formalities rather than the substance and spirit behind the laws and rules in their implementation. Mindless and mechanical application of laws and rules are the important causes for the dissatisfaction and the poor image of public servants among the people. These shortcomings and defects are remediable if there is proper understanding and desire to rectify them. Regrettably, however, not much concern is being shown to improve the conduct and behaviour of our public servants towards the general public. Their shameless indulgence in corruption is another serious fault which has lowered their image in the eyes of the public. Corruption among them has become so deep-rooted and widespread that it now appears to be as incurable as the fatal ailment of cancer in the human body. This disease of corruption though had been detected long back but not much was done for its prevention and cure. It has accordingly reached its present fatal stage. The kind of strong will and determination that are now required to curb corruption are also missing. Hopefully things may improve in days to come as ultimately truth and order in human societies are generally restored by some beneficial forces – human or divine. In the long run smooth and peaceful survival of society would depend on an honest, efficient and pro-people public service machinery of the state. The developmental goals of the government may not fructify without an effective delivery machinery of the public services. There is, therefore, serious need and urgency to improve the image and quality of our public administration and the persons engaged in it. As a proof of such improvement, the people in general should feel confident to approach the public servants for solving their administration related problems. The public servants should in their turn show that they are part of the people and have been appointed to serve them in every possible manner.

This reminds me of the advice Sardar Vallabhbhai Patel, Home Minister and Deputy Prime Minister of India, gave to a batch of IAS officers under training in New Delhi after independence. He said:

> "Perhaps you are aware of the saying which is current in India regarding the past civil service, which is known as the Indian Civil Service (ICS), that is neither Indian, nor civil, nor imbued with any spirit of service. In a true sense, it is

not Indian because the Indian Civil Servants are mostly anglicised, their training was in foreign lands and they had to serve foreign masters. Therefore, in effect the whole service was known not to be Indian, nor to be civil, nor imbued with any spirit of service, and yet it was known as Indian Civil Service. The thing is now going to change."

He hoped and expected that the IAS officers of free India replacing the ICS officers would show better behaviour and attitude towards the people and work for their genuine well-being. His words were:

"Your predecessors were brought up in the traditions in which they felt out of touch and kept themselves aloof from the common run of the people. It will be your bounden duty to treat the common men in India as your own or to put it correctly, to feel yourself to be one of them and amongst them, and you will have to learn not to despise or to disregard them. In other words, you will have to adopt yourselves to democratic ways of administration."

Concluding his talk Sardar Patel said:

"I would advise you to maintain to the utmost the impartiality and incorruptibility of administration. A Civil Servant cannot afford to and must not, take part in politics. Nor must he involve himself in communal wrangles. To depart from the path of rectitude in either of these respects is to debase public service and to lower its dignity. Similarly no service worth the name can claim to exist if it does not have in view the achievement of the highest standard of or part of them hope that you who are now starting, as it were, a new generation of Civil Servants, will not be misled by black sheep in the fold, but render your service without fear or favour and without any expectations of extraneous rewards."

The advice of Sardar Patel to the new IAS recruits would equally apply to all the civil servants of free India to whatever services they may belong and whatever high or low positions they may be holding in the states or in the Central Government. They have to be people friendly and do their best in the service of the people as they being Indians are part of them and not above them. They have to be truly "Public servants" not only in name, but in the actual performance of their public duties.

7

NEED FOR GREATER FISCAL DISCIPLINE AND ECONOMY IN EXPENDITURE

The budget documents of the Central and State Governments for the past several years show that they have been living much beyond their means violating necessary financial propriety and economy. Economists and financial experts all these years have been constantly but vainly highlighting the ever rising imbalances between the revenue receipts and non-plan expenditure of the State and Central Governments affecting adversely their economic development and growth. The non-plan expenditure has been continuously exceeding revenue receipts to such a large extent that some states at times faced problems to pay even salary and wages to their employees on time. Due to financial constraints hundreds of their schools are without buildings and teachers, many of their hospitals have no doctors, medical equipments and even medicines. In some places government vehicles find it difficult to buy petrol and lubricants on credit as the governments concerned are not considered credit worthy by the private petrol pump owners. For similar reasons private chemists hesitate to supply medicines to government hospitals on credit. Such is the poor financial image of some states. These states are virtually bankrupt and struggle to make their both ends meet through large market borrowings each year resulting in heavy debt burdens. They are to a large extent living on borrowed funds. As a result their accumulated debt burdens have become quite massive servicing of which alone is eating away bulk of the revenue receipts. Their poor fiscal health may be judged from the debt and other liability figures given below:

Outstanding Liabilities of all the States

Year	*Total Liabilities*	*As % of GDP (Rs. in crore)*
1993-94	160077	13.6
1995-95	184527	18.2
1995-96	212225	17.9
1996-97	243525	17.8
1997-98	281207	18.5
1998-99	341978	19.6
1999-2000	420132	21.7
2000-01	498092	23.8
2001-02	586687	25.7
2002-03 (RE)	688421	27.9
2003-04 (RE)	791400	28.7

Source: Reserve Bank of India Reports.

It may be seen that the outstanding debt and other liabilities of the states increased from around Rs. 1,60,000 crore (in round figures) in 1993-94 to about Rs. 8 lakh crore in 2003-04 (BE) or about five-fold because of unchecked expenditure and huge borrowings each year to balance their annual budgets. According to the 13th Finance Commission Report (Vol. II) of December 2009 the outstanding debt of all states as on 31.3.2010 would be Rs. 16,15,073 or over sixteen lakh crores. (Annexure 7.4 para 7.68)

The factors causing deterioration in the fiscal health of the states according to the *Economic Survey (2003-04)*, include growing burden of interest payment on outstanding debts; higher pension liabilities and administrative expenditure, losses of the state-owned PSUs; inappropriate user charges on supply of electricity, irrigation, and drinking water, etc. As a cumulative result of all this their *"revenue deficit"* or excess of revenue expenditure over revenue receipts increased from Rs. 5309 crore in 1990-91 to Rs. 61,240 crore in 2002-03 (RE) i.e. nearly twelve times.

So far as the Central Government is concerned the budget documents for 2010-11 and the *Economic Survey (2009-10)* reveal that its financial situation too is dismal.

The revenue receipts and revenue expenditure figures of the Central Government for the last few years i.e. from 2001-02 to 2010-11 given in *Annexures 1* and *2* (according to Budget documents) show their ever-widening gap. This gap or "revenue deficit" was only Rs. 18,562 crore in 1990-91 but rose to Rs. 100,162 crores in 2001-02 and to Rs. 3,29,061 crores in 2009-10. The Centre's revenue receipts now meet only around 70 per cent of its revenue expenditure and the balance nearly 30 per cent is met through loans and borrowings of one kind or the other involving interest payment liability. As a result the accumulated debt of the Central Government has become quite massive (as may be seen from Annexure 3) with large annual interest payment liabilities. Trends of receipts and expenditure and interest payment liability may be seen in *Annexures 1* and *2*. The revenue receipts for the year 2010-11 have been estimated to be Rs. 6,82,212 crores and the non-plan expenditure is estimated to be Rs. 7,35,657 crores. After adding the plan expenditure for the year 2010-11 the fiscal deficit would be a huge amount of Rs. 3,81,408 crores. The rising trends in fiscal and revenue deficits year after year may be seen in Annexure 4. (according to Budget documents)

The 2004-05 Budget showed the net outstanding debt and other liabilities of the Central Government to be Rs. 19,85,866.91 crores, or say Rs. 20 lakh crores (in round figures) involving interest payment liability of Rs. 1,29,500 crores for that year. These net debt and other liability figures after 5 years jumped to nearly Rs. 35 lakh crore (or nearly 15 lakh crores more) according to the budget estimates of 2009-10 with interest payment liability of Rs. 2,25,511 crore for the year (please see Annexures 1 and 2). The latest liability figures of the Central Government for the budget year 2010-11 has been estimated to be over Rs. 39 lakh crores and interest liability nearly Rs. 2.50 lakh crore (in round figures). Incidentally the total debt of the Central Government was a meagre Rs. 2,565 crore in 1950-51 which during about six decades of planned development has risen to the huge size of around Rs. 39 lakh crore. This can hardly be called "self-sustaining" development and growth as was the objective behind the Five Year Plans of economic development. Due to lack of adequate returns from past investments government has been resorting to heavy market borrowings to finance the whole of development expenditure every year. Even, as mentioned earlier, around 30 per cent of the day to day consumptive (or revenue) expenditure is also met through loans and borrowings. Thus the Central Government like the states too is living on borrowed funds. This unfortunate reality has to be kept in mind before pressing government to increase the size of development expenditure. For more expenditure would mean more borrowings and more interest payments liability. Already expenditure on interest payment accounts for about 30 per cent of the total government expenditure and more than 35 per cent of revenue expenditure. Interest payment therefore presently eats up nearly 50 per cent of the revenue receipts of the Central Government *(Economic Survey 2003-04)*. If the present high level of borrowings continue to finance a large part of the revenue expenditure and the whole of Plan or development expenditure it may not be far too long when the entire revenue receipts of the Central Government may be pre-empted for interest payment alone. For, any increase in debt will increase interest payment which in turn will necessitate further build up of debt. This vicious circle has the danger of driving the country into a serious debt trap. Therefore, there is need for greater fiscal discipline and economy in expenditure. Large scale expenditure on populist schemes for electoral gains may not therefore be in the interest of fiscal consolidation. Such a policy of "Rinam kritwa ghritam pibet" (or borrow and live well) may prove to be shortsighted.

The growing fiscal and revenue deficits all these years have no doubt been matters of concern to the successive Union Finance Ministers as may be seen from some of their budget speeches, relevant extracts of which are quoted below.

Shri Vishwanath Pratap Singh presenting budget for 1985-86 (16th March, 1985) had stated:

> "...as we enter the Seventh Plan, the resource constraint has become acute, both at the Centre, and the States. The basic problem is that our non-Plan expenditure has been increasing at a rate substantially faster than the growth of current revenues. As a result, budgetary resources for the Plan have been severely eroded. Defence, interest payments, and food and fertiliser subsidies now account for nearly 70 per cent of the non-Plan revenue expenditure of the Centre. A sizeable part of the remaining 30 per cent of such expenditure is accounted for by essential maintenance, social and community services, and grants to states. Further, the increase in non-Plan expenditures of the States has meant larger transfers to States on this account."

To finance plan expenditure he stated:

"...we have been able to finance large increases in the Annual Plan largely through borrowings, both external and internal. However, this cannot go on indefinitely. The process of pruning budgetary expenditure at the Centre and the States, however, painful, must begin so that the necessary adjustment can take place over a period of time."

Shri V.P. Singh's above warnings and advice remained unheeded as the debt burden continued to increase to meet the ever rising fiscal deficit. The basic problems causing fiscal imbalances at that time were still there for the subsequent Finance Ministers for years to express their helplessness as stated below:

Prof. Madhu Dandavate presenting the budget for 1990-91 (19 March, 1990) had stated that:

"...the management of the (fiscal) deficit will require the containment of expenditure growth. I can assure the House that we will spare no effort to reduce the burden of administrative expenditure. But the restraint of expenditure also requires careful consideration of other areas of public spending which involve implicit or explicit subsidies. We have to ask ourselves whether these subsidies are really reaching the people they are meant to serve or whether there is a better way of providing the same benefit."

After the above observation also no serious attempt to reduce administrative expenditure or expenditure on subsidies appeared to have been made as expenditure on these continued to rise as before.

Shri Manmohan Singh presenting the budget for 1993-94 (27th February, 1993) highlighted that:

"...fiscal discipline was necessary because the government had lived for too long beyond its means. The rising fiscal deficits of the Central Government were the root cause of our balance of payments problem, rising prices and high rate of interest. We have made good progress by reducing the fiscal deficit from 8.4 per cent of GDP in 1990-91 to about 5 per cent in the current year (1992-93)."

The next year while presenting the budget for 1994-95 (28th February, 1994) he again emphasised the continuing problem of fiscal deficit when he said:

"Honourable Members will appreciate that the major part of interest burden is a legacy from the past and it continues to grow because of the continued high level of government borrowing. Interest payments can be reduced only if we can implement a programme of phased reduction in the government's total borrowing requirements to meet fiscal deficit. This can become a reality only if our tax system becomes more buoyant, our public enterprises generate more internal resources and we reduce expenditure on subsidies. A bold programme for disinvestment of government equity in public enterprises and earmarking a part of the sale proceeds for debt reduction would also be of great help."

In spite of the above diagnosis of the country's fiscal ills by Dr. Manmohan Singh and the several remedial measures suggested by him, hardly any improvements took place. There was practically no higher generation of resources by the PSUs nor any reduction of expenditure on subsidies. The tax buoyancy too was at the normal average growth rate. Since, neither revenue increased, nor expenditure declined significantly, the fiscal and revenue deficits kept rising as before.

Shri Yashwant Sinha presenting the budget for 2000-01 (29th February, 2000) also voiced the usual concerns of his predecessors by saying:

"...today, we must squarely confront and overcome the critical challenge posed by a weakening fiscal situation. A long history of high fiscal deficits has left us with a legacy of huge public debt and an ever-growing bill of interest payments." He also proposed the following corrective measures:

- Stringent expenditure control of non-productive expenditure, rationalistion of subsidies and improvement in the quality of government expenditure.
- Acceleration of the privatization process and restructuring of public enterprises.
- Revenue enhancement through widening of the tax base and administration of a fair and equitable tax regime.

The following year while presenting the Budget for 2001-02 (28th February, 2001) he repeated the same old concerns:

- "Interest payments now consume over 69 per cent of the Centre's tax revenue.

- Subsidies continue to increase in unaffordable levels and do not necessarily reach the deserving beneficiaries.
- The pension liability of the Government is becoming onerous."

In sum, in spite of the warnings and concerns expressed by successive Finance Ministers in the past with regard to the problem of fiscal imbalance it continues to haunt the country even now (2010). In fact the cancer of fiscal deficit due to lack of effective remedial actions has got aggravated year after year and now appears to have become beyond easy solution. In the recent years as stated in the *Economic Survey (2003-04)* para 3.23, three-fourth of the total fiscal deficit is on account of revenue deficit leaving very limited room for the government to deploy its borrowings in a productive manner. As mentioned earlier a good part of the borrowed funds are being utilized to meet ordinary consumption expenditure like pay, pension and wages etc. and the unavoidable interest payment on heavy debts. Such large unproductive uses of national savings through borrowings is also adversely affecting growth oriented investments to meet the challenges of poverty and unemployment. Poverty alleviation and employment generation were the main objectives of our development plans. But poverty still continues to be a serious problem even after completion of ten Five Year Plans. For even now (2010) over 300 millions of our people live below the poverty line (BPL) and over 40 millions are unemployed according to official figures. The non-official figures of BPL families are of course much higher. Obviously both qualitatively and quantitatively productive or growth oriented investments have been very much less than what was required. Much more needs to be done by mobilising higher financial resources for productive investments and matching returns from such investments. The *Annual Report of the RBI (2002-03)* points out that fiscal imbalances is the main cause affecting development expenditure. It says:

> "the burden of the unrelenting expansion in interest outgoes has devolved on productive elements of fiscal spending. The overarching priority attached to reduction of expenditure to meet deficit targets has accentuated the erosion of capital outlays with serious implications for expanding the productive capacity of the economy in the future. Expenditure on subsidies has remained impervious to fiscal adjustments, while spending on social infrastructure continues to remain low."

"Moreover, the monotonic rise in public debt has eroded the Government sector's ability to generate savings and to service its internal debt. The 'quality' of the fiscal deficit has worsened, with the revenue deficit having increased substantially indicating that a larger share of borrowed fund is pre-empted by consumption expenditure."

The RBI's *Report on Currency and Finance 2002-03* (page 19) also says:

"the revenue deficit constituted 81.9 per cent of the GFD (Gross Fiscal Deficit) as against 73.1 per cent projected in the budget estimates for 2003-04 indicating that a larger share of borrowed resources is being used for current expenditure leaving a lesser amount for investment purposes."

Since various remedial measures proposed earlier by successive Finance Ministers to correct fiscal imbalance had largely remained unimplemented, the Central Government decided to enact a law to make itself legally bound to take all necessary measures to reduce fiscal and revenue deficits within a prescribed timeframe. This led to the enactment of the *Fiscal Responsibility and Budget Management Act, 2003 (FRBMA)* by Parliament.

Section 4 (1) of the **FRBM Act** required the Central Government to eliminate revenue deficit by the 31st March 2008 (which was later extended to 2009) and thereafter build up adequate revenue surplus. The new Act also required the Central Government to specify annual targets of reduction of fiscal and revenue deficits. The government's power of unlimited borrowing from the RBI was also very much restricted. In addition government was made more accountable to Parliament for sound fiscal management by requiring the Finance Minister under the new law to lay before Parliament along with the annual budget, three other statements viz., (1) Medium Term Fiscal Policy Statement; (2) Fiscal Policy Strategy Statement; and (3) Macro-economic Framework Statement. He was also required to make a quarterly review of trends in government receipts and expenditure in relation to the budget estimates and place the same before Parliament for its scrutiny and discussion. Thus the Finance Minister's accountability to Parliament to reduce fiscal deficit was more clearly laid down. However, due to the existing large revenue expenditure commitments of government the timeframe laid down for reducing fiscal deficit was found to be too short. In fact in the statement placed before Parliament on the 16th February, 2009 as required under the FRBM Act it was stated by the Finance Minister that due to certain compelling reasons the revenue deficit instead of being brought down may go up. The reasons for the failure to reduce revenue deficit were stated to be: *(a)* higher wage and pension bills on account of the Sixth Pay Commission recommendations; *(b)* increased subsidy on food, fertilizer and petroleum products; and *(c)* higher interest payment liabilities.

The Finance Minister Pranab Mukherjee in his budget speech of July 2009 stated that due to the possibility of the economic downturn (due to global economic slowdown) persisting for some time more the gross tax receipts were estimated to be lower at Rs. 6,41,079 crores for 2009-10 as against the higher estimated amount of Rs. 6,87,715 crore in BE 2008-09. He also stated that the revenue deficit will rise to 4.8 per cent pf GDP and fiscal deficit to 6.8 per cent against much lower projections i.e. 1 per cent and 2.5 per cent of revenue and fiscal deficit respectively made earlier. He admitted, like the other previous Finance Ministers, that "this level of deficit is a matter of concern and Government will address this issue in right earnest to come back to the path of fiscal consolidation at the earliest." In his budget speech for 2010-11 Shri Pranab Mukherjee stated that "...as against a fiscal deficit of 7.8 per cent in 2008-09 inclusive of oil and fertilizer bonds, the comparable fiscal deficit is 6.9 per cent as per the Revised Estimates for 2009-10." While accepting that "fiscal policy has to be guided by the required framework of fiscal prudence he provided for a lower fiscal deficit of 5.5 per cent for the year 2010-11 which works out to Rs. 3,81,408 crores. It is unlikely that this assurance of lower fiscal deficit would fructify in the near future in view of some populist schemes with massive expenditure liabilities already announced by the government and provided in the budget for 2010-11. The Thirteenth Finance Commission in para 4.26 of its Report (December 2009) has also drawn attention of the government to the need for fiscal discipline and correction as stated below:

> "The fiscal correction path, following the enactment of FRBMA was more or less on track till 2007-08, after a pause in 2005-06. A number of developments, particularly the slowdown of the economy and its adverse impact on revenue growth, increasing commodity prices, anti-recessionary

measures, farm loan waiver and implemen-tation of the recommendations of the Sixth CPC, have resulted in a worsening, going beyond the reversal of the fiscal correction achieved till 2007-08."

"Resumption of the path of fiscal correction is crucial to achieving a sustainable fiscal situation at the Centre. Though softening of international oil prices has provided some relief, reverting to the high growth path and a strategy to exit from the expansionary fiscal stance put in place as a countercyclical measure will hold the key to the fiscal correction. In recent years, off-budget liabilities of the Centre have assumed alarming proportions. In 2008-09, off-budget bonds issued to oil marketing and fertilizer companies amounted to Rs. 95.942 crore or 1.80 per cent of GDP."

The global economic slowdown from the year 2007-08 onwards undoubtedly had its adverse impact on the Indian economy too. It reduced exports of textiles, gems and jewellery, minerals, handicrafts, etc., etc. Tax revenue of the Central Government accordingly came down significantly. There was also large scale unemployment in export oriented sectors. Government had therefore to take some financial measures to stimulate the economy. These corrective measures included tax relief to boost demand for goods and services and higher government expenditure to generate employment. These measures understandably resulted in higher revenue and fiscal deficits and accordingly higher market borrowings to balance the budget. According to the 2009-10 Revised Budget figures for an estimated expenditure of Rs. 10,21,547 or say a little over ten lakh crores, Rs. 4,14,041 or a little over four lakh crores i.e. more than 40 per cent had to be found through market borrowings. Due to such financial constraints, government has limited capacity to invest in costly infrastructure projects with interest paying borrowed funds. Further if any such costly projects get delayed in their completion or suffer from cost over-runs, the fiscal problems would get aggravated. In fact this has been the sad state of affairs all these years. Again when the completed projects did not give the estimated financial returns, the fiscal deficit increased. These have been the important causes behind the financial crisis faced by the government year after year. Some illustrative examples of such cases of time and cost over-runs have been mentioned later. It is accordingly necessary that government must urgently find ways and means to control its expenditure and increase its revenue receipts. In brief for improving the present poor financial health of the government among others the following measures deserve attention:

1. The Revenue Receipts have to be significantly increased not so much by raising the present rates of taxes but by identifying and plugging loopholes in their collections fully. The unaccounted economic transactions giving rise to "Black Money" are estimated by some experts to be of the order of 40 per cent of India's GDP. If unearthed fully this huge "Black Money" could generate additional revenue income equal to if not more than the current annual revenue receipts of Rs. 6,82,212 crores estimated for the year 2010-11.
2. Thousands of persons who are well within the range of taxable income have reportedly somehow remained outside the taxation net. Such persons ought to be identified and made to pay their legitimate tax liabilities. This may require revamping of the tax administration machinery and improving its honesty and efficiency. Appropriate corruption prevention measures have to be taken.
3. Large-scale wasteful and infructuous expenditure some of which are pointed out by the C&AG from time to time in his audit reports have to be prevented. One of the latest audit report of the C&AG highlighted in the press (July 2009) revealed that more than a crore of rupees were misused by top defence officials for purchase of golf carts for their golf courses in place of wheel chairs for army hospitals. Another similar report disclosed that thousands of crores of rupees from the defence budget were misused in the purchase of unusable missiles and helicopters by the army. After purchase these were reportedly found to be duds. Another C&AG Report also found serious financial lapses in the purchase of an old Russian aircraft carrier "Admiral Gorshkov." The price paid as reported was over 60 per cent higher than the cost of buying a new aircraft carrier of the same type. Some have even called the aircraft carrier a "junk". Such deals which may have political compulsions, highlight the kind of wasteful expenditure incurred in costly defence purchases. Several cases of similar fruitless expenditure are reported from time to time in other organizations of the State and Central Governments as well.
4. There has also to be serious thinking to reduce expenditure

on subsidized sale of food, fertiliser and oil etc. as expenditure on this account is continuously rising significantly year after year.

5. The scheme to sell 25 kg. (which is being raised to 35 kg. under the proposed Food Security Act) of foodgrains (rice and wheat) at Rs. 3 a kg. by government to each poor family per month though desirable and well intended may not be affordable for too long a period of time. For if this scheme is to be seriously and honestly implemented as visualized under the proposed Food Security Act the number of eligible beneficiaries under it may run into 500 to 700 millions of poor people (the latest Tendulkar Committee calculations is that 38 per cent of the country's population or a little over 400 millions) belong to BPL. The expenditure involved on this account may be much beyond the present financial capacity of the government living on borrowed funds. The more it spends, the more it will have to borrow. Wisdom may therefore lie to invest more funds on employment generating programmes to enable the unemployed poor people to get jobs and buy foodgrains at prevailing prices out of their earned incomes. That would also add dignity to their life and living. Doles and charity are not the right way to fight poverty. In fact such schemes may perpetuate poverty by making people complacent and easy going.
6. No policy of reform with a "human face" should degenerate into cheap "populism." The announcement to supply free power to all farmers by a number of states could hardly come within the scope of development with social justice or reform with a "human face." Supply of free power makes little economic sense when practically all the electricity undertakings are undergoing losses running into thousands of crores of rupees. People would prefer to have uninterrupted power supply at reasonable rates rather than free supply with load shedding for long periods of time. At times there is no power supply for days together.
7. Similarly, when large quantities of irrigation water is wasted due to poor maintenance of canals and tube wells for lack of funds, supply of free irrigation water to farmers is a short-sighted policy. Large productive investments on water and power projects ought to give reasonable financial returns both

for making fresh investments and for proper maintenance of projects in operation.

8. Time and again waving the repayment of cooperative or bank loans or electricity dues of the farmers are financially undesirable and short-sighted measures. To facilitate regular and adequate credit flows to millions of needy farmers every year it is necessary to promote their habit of repaying old loans before taking fresh loans. To waive electricity dues (as announced by the Haryana Government in 2009) on the eve of elections may also encourage wasteful use of electricity. Farmers who paid their dues on time will also feel cheated by such waiver of dues of defaulting farmers.

There is need and scope to observe economy in many other spheres. Several study reports on expenditure control in the past have identified some such areas where economy is possible. For example, far too many commissions and committees of inquiry are appointed from time to time by Government on the slightest pretexts. But once appointed these bodies are virtually forgotten and become financial burdens for long periods of time. One such case was that of the Babri structure demolition Commission which remained in existence for 17 long years (1992-2009) costing over Rs. 8 crores to the Central Government. Its terms were routinely extended from time to time. After long lapse of time the reports of such commissions could hardly be of much use or relevance.

Similarly several committees of the state legislatures as also of parliament reportedly travel too often and too much within and outside the country involving huge expenditure on the boarding and lodging of their members. Many of such tours according to media reports in the past were hardly necessary. For example, a Parliamentary Committee on the use of Hindi in government offices reportedly went on tour to several foreign countries presumably to find out the use of Hindi in the Indian embassies abroad! Mega cabinets in the states as also at the centre are unduly costly and are also matters of public ridicule. Their sizes have only recently been fixed at lower levels depending on the membership strength of the legislatures. But still there is scope to reduce the size of the council of ministers at the Central and State levels. Recently (2010) some Ministers of State at the Centre complained to the Prime Minister (as reported in the Press) that they have no work to do as the Cabinet Ministers concerned had not allotted any work to them. One has to assume that there is no worthwhile work for them even though on grounds of coalition politics they had to be appointed.

Even if expenditure of the above nature may be a very small portion of the total government expenditure, still these need to be curtailed for the sake of observing due economy in the spending of public money. Public confidence in the government as a reliable trustee of public funds has to be ensured. There should be no room to think that public money is nobody's money and could be unthinkingly spent according to the sweet will of any person in power. It is unfortunate to know periodically through the media that huge quantities of foodgrains (rice and wheat) running into millions of tons procured annually by the Food Corporation of India (FCI) become rotten and unfit for human consumption due to their poor storage in the open. The explanation given for this utter lack of concern for public property and funds is that there is shortage of the required covered storage space. If that be so, and if there were due sensitivity to prevent wastage of public funds, the size of procurement could have been suitably reduced. Unfortunately, this long prevailing practice of wasting foodgrains and funds invested in them has not been prevented yet. This large-scale procurement is on the plea of helping the farmers by timely buying their surplus produce at the minimum support price announced by the government each year. The net result, however, is the massive wastage of foodgrains produced with hard labour of the farmers after utilizing all kinds of financial subsidies provided by the government.

When we compare the present day lack of concern in the spending of public funds with the high sense of economy and austerity observed by the political leaders and officials of the earlier years we can see the vast difference. I am reminded, in this connection, Shri Lal Bahadur Shastriji's instructions as the Union Home Minister to us in the early 60s that the petrol consumption of his official car should be regularly monitored. As a Deputy Secretary then in the Home Ministry the author was responsible as a part of his duty to ensure economy in the in-house expenditure of the Ministry. Shastriji wanted that the Home Minister's office should come within the scope of observing strict economy in expenditure in all respects i.e., appointment of his personal staff, use of staff cars, serving of tea/coffee etc. to VIP visitors to his office. Similar norms of economy in expenditure were observed by the previous Home Minister, Shri Govind Ballabh Pant, under whom also I had the privilege to work. Pantji's advice was that the tax payer's money is hard earned money and government as the trustee of the public funds must ensure that "every single pie" of it is properly spent and utilized for the fullest benefit of the citizens.

The author also remembers another important case of adhering to such strict norms of economy. It related to a proposal from the Prime Minister Pandit Jawaharlal Nehru's office to grant a third Special Pay of Rs. 75 per month to his P.A. Shri Yash Pal Kapoor. Shri Kapoor was already getting one special pay of Rs. 75 p.m. for being posted in the PM's office and one more for taking Hindi dictations. The proposal for another special pay for some other work done by him was examined in our branch of the Home Ministry which dealt with the office establishment matters of all union ministers including the P.M. These related to the number, pay, allowances, and promotion etc. of their personal staff. To grant a third Special Pay to Shri Yash Pal Kapoor was found to be against the laid down norms of propriety and economy in expenditure. It was therefore not allowed with the approval of Shastriji, the then Home Minister. In fact Shastriji called me to discuss if there was any scope to make an exception. My humble reply was that as Home Minister he could certainly make an exception and relax the existing norms of financial propriety in the case of the PM's office. However, there was the risk of citing it as a precedent for similar requests by other cabinet ministers on one ground or the other. After giving some thought Shastriji finally decided not to set an unhealthy precedent. It was realized that even "exceptions" could be viewed as precedents. The PM's office too did not pursue the matter further on being informed of the grounds for disallowing the third special pay. Incidentally Shri Yash Pal Kapoor in later years by virtue of his post in the PM's office gained much political weight. He was also nominated as a Member of the Rajya Sabha if I remember correctly.

Another important cause of the growing fiscal crisis is that many mega infrastructure development projects are suffering from considerable time and cost-over runs. There are nil or little returns for years together from the investments already made in such projects. By way of example some such long delayed projects are listed in the table below:

Sectorwise Project with Cost and Time Over-run (June 04)

(Rs. in crore)

S.No.	*Sector*	*No. of Projects*	*Latest Cost*	*Anticipated Cost*	*Time Over-run in Months*
1	*2*	*3*	*4*	*5*	*6*
1.	Atomic Energy	1	28.0	28.0	—
2.	Civil Aviation	2	103.3	111.7	—
3.	Coal	17	1312.5	1243.4	3 to 108
4.	Fertilisers	1	509.4	509.4	—
5.	I&B	1	81.6	81.6	—
6.	Mines	2	2118.8	2118.8	23 to 52
7	Steel.	2	387.8	387.9	18 to 20
8.	Petroleum	13	15874.7	16242.7	3 to 15
9.	Power	19	18517.8	22603.4	2 to 60
10.	Railways	41	11247.3	14169.4	3 to 156
11.	Road Transport & Highways	73	14475.2	14443.1	2 to 65
12.	Shipping & Ports	20	1383.4	1438.3	3 to 63
13.	Telecommunications	7	447.1	447.1	3 to 24
14.	Urban Development	3	10631.9	10644.2	6 to 38

Source: Ministry of Statistics and Programme Implementation.

It is clear from the above table that some projects in core sectors like Power, Railways, Highways and Ports have already run into time over-run of five years or more. These include projects like the Daitari-Banspani Railway Line in Orissa which was due for completion in 1997 but was still incomplete (2004); Dulhasti Hydroelectric Power Project scheduled for completion in 1990 but was still not complete until 2004. There are several other such incomplete mega projects with thousands of crores of rupees locked up in them with no returns. These do adversely affect the finances of the government significantly. Our planning process ought to ensure that the on-going projects at advanced stages of completion are not delayed on account of low allocations or shortages of funds. Tendency to start new projects with priority of fund allocations to them on political considerations even by jeopardizing the timely completion of economically more fruitful ongoing projects by denying or inadequate allocation of funds to them need to be checked. High level monitoring of on-going mega projects costing say a thousand crore of rupees or more is very necessary to prevent undue delays in their completion. Such monitoring practice had been started in the early eighties by the then Prime Minister Smt. Indira Gandhi who used to take personal interest in the monitoring reports of major infrastructure projects. The author who then held the post of Secretary Economic Coordination in the Union Government looked after this monitoring work and reported to the PM directly. On several occasions the PM Mrs. Indira Gandhi visited the states to discuss with the concerned chief ministers and senior state officials the progress of mega irrigation and power projects largely funded with grants and loans from the Central Government. The author used to accompany the PM during her such state tours to ensure proper coordination between the Centre and the States relating to the execution of the selected developmental projects. Since the Prime Minister herself took keen interest in the timely completion of major infrastructure projects it greatly helped to curtail uncalled for delays. Realising the importance of this coordination and monitoring work a separate Ministry of Programme Implementation was set up a few years later for this purpose. It appears that with the passage of time this high level monitoring and coordination work has somewhat lost its past importance. That may be one of the reasons for the huge time and cost over-run in the completion of several mega projects contributing to the present fiscal problems.

To bring about fiscal consolidation and to eliminate fiscal and revenue deficits, it is necessary: *(a)* to control expenditure, *(b)* reduce borrowings, *(c)* mobilise other financial resources and *(d)* ensure past investments to start bearing fruits without further loss of time. The problems of fiscal imbalance and their solutions have thus many dimensions all of which need to be dealt with in a coordinated manner.

In this connection it is also important to speed up disinvestment of some portions of government holdings in selected PSUs. Such disinvestment in profit making PSUs could considerably add to government's financial resources. Such disinvestment income could partly or fully be set apart for funding infrastructure projects instead of funding them out of borrowed funds with interest liability. As mentioned earlier, Dr. Manmohan Singh as Finance Minister in 1991 had himself suggested this course of action to reduce the ever growing debt burden and fiscal deficit of the Central Government. He as the Prime Minister of the country now (2010) could follow his own prescribed remedy with greater drive and dynamism. In his earlier term as Prime Minister (from 2004 to 2009) he perhaps could not implement the intended disinvestment policy because of the strong opposition of his Left Party allies. Now that Dr. Manmohan Singh's government is no longer dependent on other parties, implementation of the disinvestment policy should be comparatively easier to mobilize non-tax and non-interest paying financial resources for development expenditure. A National Investment Fund (NIF) was of course set up in 2005 to deposit disinvestment receipts. But the condition was not to utilize the corpus of the NIF for any new development expenditure. It appears government is now restructuring the NIF to enable it to utilize the disinvestment receipts up to certain amounts per year for infrastructure and social sector development projects. This should no doubt help government in reducing its fiscal deficits to some extent. As stated by the Finance Minister in his Budget Speech for the Financial Year 2010-11 he hoped to raise Rs. 25,000 crores through disinvestment in the Financial Year 2009-10 and more i.e. around Rs. 40,000 crores in 2010-11. Hopefully this policy will be duly pursued to reduce the debt burden of the government. Instead of depending on costly borrowed funds government should utilize to the maximum extent possible the disinvestment funds for the execution of important infrastructure and social sector development schemes. This shift on resource mobilisation could help in controlling fiscal deficit only if along with it wasteful expenditure is also brought under strict control. Availability of more resources through disinvestment should not lead to more wasteful expenditure. If that happens the planned remedy of disinvestment to control fiscal deficit may worsen it further. The disinvestment receipts should not also be utilized to pay off the large accumulated debt. That as some say would amount to "selling family silver to pay off debts."

ANNEXURE-1

Trends in Receipts

(in crores of Rupees)

	Actuals 2001-02	*Actuals 2002-03*	*Actuals 2003-04*	*Actuals 2004-05*	*Actuals 2005-06*	*Actuals 2006-07*	*Actuals 2007-08*	*Actuals 2008-09*	*Revised 2009-2010*	*Budget 2010-11*
Revenue Receipts	201306	230834	263813	305991	347077	434387	541864	540259	577294	682212
(a) **Tax Revenue** (Net of State's Share) (Details in Annexure 7)	133532	158544	186982	224798	270264	351182	439547	443319	465103	534094
(b) **Non-Tax Revenue** (Details in Annexure 7)	67774	72299	76831	81193	76813	83205	102317	96940	112191	148118
Capital Receipts	162500	180531	21133	200291	179549	144482	197978	299863	449833	426537
1. Internal Debt-Market Borrowings (Net)	87724	97588	88860	46031	95374	110446	131768	233630	398411	345010
1.01 Gross Market Borrowings	114213	125000	135934	80350	131000	146000	168101	273000	451000	457143
1.02 Less Repayments	26489	27412	47074	34319	35626	35554	36333	39370	52589	112133
2. External Assistance (Net)	5601	-11934	-134488	14753	7472	8472	9315	11015	16535	22464
2.01 Gross External	14790	12352	11956	21855	14470	16358	16808	21022	27766	34735

Contd...

	Actuals 2001-02	*Actuals 2002-03*	*Actuals 2003-04*	*Actuals 2004-05*	*Actuals 2005-06*	*Actuals 2006-07*	*Actuals 2007-08*	*Actuals 2008-09*	*Revised 2009-2010*	*Budget 2010-11*
Borrowings 2.02 Less Repayments	9183	24296	25444	7102	6998	7886	7493	10007	11230	12271
3. Recovery of Loans	16403	34191	67165	62043	10645	5893	5100	6139	4245	5129
4. Small Savings (Net)	8755	—	—	—	—	—	-11302	-1302	13256	13256
5. State Provident Funds (Net)	4173	4621	4892	5310	5545	5178	3897	8041	8500	7000
6. Special Deposits (Net)	8070	9326	110	-5750	487	—	—	—	—	—
7. Disinvestment of equity in public sector enterprises	3646	3151	16953	4424	1581	534	38795	566	25958	40000
8. Other items of Capital receipts (Net)	28128	43588	46841	73580	58445	13959	20405	41774	-17081	-6321
Total Receipts	363806	411365	475146	506382	526626	578869	739842	839935	1027127	1108749
Deficit on Revenue Account	100162	107879	98261	78338	92300	80222	52569	253539	329061	276512
Primary Deficit	33495	27268	-815	-1140	13805	-7699	-44118	144788	194540	132745
Bud. Deficit/Draw-down of cash	-1496	1883	-3942	-1461	-20888	4517	-27171	43834	-5581	—
Fiscal Deficit	140955	145072	123273	125794	146435	142573	126912	336992	414040	381409

Contd...

ANNEXURE-2

Trends in Expenditure

(in crores of Rupees)

	Actuals 2001-02	*Actuals 2002-03*	*Actuals 2003-04*	*Actuals 2004-05*	*Actuals 2005-06*	*Actuals 2006-07*	*Actuals 2007-08*	*Actuals 2008-09**	*Revised 2009-2010*	*Budget 2010-11*
(*a*) Non-Plan Expenditure	**261116**	**301778**	**348923**	**365960**	**365100**	**413527**	**507589**	**608721**	**706371**	**735657**
1. Interest Payments	107460	117804	1240885	126934	132630	150272	171030	192204	219500	248664
2. Defence Expenditure	54266	55662	60066	75856	80549	85510	91681	114223	136264	147344
3. Subsidies	31210	42533	44323	45957	47522	57125	70926	139708	131025	116224
4. Grants to State & U.T. Governments	15327	13305	13720	14784	30475	35734	35769	38161	46610	46001
5. Grant to Foreign Governments	402	605	688	990	1214	1294	1355	1442	1569	1688
6. Pensions	14436	14496	15905	18300	20256	22104	24261	32940	42222	42840
7. Police	7248	8163	8829	10654	12379	13541	13924	19904	24590	22154
8. Other Non-Plan Revenue Expenditure	24364	27217	31111	33520	32526	38197	47103	68241	84712	75494
9. Non-Plan Capital Expenditure (Excluding Defence)	2815	13328	46746	34748	3357	6183	47891	7271	15338	31051
10. Loans & Advances to State & U.T. Govts.	-394	2491	78	612	89	102	86	86	88	89

Contd...

	Actuals 2001-02	*Actuals* 2002-03	*Actuals* 2003-04	*Actuals* 2004-05	*Actuals* 2005-06	*Actuals* 2006-07	*Actuals* 2007-08	*Actuals* 2008-09*	*Revised* 2009-2010	*Budget* 2010-11
11. Loans to Foreign Govts.	150	533	273	283	129	103	42	833	128	—
12. Other Loans	2595	3385	1587	1599	1796	1292	1465	790	1059	960
13. Non-Plan Expenditure of UTs without Legisiature	1237	1346	1509	1673	2178	2070	2056	2918	3256	3148
On Revenue Account	1305	1402	1569	1834	2305	2242	2274	3119	3266	3190
On Capital Account	-68	-56	-60	-161	-127	-172	-218	-201	-10	-42
(*b*) Plan Expenditure	**101194**	**111470**	**122280**	**132292**	**140638**	**169860**	**205082**	**275235**	**315176**	**373092**
On Revenue Account	61657	71569	78638	87494	111858	142418	173572	234774	264411	315125
On Capital Account	39537	39901	43642	44798	28780	27442	31510	40461	50765	57967
Total Expenditure	**362310**	**413248**	**471203**	**498252**	**505738**	**583387**	**712671**	**883956**	**1021547**	**1108749**
On Revenue Account	301468	338713	362074	384329	439376	514609	594433	793798	906355	958724
On Capital Account	60842	74535	109129	113923	66362	68778	118238	90158	115192	150025

Note: *Actuals of 2008-09 are provisional.

ANNEXURE-3

Statement of Liabilities of the Central Government

(in crores of Rupees)

	Accounts					Revised	Budget
	1950-51	*2005-06*	*2006-07*	*2007-08*	*2008-09***	*2009-2010*	*2010-11*
(a) Public Debt	**2054.33**	**1484001.33**	**1647690.71**	**1920390.09**	**2151594.77**	**2477262.91**	**2898798.73**
1. Interest Debt	**2022.30**	**1389758.29**	**1544975.17**	**1808359.17**	**2028549.17**	**2337681.77**	**2736753.60**
of which under MSS	—	*29062.17*	*62973.95*	170553.77	88772.78	2737.00	50000.00
(i) Under Market Stabilisation Scheme							
(a) Dated securities under MSS	—	11000.00	22000.00	128317.00	79772.78	2737.00	50000.00
(b) 91 days Treasury Bills under MSS	—	—	14208.97	9631.77	—	—	—
(c) 182 days Treasury Bills under MSS	—	2917.21	7675.28	7605.00	—	—	—
(d) 364 days Treasury Bills under MSS	—	15144.96	19089.70	25000.00	9000.00	—	—
(ii) Market Loans (vide Annexure 4)	1444.45	862370.08	972800.89	1092467.57	1326093.61	1734504.63	2079534.63
(iii) Spl. Securities converted into Marketable Securities (vide Annex 4-A)	—	103817.95	100317.95	91317.95	86817.95	76817.95	76817.95
(iv) Spl. Securities (to Banks) converted into Marketable Securities	—	—	—	20808.75	20808.75	20808.75	20808.75

Contd...

	Accounts					Revised	Budget
	1950-51	*2005-06*	*2006-07*	*2007-08*	*2008-09***	*2009-2010*	*2010-11*
(*v*) Other Special Securities issued to Reserve Bank	—	1489.28	1489.28	1489.28	1489.28	1489.28	1489.28
(*vi*) 14 days Treasury Bills	—	39339.53	39475.31	68629.79	98662.88	98662.88	98662.88
(*vii*) 91 days Treasury Bills	358.02	16363.83	30801.70	30371.05	75594.76	735447.76	73547.76
(*viii*) 182 days Treasury Bills	—	6771.37	9255.69	9180.00	20175.00	22500.00	22500.00
(*ix*) 364 days Treasury Bills	—	29014.42	33368.70	32201.39	45545.89	41363.89	41363.89
(*x*) Compensation and other bonds	6.73	72760.38	62091.69	71321.19	47506.38	37753.33	31368.70
(*xi*) Securities issued to International Financial Institutions	212.60	25151.61	25798.49	24719.40	23085.34	20244.23	20152.17
(*xii*) Securities against small savings	—	203617.67	206601.52	195299.03	193996.55	207252.07	220507.59
2. External Debt*	**32.03**	**94243.04**	**102715.54**	**112030.92**	**123045.60**	**139581.04**	**162045.13**
(*b*) Other Liabilities	**8110.07**	**776143.72**	**890905.25**	**917035.29**	**1007583.25**	**108643.17**	**1045799.41**
1. National Small Savings Fund	336.87	413498.83	46809.62	478289.52	470140.77	473334.63	475927.31
2. State Provident Funds	95.05	66262.14	71439.92	75330.22	83377.44	91877.44	98877.44
3. Other Accounts	16.10	186920.97	220160.41	236372.57	325383.30	335938.15	341135.86
(*i*) Spl. Deposits of Non-Govt. Provident Funds, etc.	—	118256.90	117697.77	116451.90	114119.03	114119.03	114119.03
(*ii*) Other Items	16.10	68664.07	102462.64	119920.67	21164.27	221869.12	227016.83

Contd...

	Accounts					Revised	Budget
	1950-51	*2005-06*	*2006-07*	*2007-08*	*2008-09***	*2009-2010*	*2010-11*
4. Reserve Funds and Deposits	363.05	109461.78	131295.30	127042.98	128681.74	137442.95	129858.80
(*i*) Bearing interest	260.85	53649.96	62704.80	73055.56	78383.87	78076.88	83345.31
(*ii*) Not Bearing interest	102.20	55811.82	68590.50	53987.42	50297.87	59366.07	46513.49
Total Liabilities	**2865.40**	**2260145.05**	**2538595.96**	**2837425.38**	**3159178.02**	**3515905.98**	**3944598.14**
Amount due from Pakistan on account of share of pre-partition debt (approx.)	–300.00	–300.00	–300.00	–300.00	–300.00	–300.00	–300.00
Net Liabilities of the Central Government	**2565.40**	**2259845.05**	**2538295.96**	**2837125.38**	**3158878.02**	**3515605.98**	**3944298.14**
Excess of Capital Outlay and Loans over Liabilities	—	—	—	—	—	—	—
Total (Net)	**2565.40**	**2259845.00**	**2538295.96**	**2837125.38**	**3158878.02**	**3515605.98**	**3944298.14**

***Balances are according to book value.**

****Actuals of 2008-09 are provisional.**

ANNEXURE-4

Deficit Trends (घाटे की प्रवृत्तियाँ)

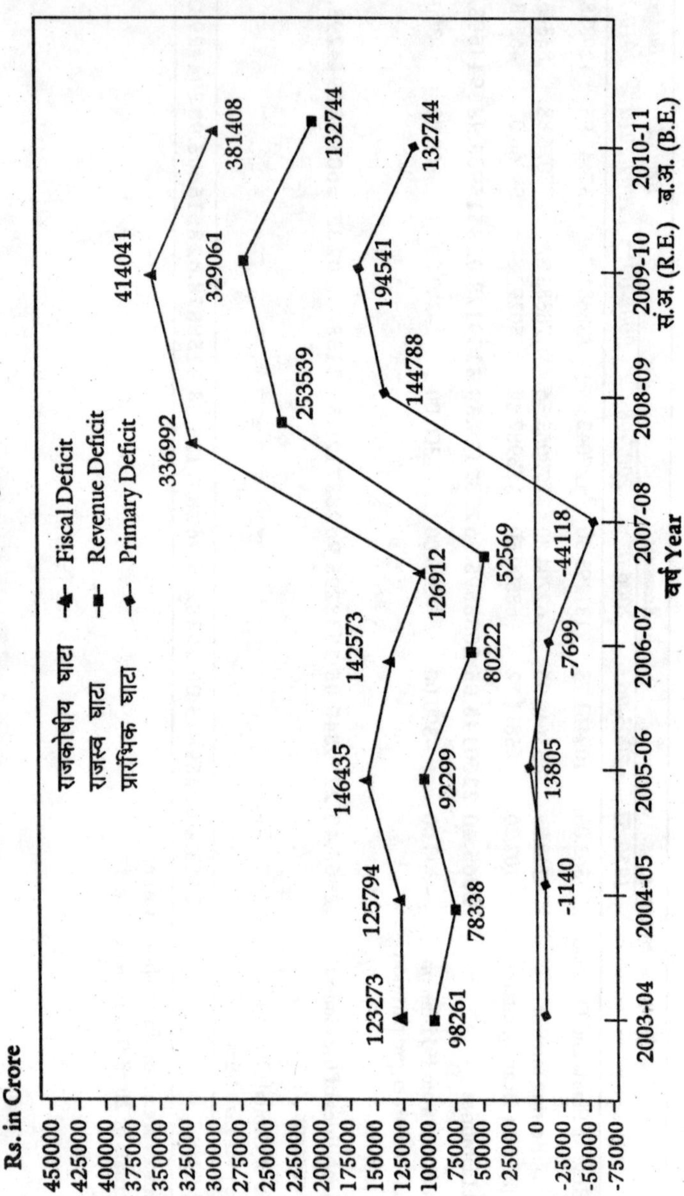

ANNEXURE-4

As a Percentage of GDP (स. घ. उ. के प्रतिशत के रूप में)

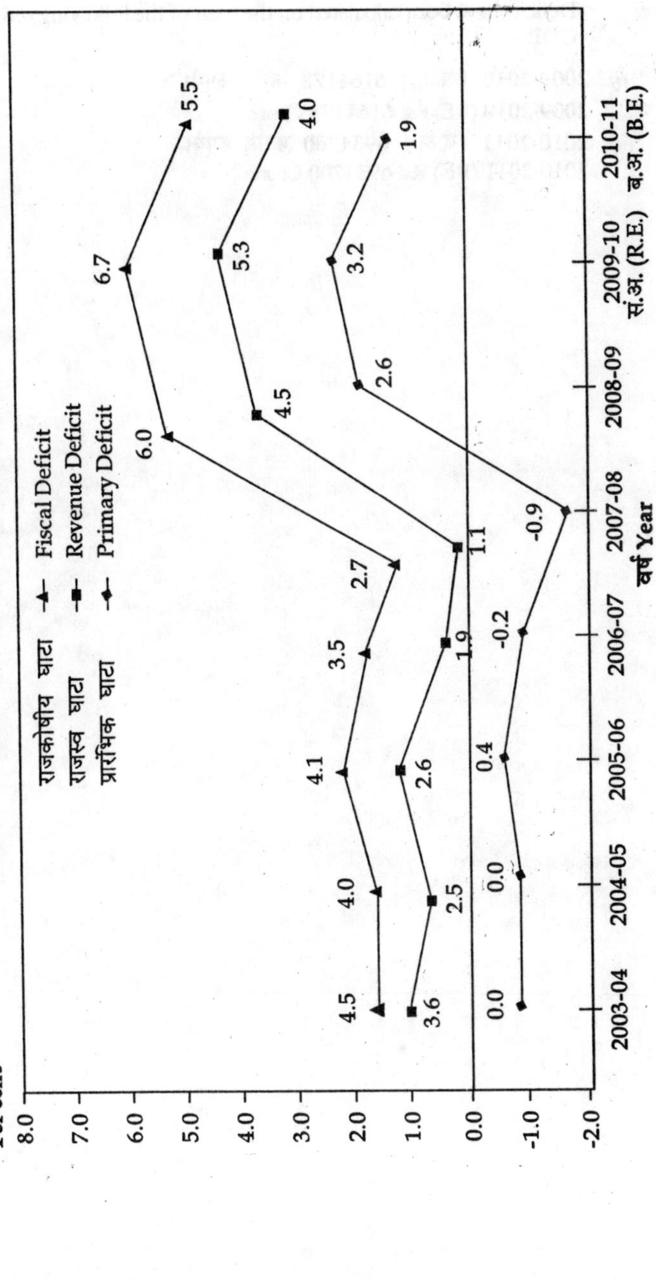

टिप्पणी: सघउ के निम्नलिखित अनुमानों के आधार पर घाटों का आकलन किया गया है।

Note: Deficits have been calculated on the basis of the following estimates of GDP.

(*i*) 2009-2010 (सं.अ.) 6164178 करोड़ रुपये।
2009-2010 (RE) Rs. 6164178 Crore

(*ii*) 2010-2011 (ब.अ.) 6934700 करोड़ रुपये।
2010-2011 (BE) Rs. 6934700 Crore

8

SOCIAL SECTOR DEVELOPMENT: "OUTLAYS VS. OUTCOMES"– AN OVERVIEW

Social Sector Development broadly refers to improvement and upgradation of basic facilities like health, education, drinking water, sanitation, housing, roads and electricity, etc. for the people. Since nearly seventy per cent of our people live in villages, Rural Development forms an important part of social development. Employment generation and poverty alleviation are also crucial to improve the social and economic conditions of the rural masses. No sustainable social development would be feasible without providing reasonable sources of income to them. Since bulk of them are dependent on agriculture and allied activities like animal husbandry, dairy farming, poultry, horticulture, fishery and forestry, etc., development of this broad agricultural sector has to have top priority to generate more employment opportunities in the villages.

An important cause of the backwardness of the rural areas is their isolation from the rest of the country. Providing road connectivity to all villages is therefore essential for their development. The problem of lack of electricity in thousands of villages too needs to be addressed. Electrification of large number of villages, through rural electrification programmes, would bring them out of darkness and isolation. The rural women would also be very much freed from the daily monotony and hard labour of fetching drinking water, fodder and fuel etc. from long distances. With availability of electricity life will not only become less taxing but will also provide more time for the people to take up additional fruitful work connected with agriculture and its many allied activities mentioned earlier. Good road connectivity and electrification of the villages are indeed the true symbols and measure of rural development. Development could also be measured on the adequacy of irrigation and drinking water supply, proper housing, higher standards of health and education available to the people. Fulfilment of all these basic needs would no doubt uplift the quality of life of the people. Higher per capita income by itself is no reliable index of higher standards of life and living. Political parties too have realized that electoral victories to a large extent depend on providing Sadak, Bijali and Pani. Ruling parties which failed to provide these facilities to a satisfactory extent lost electoral battles in a number of states in the past. "Development" is the price demanded by the people for votes.

Since the commencement of Development Planning in India from 1950, all the Five Year Plans including the last completed Tenth Five Year Plan (2002-07) did not bestow that much attention to social sector development as was called for. The financial outlays of the Central and State Governments were generally on the lower side due to various reasons including lack of adequate funds. The Expenditure figures for some years on social sector development may be seen in the Table at Annexure I. From the Financial Year 2004-05 onwards there has been higher allocation of funds and higher expenditure but there are complaints that good portions of such expenditure have not been well utilized due to leakages of funds and corruption in the execution of important schemes.

Development in areas like health, education, drinking water, housing, agriculture, roads and electricity largely fall within the sphere of the states. Their development, therefore, is dependent on the financial resources of and the allocations made by the states in their respective Five Year Plans. However, the Central Government too has been making large financial allocations for a host of social sector programmes like welfare of the SCs/STs health and family planning, and several educational programmes and schemes. Plan schemes falling under soil conservation, water harvesting and water conservation, rural roads and rural electrification, food for works programmes, and the latest NREGP etc. also get substantial Central plan assistance. In fact, in many social sector developmental activities, the Central Government not only provides financial assistance to the states but also provides technical guidance and coordination. The Central Planning Commission is supposed to continuously evaluate performance of various central and state development programmes to assess if the "outlays" on them have resulted in matching "outcomes." Large financial allocations alone are no guarantee of higher development unless the budgeted amounts are efficiently and economically utilised to achieve the desired goals.

While presenting the Central budget for the year 2005-06 the Finance Minister, Shri P. Chidambaram in his speech (dated 28th February 2005) in the Lok Sabha had stated that (paras 99 & 100) "we must increase our revenue and reorient expenditure to pay for more outlays on education, health and infrastructures." At the same time he also cautioned that "outlays" do not necessarily mean "outcomes."

The planned efforts so far, according to official figures, have reduced the incidence of poverty from 50 per cent in the 1950s to less than 30 per cent in 1999-2000. (Economic Survey–2004-05, p. 227) It is also stated that the number of BPL (Below Poverty Line) persons has come down from 328.9 millions to 260.3 millions. Literacy rates too have increased from 18.3 per cent in 1951 to 64.8 per cent in 2001. Similarly, in the health sector, life expectancy at birth (male) has gone up from 37.2 years in (1951) to 63.9 years (2001-06) and for females from 36.2 years to 66.9 years (Economic Survey 2004-05, p. 238). Infant, child and maternal mortality rates too have considerably come down. However, the country has still miles to go to catch up with the quality of life of many other developing and developed countries. For example, according to the latest (2009) World Bank Report India is "one of the most mal-nourished nation in the world". Further according to the Economic Survey 2004-05 (p. 231) the adult literacy rates in China and Sri Lanka in 2002 were 99.9 per cent and 92.1 per cent respectively as against India's 64.8 in 2001. It is seen that even after over 50 years of Planning, India ranks quite low globally on human and gender development according to the UNDP's Human Development Report. Though in terms of GDP India ranks among the top ten countries in the world, in terms of human development it occupied a very low position of 127 out of 177 countries (in 2002) as against Australia ranking 3, China 94, Sri Lanka 96 and Indonesia 111 (please see tables of Annexures II, III and IV). In terms of GDP India presently ranks among the top 10 countries of the world and according to Purchasing Power Parity (PPP) calculations India is the fourth wealthiest country in the world. It is also rated as an emerging economic super power. But in spite of this high economic ranking, in terms of human development or the quality of life of its teeming millions India presents a very gloomy picture. India has the largest number of illiterate people in the world–numbering 306 million in 2001 (Planning Commission Report). As mentioned earlier people suffering from extreme poverty (BPL) number over 260 million or nearly 25 per cent of the total population of the country. People struggle and at times fight to get safe drinking water not only in thousands of villages but also in many cities and state capitals as also in the National Capital Delhi. 24-hours uninterrupted electricity supply continues to be a distant dream—even in major towns and mega cities let alone thousands of villages. 25 to 50 per cent load shedding in most parts of the country is a normal feature which at times lead to public disturbances and breach of peace. During hot summer days people start abusing and even physically assaulting power sector employees on being deprived of power supply.

Most Government schools and hospitals are in poor condition lacking even the minimum required facilities. Condition of public roads is no better. All said and done India looks pretty shabby not only to foreign visitors but also to its own people. With ever declining qualities of governance and massive corruption in most spheres of public activities life of the people has indeed become nasty and taxing. What is more shameful is that presently India is considered to be among the top ten (10) most corrupt countries of the world.

To make up for the deficiency in the social sector development the Common Minimum Programme (CMP) of the UPA Government (2004-08) had accorded very high priority to it. Under its "Bharat Nirman" schemes large financial spending of around 1,74,000 crores of rupees had been planned. The focus was to build rural infrastructure by speedier development of irrigation, road, housing, water supply, health, education, electrification and telecommunication connectivity, etc. The targets set for the "Bharat Nirman" activities for a few years (ending 2007) as stated in budget speech (2005) of the Finance Minister were as below:

- To bring an additional one crore hectares agricultural land under assured irrigation;
- To connect all villages that have a population of 1000 or more (or 500 in hilly/tribal areas) with a road;
- To construct 60 lakh additional houses for the poor;
- To provide drinking water to the remaining 74,000 habitations that are uncovered;

- To reach electricity to the remaining 1,25,000 villages and offer electricity connection to 2.3 crore households; and
- To give telephone connectivity to the remaining 66,822 villages.

The "outlays" planed for the social sector projects though very necessary however, appeared to be beyond the financial capacity of the State and Central Governments. Some viewed these proposed massive outlays to be mere wishful thinking. As stated more elaborately in the previous chapter low revenue receipts and high non-plan expenditure of the Central and State Governments for several years in the past compelled them to resort to heavy market borrowings year after year. This resulted in mounting interest payment liabilities on the accumulated debt burdens. A large part of the revenue receipts of the Central and State Governments are therefore spent on interest payments alone. The states and the Centre are by now virtually sinking in debt and have no revenue receipts available for development work. For whatever development work is to be done all the money has to be borrowed from the market. The new legislation of National Rural Employment Guarantee Act envisages 100 days of employment in a year to at least one member of each rural household. A very desirable proposition indeed but this appears to be financially an over-ambitious plan. This guaranteed employment scheme is estimated to cost several thousand crores of rupees annually. Its implementation with borrowed funds for long would necessarily result in increasing the debt burden of the government further and may also harm the fragile financial health of the Central Government. Normally employment should be in asset building work and not for just digging holes or trenches and filling them up. Employment generation in the rural areas should appropriately be linked to different growth oriented and asset building development projects included in the Five Year Plans. Unless employment is for productive plan schemes it may only increase the debt burden and widen the scope for corruption by showing employment on paper to thousands of fictitious persons. Already there are several complaints of fudging of employment figures under the NREG programme. Greater vigilance is therefore required in the implementation of this programme.

Considering the crucial role of the implementing agencies for the success of the Bharat Nirman schemes the Prime Minister Dr. Manmohan Singh had called a Conference of all district collectors on 20th May 2005 to speak to them directly. In his address he said:

" The government is in the process of finalizing a focussed programme called Bharat Nirman. Under Bharat Nirman, we have a target of providing 100 per cent connectivity to India's villages through roads, electricity and telecommunications and ensure 100 per cent coverage under safe water supply by 2009. In addition, we aim to create one crore hectares of additional irrigation and 60 lakh houses through the Indira Awas Yojana. You are the critical agents for ensuring that the new deal to rural India genuinely transforms rural lives and livelihoods." He further said:

"We have similarly targeted programmes for universal elementary education. Improvement of rural health through the National Rural Health Mission, universal coverage of mid-day meal, expanded coverage of the ICDS, agricultural transformation through the National Horticultural Mission and addressing food security through the Antyodaya Anna Yojana—all of which have adequate funds and are to be managed at the district level."

The Common Minimum Programme (CMP) of the UPA–I Government had highlighted the special importance being accorded to Education and Health by taking measures briefly mentioned below:

Education

- 2 per cent education cess levied to raise more funds for public spending on education.
- Scope of the cooked mid-day meal programmes widened.
- National Mission for Sarva Shiksha Abhiyan constituted under the Chairmanship of the Prime Minister, for the first time.

Health

- National Rural Health Mission was launched to improve access to health care at district level for the weaker sections of rural society.
- A cadre of health activists was to be developed to ensure effective health care and to set up good quality functional hospitals for every 1 lakh and above of population.
- Funding for National Campaign for HIV/AIDS Awareness being increased.
- Health and population programmes to be integrated, so that

improvements in the health status of women and girl child encourage preference for small families.

World Bank's World Development Report 2004 considers funding and providing for Education and Health Care for its people to be the fundamental responsibility of the Governments concerned. It says:

"By financing, providing, or regulating the services that contribute to health and education outcomes, governments around the world demonstrate their responsibility for the health and education of their people. Why? First, these services are replete with market failures—with externalities, as and when infected child spreads a disease to play-mates or a farmer benefits from a neighbour's ability to read. So, the private sector, left to its devices, will not achieve the level of health and education that society desires. Second, basic health and basic education are considered fundamental human rights. The Universal Declaration of Human Rights asserts an individual's right to "a standard of living adequate for health and well-being of himself and of his family, including ...medical care ... and a right to education that is ... free at least in the elementary and fundamental stages." No matter how challenging the problems of delivery may be, the public sector cannot overlook development of health and education facilities for its people. The challenges are to see how the government–in collaboration with the private sectors—can meet this fundamental responsibility."

Some causes for the slow progress in the social sector development so far appear to be due to:

- Low level of budgetary allocations as % of total public expenditure (both plan and non-plan) by the Central and State Governments.
- Under-spending of allocated funds leading to their lapse-partly on account of delayed sanctions and partly due to organisational shortcomings. Sometimes sanctions for expenditure are issued in the last month of the financial year, i.e. March allowing little time to start work on any approved scheme. At times such late sanction of funds leads to hasty expenditure on purchase of many un-required items to avoid lapsing of funds.
- Often more expenditure is incurred on salaries and

establishment than on substantive work. Corruption, waste and negligence on the part of the implementation agencies too have become rampant. Accordingly Rajiv Gandhi as Prime Minister had once lamented that only 15 Paisa of a rupee is utilised for actual work, the rest being either wasted or misused otherwise. The general belief now is that corruption has worsened in recent years and has become the main road block to all developmental activities. Influential politicians, contractors and personnel of the implementing agencies allegedly siphon off large parts of money sanctioned for development. "Food for Work" programme is alleged to have been turned into "Loot for Work" programme. In executing most development projects leakages of funds through corruption have increased substantially leaving very little for actual development work. Therefore, without corruption prevention the planned developmental activities may not be quite fruitful.

- No day passes when one or more cases involving waste of public money are not reported in the media. Year after year many cases of wasteful expenditure are brought to notice by the C&AG in his audit reports to the state legislatures and the Parliament. Unfortunately, these reports on the accounts of the Central and State Governments no longer appear to receive the required official notice for taking any preventive or punitive measures.
- Frequency of transfers of personnel engaged in developmental works too make them indifferent in their work leading to slowdown of developmental projects. The officials also remain unaccountable for their low performance due to their short tenures. Sometime honest officers are removed at the behest of contractors to facilitate grabbing of public funds by them without any matching work or even no work at times. There are also allegations of corruption with regard to postings and transfers of project officials often at the behest of the concerned contractors or persons with other vested interests.
- Lack of adequate and effective monitoring and evaluation of the development projects often lead to time and cost over-run in many incomplete projects. Large amounts of funds invested in incomplete projects remain blocked without any returns. These are cases of "outlays" without "outcomes" for long

periods. This has been discussed in the previous chapter with specific examples. There may be several other causes for low performance and low outcomes in the developmental sector. All such causes ought to be probed to take effective corrective steps. Knowing the ills of the system is not enough unless there is the required will and determination to eliminate them and set things right. Unfortunately, this has not been happening to any significant extent resulting in huge wastage, blockage and leakage of developmental funds.

Frequently complaints are made by the public that the rural hospitals, dispensaries, schools etc., new or old, remain without doctors, and teachers for long periods thus making their existence fruitless. Empowering Panchayats in the management of these institutions may therefore be a desirable alternative. This is also the view expressed in the Economic Survey (2007-08) in para 2.34 quoted below:

> "Available information shows that, despsite the clear Constitutional directions handed out through the 73rd and 74th Amendments, there are wide inter-state variations in the degree of effective decentralization achieved. Evidence suggests that the success of decentralized programme implementation depends on effective transfer of functions; functionaries and finances to local-self governments and creation and patronage of grassroots level participatory institutions like Gram Sabhas, people's bodies for project formulation, implementation and monitoring, and watershed-based institutions. The success stories of participatory project implementation and devolution of plan and non-plan funds must be systematically studied, recorded and replicated elsewhere with appropriate region-specific adaptations."

The Economic Times in its editorial of 4th June 2005 with the heading "Lower Fiscal Deficit is Good: But It Does Not Mean Wiser Spending" wrote: "The CMP assumes wrongly that India's pathetic performance in education and health can be improved by higher outlays. But Indonesia and Sri Lanka have achieved 90 per cent literacy while spending 1.8 per cent of GDP on education. Whereas India has been spending 4 per cent and yet achieved only 65 per cent literacy. So the CMP pledge to raise spending to 6 per cent of GDP is really a promise to waste more." What the editorial emphasized was that unless the quality of implementation was improved, higher expenditure may only lead to higher level of wastage and corruption.

Truly, "Outlays" alone are no guarantee of higher "Outcomes." Efficient and corruption free implementation is the prime necessity to get the matching return from every rupee of investment. That was perhaps the intention why the Prime Minister Dr. Manmohan Singh wished to address the collectors directly as they are the king pin for developmental activities in the social sector in the field. Their enthusiasm and commitment are, equally if not more, important than higher budgetary allocations. To convert "outlays" into matching "outcomes" honest, sincere and committed implementation agencies are required. Public administration must aim to provide man-power of the required qualities and capabilities.

The Finance Minister Pranab Mukherjee also in his 2010-11 Budget Speech drew attention to some of these challenges that came in the way of India's speedier development and progress. In para 9 of his budget speech he stated that the country's considerable dependence on timely and adequate rainfall for agricultural productivity was the first challenge. The second was how to make development more inclusive. The third and most important challenge according to him "relates to the weaknesses in government systems, structures and institutions at different levels of governance. Indeed, in the coming years, if there is one factor that can hold us back in realising our potential as a modern nation, it is the bottleneck of our public delivery mechanisms." Efficiency, honesty and effectiveness of our administration has to substantially increase to speed up progress and for making development more inclusive.

No less important a factor for this purpose is that government should inspire confidence in its sense of justice and fair play among the vast number of administrative personnel engaged in the execution of various development works. While the dishonest persons need to be penalised, the honest and committed individuals deserve to be encouraged and assured of protection from false allegations, if any, made against them by persons with vested interests. Let not all public servants be viewed with suspicion.

Rendering Social Justice is another important aspect of social sector development. Social justice requires to take special care of the weaker sections of society in matters of their education, health, employment, housing etc. It is not enough for a state to be an economic power house unless its money power is utilized for the good of all the citizens, specially the weaker and poorer sections of the society. Prosperity of the few and poverty of the many are not conducive to social harmony and stability. Development has to be all-inclusive. It must take care of all the people living in urban and rural areas. This is a financially challenging task as pointed out by the Finance Minister in para 8 of his 2010-11 budget speech as stated below:

> "We have to strengthen food security, improve education opportunities and provide health facilities at the level of households, both in rural and urban areas. These are issues that require significant resources, and we have to find those resources."

The Economic Survey of 2007-08 of the Ministry of Finance on page 263 under the heading "Outlook and Challenges" relating to Social Sector Development while highlighting some gains has also mentioned what more needs to be done as quoted below:

> "Along with higher economic growth and poverty reduction, there has been an improvement in many important social indictors like life expectancy, infant mortality rate and gross enrolment ratios at primary level of education. However, disparities continue at the state and regional level. Better governance and improved service delivery are essential to ensure that leakages are plugged and the funds under the welfare schemes reach the intended beneficiaries to the maximum extent. Local governments and panchayati raj institutions as well as social and non-government organizations can play an important role in this area."

A positive development for monitoring social sector development is that in addition to "outlays (or expenditure) budget" the Finance Minister is now required to present to Parliament an "Outcome budget." This would lay down the physical targets to be achieved in each quarter of the financial year by different ministries. At the end of the Financial Year information on "outcome" or actual performance by the ministries will also be placed before Parliament by the Finance Minister. Hopefully, these progressive developments in the Budgetary process may lead to better utilization of public money. The implementation agencies have been made more accountable and thus may take their responsibilities more seriously to achieve better results. Time alone will, however, show how far the new promises and procedures would give the desired results.

The Economic Survey 2009-10 in para 11.71 outlines in the following words shortcomings in achieving the targeted goals of Social Sector Development and how these are to be dealt with:

> "In spite of increased Government outlays in the social sector in recent years, lack of identity proof results in harassment and denial of services to the poor and marginalized. As a result, there are still leakages in the programmes/schemes and the benefits do not reach the intended target groups of individuals/people in full. Providing identity proof to the poor and marginalized through the UIDAI will enhance their access to Government services, both at State and Central levels, and will enable smoother delivery of direct benefits to the poor and underserved. Specially it will improve the delivery of the flagship schemes of the Central Government. This will also prevent leakages as well as wastages in the implementation of these schemes. Success in reaching this objective can be further assured through involvement of local communities and PRIs."

Thus various special steps need to be taken to achieve inclusive development and growth to benefit the weaker sections of our people whose number presently runs into several hundred millions.

Annexure-I
Social Sector (Social Services and Rural Development) Expenditure by Centre and States

	Social Sector Expenditure (Revenue and Capital)		
	As % of GDP	*As % of agg. pub. exp. (rev. + capital)*	*Per capita exp. (in Rs.) in 1993-4 prices*
1987-88	7.26	25.29	564
1988-89	6.95	25.22	585
1989-90	7.17	25.19	635
1990-91	6.78	24.85	623
1991-92	6.58	24.28	599
1992-93	6.38	24.06	594

Contd...

	Social Sector Expenditure (Revenue and Capital)		
	As % of GDP	*As % of agg. pub. exp. (rev. + capital)*	*Per capita exp. (in Rs.) in 1993-4 prices*
1993-94	6.46	24.58	622
1994-95	6.39	25.01	632
1995-96	6.40	25.95	674
1996-97	6.30	26.46	716
1997-98	6.41	26.18	763
1998-99	7.01	27.36	882
1999-2000	7.14	26.56	951
2000-01	7.45	26.56	988
2001-02(B)	7.18	25.31	986

Source: Computed from the data available in Indian Public Finance Statistics, Ministry of Finance, GOI, 1995, 2000.

Annexure-II

India's Global Position on Adult and Youth Literacy Rates

Country	*Adult Literacy Rate (per cent 15 years & above)*		*Youth Literacy Rate (per cent 15 years-24)*	
	1990	*2002*	*1990*	*2002*
China	68.3	90.9	95.3	98.9
India	49.3	61.3	64.3	73.3*
Nepal	30.4	44.0	46.6	62.7
Pakistan	35.5	41.5	47.4	53.9
Sri Lanka	88.7	92.1	95.1	97.0
Bangladesh	34.2	41.1	42.0	49.7

Figures relate to 2001.

**Source:* UNDP, Human Development Report, 2004.

Annexure-III
Selected Health Indicators

(Person Years)

S.No.	*Parameter*	*1951*	*1981*	*1991*	*Current Level (2002)*
1.	Crude Birth Rate (Per 1000 Population)	40.8	33.9	29.5	25.0 (2002)
2.	Crude Death Rate (Per 1000 Population)	25.1	12.5	9.8	8.1 (2002)
3.	Total Fertility Rate (TFR) (Per woman)	6.0	4.5	3.6	3.1 (2001)
4.	Maternal Mortality Rate (MMR) (Per 100,000 live births)	NA	NA	437 (1992-93) NFHS	407 (1998)
5.	Infant Mortality Rate (IMR) (Per 1000 live births)	146 (1951-61)	110	80	63 (2002)
6.	Child (0-4 years) Mortality Rate (Per 1000 children)	57.3 (1972)	412	265	19.3 (2001)
7.	Couple Protection Rate (per cent)	10.4 (1971)	228	44.1	48.2 (1998-99) NFHS
8.	Life Expectancy at Birth				
	Male	37.2	54.1	59.7 (1991-95)	63.9 (2001-06)
	Female	36.2	54.7	60.9 (1991-95)	66.9 (2001-06)

Note: The dates in the brackets indicate years for which latest information is available.

NFHS: National Family Health Survey.

NA: Not Available.

Source: Ministry of Health and Family Welfare and Office of the Registrar General, India.

Annexure-IV
India's Global Position on Human and Gender Development

Country	*Human Development Index (HDI)*		*HDI Rank*		*Gender Development Index (GDI)*		*GDI Rank*	
	1997	*2002*	*1997*	*2002*	*1997*	*2002*	*1997*	*2002*
Norway	0.927	0.956	2	1	0.927	0.955	2	1
Australia	0.922	0.946	7	3	0.921	0.945	4	3
Sri Lanka	0.721	0.740	90	96	0.712	0.738	76	73
China	0.701	0.745	98	94	0.699	0.741	79	71
Indonesia	0.681	0.692	105	111	0.675	0.685	88	90
India	0.545	0.595	132	127	0.525	0.572	112	103
Pakistan	0.508	0.497	138	142	0.472	0.471	116	120
Bangladesh	0.440	0.509	150	138	0.428	0.499	123	110
Nepal	0.463	0.504	144	140	0.441	0.484	121	116
Mozambique	0.341	0.354	169	171	0.326	0.339	138	139
Niger	0.298	0.292	173	176	0.286	0.278	143	144

Source: UNDP Human Development Report (HDR) 1999 and 2004.

9

THE OMBUDSMAN INSTITUTION: ITS RELEVANCE FOR INDIA

Neither anarchy, due to lack of effective political authority, nor dictatorship with absolute power in one hand is to man's liking. By nature, man is a social animal and for peaceful existence he is tolerant of reasonable restrictions on his freedom. In the process of political evolution in the first phase, power of the state in most countries came to be exercised by kings and monarchs some of whom were dictatorial. The citizens felt suffocated and chained in such regimes. Autocratic regimes in France led to the French Revolution (1789) and the beheading of the unpopular Bourbon dynasty monarch of that time. Political thinkers also championed the cause of freedom through their writings and hastened the fall of monarchies and other dictatorial regimes world over. Lock and Rousseau were among the ideological fathers of the French Revolution which, with its slogans of "liberty, equality and fraternity" smoothened the path of democratic regimes. The new era of republicanism influenced by the writings of the French political thinker Montesque also devised a system of "separation of powers" by distributing state powers between its three organs i.e. the Legislature, the Executive and the Judiciary. This device was considered necessary to safeguard the freedom of the citizens. The various institutions of governance and public officials exercising state powers were kept under suitable legal checks and control to protect the citizens from arbitrary exercise of powers by any of them.

The Swedish Constitution of 1809 in addition to "separation of powers" also provided for a unique institution called "Ombudsman" to protect the citizens against administrative injustice or abuse of power by public officials. The Swedish word, "Ombed" refers to a person who acts as a spokesman or the representative of another person. The Ombudsman in Sweden is appointed by Parliament to supervise, as an independent authority, the functioning of all public officials. He is to protect the citizens from undue interference, negligence and errors of all public officials exercising the state powers. He is thus a peoples man who protects them from any wrong doings of public officials'.

Under the Swedish Constitution, Parliament (Riksdag) has to elect one or more Ombudsmen. Now there are four of them–one of whom is designated as Chief Administrator or Chief Ombudsman. Each of them has a demarcated functional area to look after.

Article 6 under Chapter 12 entitled "Power of Control", the Swedish Constitution lays down that—

> The Riksdag shall elect one or more Ombudsmen for the purpose of supervising , under instructions determined by the Riksdag, the application in public service of laws and other statutes. An Ombudsman may initiate legal proceedings in such cases as are indicated in the instructions.
>
> An Ombudsman may be present at the deliberations of a court or an administrative authority and shall have access to the minutes and documents of any such court or authority. Any court or administrative authority as well as any civil servant of the State or a municipality shall provide an Ombudsman with such information and reports as the latter requests. An obligation to this effect shall be incumbent also on any other person who is under the supervisory authority of the Ombudsman. Any public prosecutor shall on request assist the Ombudsman.

Some provisions of the Act of Instructions to the parliamentary Ombudsmen laying down their powers and functions are–

> ***Section 1***
>
> The Parliamentary Ombudsmen shall... supervise the observance of laws and other statutes by those exercising public activity and that they in all respects properly fulfil their obligations.
>
> ***Section 3***
>
> It is the particular duty of the Ombudsman to ensure that courts of law and administrative authorities observe the

provisions of the Instrument of Government concerning objectivity and impartially and that the fundamental rights and freedoms of citizens are not encroached upon in the process of public administration.

Section 6

Should an Ombudsman deem it necessary for the official to be dismissed or debarred from performing his duties on account of criminal act or grave or repeated negligence of duty, he may make a report thereon to the person or body which has the authority to decide on such measures.

It may be seen from the above constitutional and statutory provisions that an Ombudsman in Sweden elected by the Parliament has very wide powers of supervision over all public officials (i.e. the executive). Even courts and judicial officers (i.e. the judiciary) are not excluded from his purview. He can remain present during deliberations of an administrative authority or during hearing of the case in a court of law. He has access to all official records also. He is to generally ensure that administration is carried on in accordance with laws and statutes; that public authorities do not exceed or abuse their powers; that justice is rendered fairly and impartially; and that the rights and freedoms of the citizens are not violated. An Ombudsman has also been given the power to prosecute any erring public official or recommend departmental action for his removal or dismissal for any grave negligence in the performance of his duties. Even judges of the Supreme Court can be prosecuted by him. He is indeed a very powerful parliamentary official appointed to protect the citizens against injustice, abuse of power or any other act of misadministration, which he may himself consider to be such.

He can prosecute an official in a court of law but punishment will depend on the court's decision. He cannot also reverse or amend a decision already taken by any official, but he can recommend or advise for modification or even cancellation of any faulty order or decision to the competent higher authority of the official concerned. Thus he is neither a super-administrator nor a super-judge but as a Parliamentary supervisory official under the constitution, if he comes across any fault, deficiency or shortcoming in the work or decisions of other public officials he is to report to the appropriate higher authorities for corrective action and, where necessary, for initiating suitable penal or departmental action against an erring official. He is not a superior officer in the official hierarchy but a supervisory officer of the country's Parliament. In his supervisory role he has, however, the power to admonish or criticize an official. He has also the power, not only to recommend correction of individual defects, but also to suggest amendment of laws, rules, procedures and practices if any of these are found to be faulty or injurious to public interest. He is thus a standing administrative reforms Commissioner. The advice and recommendations of the Ombudsmen are generally accepted by virtue of the power and prestige attached to the office.

The Ombudsman can initiate action either on the basis of an individual complaint, or *suo moto*. He can also dismiss a complaint summarily if he finds it to be unfounded, vexatious or trivial. With regard to the courts, his role is primarily to ensure that cases are not unduly delayed and there are no breaches of duties on the part of Judges. Normally, he does not interfere with the merits of any judgment unless it is grossly violative of justice, in which case he writes to the appropriate appellate court for necessary action.

Strangely, although the judiciary comes within the purview of the Swedish Ombudsman, members of Parliament and Cabinet Ministers have been excluded. This, it appears, was done to make the institution non-political and non-controversial and also due to the fact that in Sweden, Ministers cannot give administrative officials binding orders when dealing with individual cases. As the level of corruption in Swedish administration is very low the number of corruption cases prosecuted on the advice of the Ombudsman constitute a very small fraction of the total number of all cases handled in a year by the Ombudsman. The main activities of the Ombudsman are to deal with the complaints of citizens involving maladministration like delay, negligence, improper or misapplication of laws and rules, harsh or unjust decisions, etc. Although the Ombudsman is empowered to deal with corruption and other types of wrong doings of public officials his workload is more due to complaints relating to maladministration.

The Ombudsman is independent of the legislature, the judiciary and the executive. He has the power to investigate any case of violation of laws or negligence of duties by public officials. He has the power to submit special report in addition to his annual report on any important case of maladministration or where his advice was not accepted. The annual report and special reports, submitted by him, are examined and discussed in one of the committees of the Parliament.

The Press is an important ally of the Ombudsman as fear of adverse publicity of the work of any official makes him more careful and cooperative. All important decisions of the Ombudsman are well reported and commented upon in the Press. Sometimes, even the Ombudsman is criticized if his handling of a case is viewed to be defective. This ensures his own objectivity and impartially. Under the Swedish law, all official records are accessible to the public, except a few which are declared to be secret.

The experience of Sweden over a period of many decades is reported to be that the institution of Ombudsman has proved to be an effective guardian of the rights and interests of the citizens against misadministration of any kind. In this institution Swedish people have found an informal, impartial, powerful, inexpensive and speedy parliamentary agency to investigate their complaints against all categories of public officials. Complaints could be made by simply writing a letter to the Ombudsman. The institution also acts as a friend of officials when it clears them after investigation of any false complaint or unfounded criticism in the Press. There is no penalty laid down for any false complaint.

For over a century, this institution of Ombudsman of Sweden remained unnoticed by outsiders. But during the fifties and sixties of the twentieth century this simple but effective institution attracted world-wide attention. Following the Second World War, the need for massive socio-economic development programmes arose to revive the war-devastated economies. Consequently, there was enlargement of government functions and its machinery. As a result, people had greater and frequent inter-actions with public officials. Their complaints and grievances against officials relating to injustice, malpractices, and mal-administration also increased in numbers. For many of such complaints, they found the traditional complaint resolving arrangements like the higher administrative officials, administrative and other quasi-judicial tribunals very slow, inadequate and ineffective. Parliament and their committees as also the judicial courts, were either not available for many complaints for relief or were found to be too expensive, formal, and time-consuming. The need was, therefore, strongly felt for a less costly, less formal, but effective, impartial and speedier, machinery. The Ombudsmen Plan of Sweden satisfied all these requirements to a large extent. It accordingly caught the attention of the constitutional experts and policy-makers in many democratic countries. Consequently, this institution got installed rapidly in many countries, and is under consideration for adoption by many others. The Swedish institution however, has not been adopted as such in its totality as administrative practices and culture greatly varied from country to country. They adopted the Swedish Plan with suitable variations and modifications to suit their constitutional arrangements and administrative practices.

By mid-eighties of the 20th century more than 35 countries around the world had adopted the Ombudsman system. Some of these countries were Australia, Denmark, Finland, France, New Zealand, Norway, the United Kingdom, etc. In Canada and the United States, while the establishment of Ombudsman at the national level has been under discussion in the meanwhile state-level Ombudsmen have been set up in some of their states. Some of the developing countries like Fiji, Guinea, Mauritius, Jamaica, Ghana, Zambia, Nigeria and Pakistan have already appointed Ombudsmen in those countries. The Pakistani Ombudsman is designated as Wafaqi Mohtasib and the author had the opportunity to discuss his work with him while attending the World Ombudsman conference in New York in 1986 as India's representative. I was then holding the post of Central Vigilance Commissioner of India who was in a way doing the work of an Ombudsman in settling public grievances against Central Government officials particularly relating to allegations of corruption.

In the United Kingdom, in addition to the Parliamentary Commissioner for Administration (Ombudsman), there is a separate Ombudsman (National Health Service Commissioner) to deal with complaints relating to local administration and health services. In some other countries also, particularly, Canada, there are specialized Ombudsmen to deal with specific areas of administration like local administration, health, etc. Even some city administrations and local bodies have set up independent Ombudsman type bodies to handle complaints and grievances of the affected parties. The Ombudsmen institutions established in most other countries outside Sweden, however, do not have equal powers, functions and effectiveness as that of the Swedish institution which is now described as the "classical" Ombudsman. The powers and functions of Ombudsmen elsewhere have been somewhat restricted. But even so they are independent of the Executive, the Legislature and the Judiciary. By and large, they report to the Parliament directly. For example, the Ombudsman in Denmark has no jurisdiction over the courts but has jurisdiction over Ministers. Like his Swedish counterpart, the Ombudsman in Denmark is required under the law "to supervise the civil and military administration of the state." The law further empowers him "to keep himself informed as to whether any person under his jurisdiction pursues unlawful ends, makes arbitrary or unreasonable decisions or otherwise commits mistakes or acts of negligence in the discharge of his duties." The law thus gives him a free hand in examining cases of unlawful or arbitrary use of power, mistakes , negligence or delay in handling public business. The Danish Ombudsman, however, cannot prosecute any erring official himself but has to ask the Public Prosecutor to do so. He can also recommend departmental action against erring officials to higher authorities. In case of a Minister, the Ombudsman is required to submit his recommendation regarding civil or criminal action to be taken against him, to the Parliamentary Committee on Ombudsman. The Norwegian Ombudsman has powers similar to that of Denmark. The courts are excluded but Ministers are included in his jurisdiction. New Zealand was the first country outside the Scandinavian countries to adopt the Ombudsman system in 1962. His functions as laid down under Section 13 (1) of the Ombudsman Act of 1975, are:

> "To investigate any decision or recommendation made, or any act done or omitted relating to a matter of administration and affecting any person or body of persons in his or its personal capacity...by any officer, employee or member of any such Department or organization in his capacity as such officer, employee or member."

The expression relating to "a matter of administration" has not been defined. This gives the Ombudsman a free hand to deal with any acts of commission or omission, on the part of public officials, which, according to him, are unjust, unfair or discriminatory. Service matters of public officials are, however, excluded from his jurisdiction. The Ombudsman in New Zealand, like in Denmark, has no power himself to take any action against a defaulting official but can report any such matter to the appropriate higher authority if he has noticed "significant breach of duty or misconduct." If no action is taken on his recommendation by the competent higher authority, then the

Ombudsman can bring it to the notice of the Prime Minister, and later to that of the Parliament. Like the Ombudsmen elsewhere, he cannot himself reverse or modify any decision of an official but can only recommend for the same to the appropriate higher authorities. He has also the power to suggest improvements in administrative procedures or practices or even amendment to laws and rules in order to secure justice and fairness to the people. He can act on the basis of complaints as well as *suo moto*. A complainant should, however, have sufficient personal interest in his complaint to merit investigation. Any committee of the Lower House can also refer any petition pending before it for investigation by the Ombudsman. The Prime Minister also can refer any matter with the consent of the Chief Ombudsman for investigation by the Ombudsman.

The New Zealand model, in preference to the Scandinavian model, has been adopted by many countries. The institution of Parliamentary Commissioner for Administration in the United Kingdom set up in 1967 is more or less based on the New Zealand model but with much restricted jurisdiction. He is empowered to investigate complaints from any member of the public who claims to have sustained "injustice in consequence of misadministration" as a result of "any action taken by on or behalf of a Government Department or other authority" covered under the Parliamentary Commissioner Act of 1967. The expression "misadministration" has not been defined. A complainant can, however, approach the Ombudsman in U.K. only through a member of Parliament and not directly. The investigation report of the Ombudsman is also sent to such member of Parliament who may, in turn, inform the complainant suitably. A complainant has thus no direct access to the Ombudsman in UK. His investigation cannot question the merits of any law, rule or policy. He can only go into the implementation aspect, i.e. delay, negligence, arbitrariness, and incorrect decisions, etc. He cannot investigate into service matters of civilian or defense forces and action taken for the purpose of investigating any crime or for the security of the State. Some sections of the British Press had described the British Ombudsman as "a muzzled watchdog" or "a crusader without a sword", while others sarcastically laid emphasis on the date when the British Parliamentary Commissioner took over his office, i.e. on the 1st of April (or all Fools Day) in 1967. The British Parliamentary Commissioner can report to the Parliament if any case of injustice or misadministration has been established after his investigation and he feels that such "injustice has not been or will not be remedied." He has himself no power to prosecute or recommend departmental action, admonish or criticize any official or reverse any decision or action. Discretionary matters are also outside his jurisdiction unless any guidelines have been violated in taking decisions.

The Administrative Reforms Commission (ARC 1966-69) headed by Moraji Desai which had examined the question of establishing the Ombudsman type institution in India to deal with public complaints came to the following conclusions:

> "Our study of the institution of Ombudsman in Scandinavian countries and of the Parliamentary Commissioner in New Zealand and of the working of these functionaries convinces us that we can suitably adapt these institutions for our needs. These institutions are, generally, a supplement to the Parliamentary control, independent of any political affiliations, outside the normal administrative hierarchy, and free from the formalism, publicity and delays associated with governmental machinery."

When the ARC examined this matter, the Parliamentary Commissioner Act 1967 of U.K. had not yet been passed, although the issue was under consideration for adoption in Britain. After taking into account the federal character of our polity, the vastness of the country, the size of the population, the large involvement of Government in public affairs, the existing judicial system with extensive writ jurisdiction of the higher courts, existence of various semi-judicial Tribunals and the normal departmental grievance handling agencies, the ARC had recognized the difficulties to be encountered in the way of establishing Ombudsman-type institutions in India. The ARC however still felt that–

> "The vastness of the country and its population need not be a deterrent to the establishment of such an institution. Our administrative system already provides for the functioning of the judiciary and administrative tribunals and for a hierarchy of appeals against the orders of subordinate authorities to superior authorities. We do not intend the system we envisage should clash with these institutions and wish, therefore, to provide for the functioning of that institution only in respect of matters for which such remedies are not available or where

in some cases it might not be reasonable to expect a citizen to take recourse to legal proceedings. This would substantially reduce the number of complaints eligible for investigation and thus enable the institution to devote its attention and energies only to those cases in which *prima facie* the need for redressing an act of injustice or misadministration exists."

The need for an independent, informal and speedy citizens' grievance redressal machinery was thought to be a *sine qua non* in a democratic form of government by the ARC. In doing so it had taken due note of the fact that in the years to come more developmental activities under the Five Year Plans will be taken up by the government with the possibility of numerous complaints of corruption, nepotism, waste, fraud, injustice, etc. The work relating to citizens' grievances thus could be stupendous for any single Ombudsman to do justice to the same within reasonable time limits.

The ARC, however, finally recommended that the complaints against Ministers and Secretaries to Government may be dealt with by an Ombudsman type authority to be designated as *Lokpal* and that another Ombudsman type authority may be empowered to deal with complaints against officials below the level of Secretary and may be designated as *Lokayukta*. There have to be separate Lokpals and Lokayuktas for the centre and the states. The main features of these institutions of Lokpal and Lokayukta, as recommended, were more or less like that of the Ombudsmen type institutions elsewhere with regard to their independence, status, mode of appointment and removal. They were to deal with matters involving acts of injustice, corruption or favouritism. Judiciary was to be kept out of their purview to ensure its independence as provided under our Constitution. As in the case of the Parliamentary Commissioner in U.K. certain matters were kept out of the purview of the Lokpal and Lokayukta, e.g. service matters of civil and defense personnel, in respect of which remedy was available by reference to normal courts or tribunals, certain commercial or contractual dealings of the Government with private parties, etc. etc.

In brief the following were to be the main features of the institutions of Lokpal and Lokayukta recommended by the ARC:

(a) They would be demonstrably independent and impartial;
(b) their investigations and proceedings should be conducted in private and should be informal in character;

(*c*) their appointment should, as far as possible, be non-political;
(*d*) their status should compare with the highest judicial functionaries in the country;
(*e*) they should deal with matters including those in the discretionary field involving acts of injustice, corruption or favouritism;
(*f*) their proceedings should not be subject to judicial interference and they should have the maximum latitude and powers in obtaining information relevant to their duties; and
(*g*) they should not look forward to any benefit or pecuniary advantage from the executive government.

In the Indian context, investigation of corruption matters received much greater attention rather than ordinary cases of injustice, harassment, neglect and delay in some states where Lokayuktas were appointed. The Ombudsmen institutions in other countries, on the other hand, mainly concern themselves with non-corruption grievances involving misadministration. Although no institution of Lokpal or Lokayukta has yet been established at the Centre, some of the States like Maharashtra, Madhya Pradesh, Karnataka, Bihar, Orissa etc. did appoint Lokayuktas for dealing with public complaints on the lines suggested by the ARC. The earliest legislation was that of Maharashtra—The Maharashtra Lokayukta and Upalokayuktas Act, 1971. The other State legislations were more or less based on the Maharashtra legislation. The Lokayukta in Maharashtra has exclusive power to look into complaints against State Ministers, Secretaries and other senior officers, while Upalokayukta deal with complaints against other lower level officials. There is no separate institution of Lokpal. A complaint, under the law, includes both "grievance" relating to misadministration and "allegation" relating to corruption. Under Section 6 of the Act, complaints are not to be entertained, save in exceptional cases, if the complainant has or had any remedy by way of proceedings before a tribunal or a court of law. The complaint has also to be accompanied by such affidavits as may be prescribed. There is also a penal provision under Section 9 of the Act for anyone who wilfully or maliciously makes any false complaint. Donald C. Rowat, an internationally-renowned expert on the Ombudsmen institutions in the world, (whom I had met while attending the World Ombudsman conference in Newyork in 1986) had commented on this legislation as below:

> "The main defect in the Indian plan (Ombudsman type) has been the attempt to combine the Ombudsman institution with the machinery for fighting corruption, and the consequent treatment of grievance/complaints (i.e. involving maladministration) in almost exactly the same way as allegations of misconduct and corruption. This has had two unfortunate results. The fear by senior officials and ministers of allegations against themselves or their colleagues has meant that they have given the plan weak support bordering on actual sabotage of its effective working. Secondly, the threat of punishment to the complainant unfortunate enough to have made a false statement. The Ombudsman elsewhere is widely regarded as the little man's friendly helper and defender against the bureaucratic juggernaut of the modern state...."

The Ombudsman institutions elsewhere, as mentioned earlier, mainly concern themselves with public grievances relating to misadministration rather than complaints about corruption. Investigation relating to complaints of corruption are procedurally lengthy and accordingly time-consuming. Allegations of corruption involve stigma and possibility of imprisonment in case an official is found to be guilty. A complainant has, therefore, to be deterred from making a false complaint out of fear of punishment in case his complaint is found to be false. False corruption complaints should not be allowed to undermine the morale and dynamism of honest officials. Non-corruption complaints relating to delay, negligence, unfair or arbitrary decision etc. on the other hand stand on a different footing and could be treated differently and more simply. There need not be any prescribed forms for making such complaints nor any formal or elaborate procedure for their investigations. No penalty need also be prescribed against a complainant for making such complaints even when the same are found to be baseless on enquiry.

In some countries, Ombudsmen quite often get the grievances redressed by telephoning the concerned officials and hardly any formal investigation as such is involved. The normal practice is for the Ombudsman to write to the officials complained against in cases of delay, negligence or arbitrariness, etc. and get the problem resolved. Often a simple letter from him to the concerned official about the case of an aggrieved citizen leads to prompt action without any further enquiry. Cases of complaints relating to inefficiency, discrimination, favouritism, departure from laws, rules or regulations, unjust or biased decisions, administrative excesses and abuses, not involving corruption are dealt with by the Ombudsman more speedily and satisfactorily. Most of such complaints are usually dealt with by the Ombudsman either after calling the complainant and the accused official to his chamber or himself visiting his office and discuss the case. Relief is provided immediately in case of genuine complaints and those not found to be of any merit are closed with suitable intimation to the parties. In dealing with public complaints, an Ombudsman's first priority is to provide relief to the aggrieved party wherever it is due. Punishment of the erring officials by their higher authorities comes next, in case of deliberate delays, negligence or any other fault or shortcomings on their parts. If anyone was found to be habitually negligent, the Ombudsman has the power to write to the higher authorities for taking disciplinary action and he himself could send an adverse report on the officer after obtaining his explanation, for being placed in his Confidential Rolls. Cases involving corruption are passed on to a separate agency dealing with corruption cases, for formal investigation and inquiry under the law. This appears to be the most practical way of dealing with ordinary complaints and giving relief to a genuinely aggrieved party. The important point is to have two separate machineries for dealing with public complaints–one involving corruption and another involving misadminis-tration. The combining of these two types of complaints to be handled by a single institution, under the ARC's recommendation, (of *Lokpal* and *Lokayukta)* did not find favour at the Central level and in many states too. Hence at the Centre there is neither a Lokpal nor a Lokayukta as yet. There is, therefore, need to re-examine this matter and provide for two separate complaint-handling machineries. Complaints involving ordinary grievances can be dealt with by one specific grievance-handling authority (Ombudsman type) at the Centre. It may consist of one or more Ombudsmen who could be designated as Lokadhikari, as distinct from Lokpal and Lokayukta whose roles may be confined to investigation of corruption cases only. Lokpal may deal with corruption allegations against ministers, and Lokayukta with corruption allegations against all other public officials. In fact, the latest Lok Pal Bill (1998) of the Central Government (which is still pending) realized this important aspect and accordingly deals only with complaints involving corruption against Central Ministers. Complaints of misadministration relating to inefficiency, misapplication of laws and rules, harsh or improper decisions, etc. on the part of Ministers or officials, have been kept out of the jurisdiction of Lokpal. However, at present there is no independent non-corruption grievance handling machinery either at the Centre or in the States. The Central Vigilance Commission deals with this problem to some extent relating to public officials. But here also corruption cases take much of the CVC's time. There are of course departmental agencies to handle public grievances under the control of the departments concerned. Aggrieved citizens dissatisfied with the acts of omissions and commissions of public officials now mostly knock the doors of the judiciary for relief. That has overburdened the judiciary with massive load of cases millions of which remain pending for long periods. There is accordingly need to have an Ombudsman type of independent grievance redressal body which could be designated as mentioned earlier as Lokadhikari. The Lokadhikari, like the Ombudsman, is to be independent of the executive, the legislature and the judiciary. He may be required to investigate complaints of citizens and recommend suitable action for redressal to competent authorities. His functioning need to be open and informal without any rigid procedures. To keep his workload within manageable limits he may deal with complaints of general nature concerning the public at large rather than complaints of wrong doings against any single individual barring exceptional cases of gross injustice or hardship. The complaints of general nature may relate to matters like lack of water supply, power supply, faulty maintenance of institutions like schools, hospitals, roads–sewerage, transport facilities, allotment of land, houses, etc. in any area (village, town, city etc.). The Lokadhikari may visit schools, hospitals, jails, police stations, orphanages, etc. to see if these are functioning satisfactorily in accordance with the prescribed rules, procedures and guidelines. If he comes across cases of corruption he may report the same to the Lokpal/Lokayukta as the case may be. Individual complaints except cases of gross injustice may be dealt with by the departmental agencies. Important complaints involving chronic or large-scale faults of a general nature need alone to be dealt with by the Lokadhikari. He should exercise his powers of supervision and inspection of public dealing offices effectively to prevent any wrong doing. He should have like Ombudsman elsewhere the power to recommend amendment of laws, rules, procedures etc. where any such change may be beneficial to the citizens. It may be necessary to have more than one Lokadhikari as a single person may find the work to be too heavy.

One of the Lokadhikaris (where there are more than one) may be designated as Chief or Mukhya Lokadhikari to coordinate and distribute work among them on departmental or functional basis. In due course, the States may have their own Lokadhikaris to deal with citizens' non-corruption grievances in their areas of administration. The appointment and removal of a Lokadhikari at the Centre and in the states may be in the same manner as that of the Comptroller and Auditor General of India (C&AG). His status and other service conditions could also be similar. In a sense, a Lokadhikari may perform analogous functions in the administrative field as the C&AG does with regard to the financial dealings of Government being above board. He may thus in a way function as the "Efficiency Auditor" of public officials. Lokadhikari may investigate acts of omissions and commissions of officials on his own initiative or on the basis of complaint from aggrieved citizens. Like the Ombudsmen elsewhere, the Lokadhikarihe may, after investigation, recommend appropriate remedial steps where necessary, to competent higher authorities. He himself should have no power to reverse or modify any action or decision of any public official. By virtue of the power and prestige attached to his office and also by convention, his advice and recommendations should generally be accepted. To make the institution of Lokadhikari strong and effective, in investigating cases of misadministration on the part of public officials, it should have the following features which are broadly similar to the Ombudsman systems in countries like Denmark, New Zealand and the U.K. etc.:

(i) A Lokadhikari should be a constitutional body of the rank and status of the C&AG. Constitutional appointment will give him the prestige necessary for effective discharge of his functions.

(ii) He should have the power to take up investigation, on the basis of a complaint as well as on his own initiative *(suo motu)*.

(iii) He should have the power to recommend or advise suitable remedial or corrective action in important cases involving the general public, as also to suggest changes, improvements in policy, procedures or practices in administration or amendment of laws, statutes etc., where called for.

(iv) Decisions should be taken on his advice, recommendations, etc., by the competent authorities within a specified time-limit.

(v) A Lokadhikari should have the power to publicize cases of

serious misadministration where his advice was disregarded after due intimation to the agencies concerned.

(*vi*) A Lokadhikari should have the power to send special reports to Parliament in addition to the annual report with copies to the Prime Minister. These reports should be discussed in a Committee of Parliament in the same way as the C&AG's reports are discussed by the Public Accounts Committee.

In keeping with our political, judicial and administrative arrangements, certain areas of administration like service problems of civil and defense employees, matters involving security of the State or issues where remedy is available through normal courts or tribunals etc., be kept out of the purview the Lokadhikari. In special circumstances, a Lokadhikari may deal with complaints relating to such matters, where an aggrieved party for good and adequate reasons is not in a position to approach a court or a tribunal.

There is no doubt that with the growing dissatisfaction of the people with government due to lack of sensitivity, efficiency, impartially and fair play of public officials, an Ombudsman-type independent supervising and investigating authority will go a long way in restoring public confidence in administration. The findings of an independent investigation authority would also protect public officials in cases of false or baseless complaints against them.

The new institution will also, to a large extent, lessen the burden of the higher courts relating to Public Interest Writ Petitions (PIL). At present, much time of the High Courts and the Supreme Court is taken away on the hearing of many complaints of misadministration like patients not getting proper food or medicine in Government hospitals; mine labourers not getting required facilities of drinking water; inefficient administration of protective homes, jails and hospitals; irregularities in admissions or conduct of examinations in engineering or medical colleges, torture of persons in police custody, etc. etc. Doubts have been raised and strong criticisms voiced against the higher courts to spend so much of their time for such work. The Lokadhikari could deal with most of such cases of public interest litigation (PIL) with greater speed and informality. That will save the valuable time of the higher judiciary to deal with constitutionally more important matters. As in other countries, fear of adverse press publicity in not accepting recommendations of the Lokadhikari will force the concerned public authorities to positively respond to them. In a democratic system of Government like ours, this would be a more reasonable and practical way to render social justice.

The new institution of Lokadhikari will also be a boon to public administration from another angle. There is increasing criticism of outside interference, pulls and pressures, in taking objective and impartial decisions by public officials. Investigation of any such complaint by an independent, non-political, non-partisan authority like the Lokadhikari will be of great advantage. The Lokadhikari can publicly expose and criticize any influential person who may have exercised undue, unhealthy, or partisan pressure on a public official in the discharge of his lawful duties. The risk and possibility of such investigation and publicity will make officials more careful and this will also strengthen their hands in resisting outside pressures of influential persons. A Lokadhikari should be empowered to call and go through any official records to verify the truth and soundness of reasons in arriving at a decision. Even a Minister's orders could be subject to his scrutiny in case of complaints of arbitrariness, nepotism or favouritism. The very existence of such an institution will have great preventive value in checking misadministration and malpractices.

To make a beginning as in some Canadian states, one or more specialized Lokadhikaris may be appointed for dealing with specific areas of administration, like the police, roads, electricity boards, Railways, Banks, etc. Presently *Sadak, Bijli* and *Pani* are the main problem areas of the people. Grievances relating to these may receive priority of attention of the Lokadhikaris in the states as also at the Central level. The success of the institution of Lokadhikari will, however, ultimately depend on the caliber, character and competence of the persons so appointed. Over-zealousness, exaggerated sense of self-importance, or an undue fault-finding mentality may pose a danger to the success of the Plan. There should be no attempt to find fault where there is none or the fault is of a minor or technical nature. Official view-points should also be given utmost consideration. It has to be recognized that, despite wide-spread criticism of administration and public officials, there are still many honest and competent officials. One of the strong arguments against introduction of Ombudsman system in some countries is that any indiscriminate fault-finding and giving injurious Press publicity of administrative actions, by an external agency lacking understanding of prevailing circumstances, may weaken and demoralize public officials. Hence, the need to select the right type of persons for this office. A Lokadhidkari must not only be impartial, objective and fair-minded but also refrain from the temptation of false image-building, or projecting self-importance through media publicity. He must not have the faults he is empowered to probe among others.

10

JOB RESERVATION FOR OBCs: CONSTITUTIONAL PROVISIONS AND JUDICIAL VERDICTS

Backward class reservation issues keep coming to the forefront again and again generally on the eve of Assembly or Parliamentary elections. This is because the Constitution has left scope for the Government to decide as to which category of persons could be treated as the "backward class" deserving benefits of reservation and what should be the size of such reservation for them. Most political parties to placate various castes and communities for getting their votes and electoral support, vie with each other to enlarge the list of backward classes unmindful of the real scope and purpose of reservation. Brahmins, Vaisyas, Kshatriyas, Marathas, Jats, Rajputs, etc., who were considered by the Mandal Commission on OBC reservation, to be higher social classes and outside the scope of reservation are also agitating to get the benefit of reservation on economic considerations. In some states Jats have already succeeded in getting their reservation claims accepted – on grounds of social and educational backwardness. Now the Rajputs and Gujjars have mounted their campaign particularly in Rajasthan for being treated as 'backwards'. Brahmins too have claimed reservation benefits on grounds of poverty. Every caste and class earlier excluded from reservation benefits now want the doors of reservation to be opened for them too. Virtually all castes and communities, including Muslims, are claiming to be "backwards" to become entitled to reservation.

Keeping these developments in mind it may be useful to examine the legal and rational aspects of reservation. The relevant constitutional provisions and the judicial verdicts thereon have to be taken into account. The subject of reservation with its social and economic dimensions has been comprehensively dealt with in various judicial verdicts. It goes to the credit of our higher judiciary that it has generally interpreted the reservation provisions in the Constitution in a manner as would make them equitable and rational in their implementation. Through their various judgments the High Courts and the Supreme Court have been able to limit the size and scope of reservation to be broadly in tune with the spirit of the Constitution. For this purpose the important goals and objectives of the Constitution, more particularly those laid down in the Directive Principles of State Policy in Chapter IV, have been kept in view.

Reservation of seats in educational and technical institutions under Article 15(4) and in public services under Article 16(4) of the Constitution had presented little problem for those "backward" classes who belonged to the Scheduled Castes and Scheduled Tribes. These Castes/Tribes are in fact notified as such under Articles 341 and 342 respectively of the Constitution for each state. Article 335 also provides that "the claims of the members of the Scheduled Castes and Scheduled Tribes shall be taken into consideration, consistently with the maintenance of efficiency of administration, in the making of appointments to services and posts in connection with the affairs of the Union or of a state." Here the only caution to be exercised was the need to maintain "the efficiency of administration" while specially considering the claims of the SC/ST for public services. There is no mention of any size or percentage of reservation as such for the SCs/STs.

This general provision under Article 335 only implied that relaxed or somewhat lower standards could be applied in assessing the suitability of SC/ST candidates for public posts and services in comparison to the general category candidates. The in-built check or restraint also implied that in adopting lower norms, the need to maintain efficiency of administration has to be given due importance. This meant that the norms or the benchmark in assessing suitability of SC/ST candidates should not be too low nor the size of reservation too high as that might adversely tell upon the efficiency of administration. The scope of clause (4) of Article 16 of the Constitution was however very much wider as besides the Scheduled Castes/Scheduled Tribes, it also permitted reservation being made in favour of "any backward class of citizens which, in the opinion of the state, is not adequately represented in the services under the state." In the original draft of this clause even the phrase 'backward' was absent. It was inserted later in the final draft. The justification for this addition, as explained in the Constituent Assembly by Dr. Ambedkar, the Chairman of the drafting Committee of the Constitution, was that "unless you use some such qualifying phrase as 'backward' the exception made in favour of reservation will ultimately eat up the rule altogether. Nothing of the rule will remain" as very large number of people may demand reservation. The 'rule' which Dr. Ambedkaar referred to was clause (1) of Article 16 providing that "there shall be equality of opportunity for all citizens in matters relating to employment or appointment to any office under the state."

The intention of the founding fathers of the Constitution, as may be seen from the debates in the Constituent Assembly relating to Article 16 was to reconcile the viewpoints of those who wanted absolute equality for all citizens without any reservation for any class and those who wanted a suitable provision "in favour of certain communities which have so far been outside the administration" in making appointments to services under the state. Accordingly, Article 16 with its clauses (1) and (4) tried to harmonise these two opposing viewpoints. While clause (1) emphasized "equality of opportunity" for all citizens, clause (4) by way of special provision permitted some reservation in favour of any "backward class" of citizens, who in the opinion of the state are not adequately represented in government services. This conditional reservation as stated by Dr. Ambedkar was meant for only a "minority of seats" so that the importance of the main provision of "equality of opportunity" is not unduly undermined. Even though 'backward class' was not defined in the Constitution, it was clarified during the debates that among others this 'class' would certainly include the Scheduled Castes and Scheduled Tribes. Dr. Ambedkar further stated that a backward community is one which is "backward in the opinion of the government." Thus it was left to the state and Central governments to specify who besides the Scheduled Castes/Scheduled Tribes are to be the 'Other Backward Classes' (OBCs) and the criteria for their being so treated or identified. The size of reservation to be made for them was also left to the governments (Central or States) concerned to decide for posts and services under them. Since the conditions and levels of backwardness and the numerical size of the backward people varied from state to state and they were yet to be properly identified, the framers of the Constitution did not wish to lay down any specific or uniform percentage of reservation for the OBCs for the state or the Central services and posts.

For those classified as Scheduled Castes/Scheduled Tribes under the Constitution reservation in Central services was in vogue since long. In fact for the Scheduled Castes (some of them earlier referred to as 'depressed' classes) reservation of 8.33 per cent in 1943, which was raised to 12.5 per cent in June 1946 was in vogue for Central Government posts. Thus for them there was reservation even before independence. For some of the Scheduled Tribes earlier referred to as "Primitive Tribes" five per cent reservation in Central posts was introduced for the first time only in 1950. After the 1961 census reservation for the Scheduled Castes was raised to 15 per cent and for the Scheduled Tribes to 7.5 per cent in Central Government posts and services. This was nearly in proportion to the percentages of their population in the country. There was no reservation in the Central services for any category of persons later described as "OBCs." In some southern states, however, some such OBCs had reservation of varying percentages in their respective state services even prior to the adoption of the Constitution in January 1950. The definition of 'backward class' and their lists, however, varied from state to state.

As required under Article 340 of the Constitution, the Central Government had set up a Backward Class Commission in January 1953 under the Chairmanship of Kaka Kalelkar "to investigate the conditions of the socially and educationally backward classes and to recommend the steps that should be taken to improve their conditions." This first Backward Class Commission submitted its report in March 1955 listing 2,399 castes and communities as "backward." It recommended reservation of posts in government services as one of the ways to help to remove their social, educational and economic backwardness. The Central Government then headed by Pt. Jawaharlal Nehru, however, did not accept this recommendation for Central Government posts as identification of backwards was primarily based on caste considerations. In rejecting the Commission's recommendation the Central Government order stated that caste system is the greatest hindrance in the way of India's progress towards an egalitarian Society and as such caste cannot be permitted to be a basis for any reservation for Central Government posts. State Governments, however, were left free to decide on reservation for posts under State Governments according to their own thinking and policy. Some State Governments thereafter appointed their own separate state level commissions to identify socially and educationally backward classes to consider the scope and size of reservation for them. Following the recommendations of such state level commissions, reservations were made in some state services for the OBCs of those states. On the basis of some judicial verdicts like *Balaji* vs. *State of Mysore* 1963 (Supp. 1 SCR 439: AIR 1963 SC 649) these state level reservations were, however, kept within the upper limit of 50 per cent of the vacancies to be filled so as to be fair to the general category candidates and thus satisfy the basic philosophy of the Constitution relating to "equality of opportunity." Any reservation higher than 50 per cent was judicially held to be violative of the constitutional mandates of Article 16(1) and (4) as it would amount to reverse discrimination.

Later, the Central Government, during the Janata regime of Morarji Desai, appointed another Backward Class Commission in 1979 under the Chairmanship of B.P. Mandal which submitted its report in 1980. This Backward Class Commission, better known as Mandal Commission, identified 3,743 castes as socially and educationally backward (SEBCs) and recommended 27 per cent job reservation for them in Central Government posts. In doing so it kept in view the existing 22.5 per cent reservation for Scheduled Castes and Scheduled Tribes and the judicial verdicts to limit the total size of reservation to 50 per cent. According to the Mandal Commission 43.7 per cent among Hindus and 8.40 among non-Hindus or nearly 52 per cent of the Indian population belonged to OBCs. Thus, together with the 22.56 per cent SC/ST population, about 75 per cent of the Indian population was treated to be of 'backward classes' category to be eligible for reservation under clause (4) of Article 16. This obviously was too large a size of the population to improve their social and economic conditions through job reservation in public services. The Mandal Commission had in reality failed to identify such of the fewer genuinely 'backward' classes who would have deserved to come under the scope of Article 16(4) to improve their social, educational and economic conditions through the mechanism of job reservation in government services. Accordingly, for nearly a decade the Mandal Commission Report had not been accepted by the Congress Governments of Indira Gandhi and Rajiv Gandhi (1980-89). The Report had remained under discussions and debates between the Central and state governments to give it a more practical shape and help the real backwards. The thinking was not against OBC reservation as such but to make it more meaningful by limiting the number of OBCs deserving of reservation. As provided under Article 335– "administrative efficiency" had also to be given due importance along with considerations of "social justice." To accept the Mandal Report without any refinements, limitations or modifications especially its caste based eligibility criteria for OBCs would have added fuel to the fire of casteism and communalism in the country. The view at that time therefore, was (the author was the then Secretary to Government of India in the Ministry of Personnel, and Administrative Reforms dealing with civil services) to restrict reservation to fewer and more deserving backward classes identified on social, educational and economic criteria rather than on caste criteria alone. However, after the change of government at the Centre in 1989 and V.P. Singh as the new Prime Minister, for political expediency the Mandal Report was immediately accepted by his government in its totality without modifications. Government orders were also hastily issued in August 1990 reserving 27 per cent vacancies in Central posts and services for the OBCs as listed in the Mandal report in addition to the existing reservation of 22.5 per cent for the SCs/STs. The size of the total reservation thus became 49.5 per cent or a fraction less than the upper limit of 50 per cent decided in the *Balaji* vs. *State of Mysore* judgment. Thus, though the upper limit of reservation as decided by the Judiciary was technically adhered to the spirit behind the upper limit of 50 per cent was not kept in mind so as to bring it down to a more reasonably lower level. It appears that the motive of caste based electoral politics outweighed prudent and rational policy of "social justice" for the benefit of the truly "backward" classes. It was thought that if more castes were included in the "OBC" list more would be the political gain to the ruling party.

The order accepting the Mandal Commission Report was issued so hastily by the V.P. Singh Government that it came as a bolt from the blue to the general category of students. No wonder that it provoked widespread protests, and riots, causing large-scale damage to private and public properties and loss of many young lives through self-immolations. The government job minded younger persons of the non-OBC class saw their future to be bleak and gloomy. The general feeling was that merit was being sacrificed at the altar of casteism on malafide political considerations of building vote bank. The legality of the order was accordingly immediately challenged through several writ petitions in the Supreme Court.

All the writ petitions were combined and the matter was heard by a Special nine-Judge Bench of the apex court "to finally settle the legal position relating to reservation" as the judgment of the case stated. In this case ((*Indra Sawhney* vs. *Union of India* 1992 SCC (L&S) Duppl: popularly known as the Mandal Judgment the apex court dealt with most of the ongoing major reservation issues. These among others included *(a)* the question of Constitutional validity of reservation; *(b)* its scope and upper limit; *(c)* how to ensure that it does not impair the efficiency of administration; and *(d)* how to identify the 'backward classes' without solely relying on caste, etc. While considering these important issues the apex court had kept in mind, (as the judgment says) that "the law is not an abstract concept removed from the society it serves, and that judges must constantly strive to narrow the gap between the ideal of equal justice and reality of social inequality." In simple language it meant that at times ground realities may require some compromises to be made in following theory of equal justice for all. With regard to the Constitutional validity of reservation, the judgment elaborately dealt with the real meaning and intentions behind Articles 14, 15 and 16 of the Constitution dealing with "equality", "equal opportunity" and "non-discrimination" between citizens to decide on the legality of reservation for some classes of people. It was explained that the expression "equality before law" and the "equal protection of laws" in Article 14 not only permitted but required that "unequals be treated unequally" to bring about real equality before law for them. The intention of the Article was not mere theoretical or academic equality but to ensure real and substantial equality. If the weaker sections or the backwards are treated on equal footings with the better placed persons or the advanced classes they will be unable to compete with them. That would amount to denial of justice to the backwards and would perpetuate, if not aggravate, their inequality and backwardness. To bring about equality between the unequals, therefore, it would be obligatory to adopt special and positive measures in favour of the back ards to minimize or eliminate their inequality. Articles 15(4) and 16(4) more explicitly provided for special treatment for the disadvantaged sections of society and thus supplemented and strengthened Article 14. Again, while clause (1) of Article 15 prohibits discrimination against any citizen on grounds only of religion, caste, sex, etc. Clause (4) of this very article permitted the state to make special provision for any 'socially and educationally' backward classes as also for the Scheduled Castes/Scheduled Tribes.

This clause (4) in Article 15 was in fact inserted by way of the Constitution First Amendment Act, 1951. This enabled the state to reserve seats for the backward class of citizens including the Scheduled Castes and Scheduled Tribes in public educational institutions for their advancement. The necessity for this constitutional amendment arose, as in a case before it (*State of Madras* vs. *Champakam*–1951) the apex court had held the communal G.O. of 1927 of the then Madras Government reserving seats in Medical and Engineering Colleges on communal basis, i.e. separately for Hindus, Christians, Muslims, etc., and not on specific considerations of social backwardness to be invalid under the new Constitution after it came into force in 1950. Accordingly a new clause (4) in Article 15 had to be inserted by way of the First constitutional amendment to make it constitutionally permissible for reservation of seats for 'socially and educationally backward classes' as also for Scheduled Castes and Scheduled Tribes.

Similarly, while clause (1) of Article 16 provides for equality of opportunity in matters of employment under the state and clause (2) prohibits discrimination between them on grounds only of religion, race, caste, sex, etc., clause (4) of the Article which was there from the beginning allows the state to make reservation for any backward class of citizens, which in the opinion of the state is not adequately represented in the services under the state.

Apart from Articles 14, 15, and 16 which constitutionally permit special consideration or positive action by way of reservation being made in favour of the backward classes of citizens, several other Articles, like 38, 39A, 41 and 46 falling under the Directive Principles of State Policy also call upon the state to take ameliorative measures to remove inequalities among citizens and improve the lot of those who suffer from social, educational and economic disabilities. Article 38(2) for example, wants the state "to strive to minimize the inequalities in status, facilities, and opportunities not only among individuals but amongst groups of people." Similarly, Article 39A wants the state to ensure "that the operation of the legal system promotes justice." Article 46 says in more positive terms that "the state shall promote with special care the educational and economic interests of the weaker sections of the people, and in particular, of the Scheduled Castes and the Scheduled Tribes and shall protect them from social injustices and all forms of exploitation." All these important provisions in the Constitution were undoubtedly made to minimize inequalities among citizens. It was obviously realized that where there are glaring inequalities among the people there would be no room for real equality under the law if they are treated on equal footings. To treat every one–backwards and forwards-with equality would have amounted to perpetuating inequality of the backwards. The socially handicapped had therefore to be given special support for real justice and for meaningful equal treatment. Thus the apex court held reservation for the OBC including SCs/STs to be constitutionally valid and justified. The size of reservation to bring about equality however had to be fair and reasonable and was accordingly comprehensively deliberated to be finally fixed at 50 per cent. The rationality of this has been explained in subsequent paragraphs:

> Justice Sawant, a member of the nine-judge bench in the *Indra Sawhney* case, in his separate judgement, stated that "inequality ill favours fraternity" and that the constitutional goals of assuring the dignity of the individual and the unity and integrity of the nation would remain unattainable so long as the equality of opportunity is not ensured to all. Justice Pandian, another judge of the bench, too was of the view that Article 16(4) was designed and purposely introduced for providing special preferential treatment to the backward class "in order to make the unequal equal." Justice Sahai, also a member of the nine-judge bench, was of the view that "abstract equality is neither the theme nor the philosophy of our Constitution. Real equality through practical means is the avowed objective." He also stated that the principle of equal protection of law does not mean that "every law must have universal application to all persons who are not by nature, attainment or circumstance, in the same position." Special treatment by way of reasonable reservation for the classes that genuinely require special treatment was accordingly not violative of "equality before the law" or "the equal protection of the laws" under Article 14 of the Constitution. Similarly, positive discrimination in favour of the weaker sections of society is permissible under Articles 15 and 16 provided it is reasonable and fair in its reach and scope.

The resentment and large-scale disturbances on the acceptance of the Mandal Report were really not against the policy of reservation and its application in favour of the Scheduled Castes and Scheduled

Tribes. The agitations and the writ applications were provoked on the grounds of reservation being made applicable to "OBCs" and that too being excessive due to indiscriminate classification of hundreds of undeserving castes as 'backwards' with malafide political motives of gaining their electoral support. 'Poverty' or economic criteria for reservation of a reasonable percentage of vacancies under clause (4) of Article 16 may not have been unacceptable to the young students of the general category. As mentioned earlier, even before Independence there was reservation and it had been accepted to help the real backwards i.e. the "depressed" and the "primitive" classes. What was new and considered to be unjust in the latest reservation order was the political twist given to reservation by extending its scope to include hundreds of castes by treating them as OBCs on the basis of the Mandal Commission Report. "Caste" was treated as synonimous to "class" by Mandal Commission for reservation under Article 16(4) which was not the intention of the Constitution makers for they were well aware of the difference between the words "caste" and "class" and had used the later terminology for reservation in clause (4) of Article 16. The word "caste" was not deliberately mentioned in the Article, with a view that it should not be the only basis for reservation purposes.

With regard to the size of reservation under clause (4) of Article 16 the apex court had held that "the power of reservation like any other legal power should be exercised in a fair manner and within reasonable limits and what is more reasonable than to say that reservation under clause (4) shall not exceed 50 per cent." In justification of this decision the apex court further explained that while Article 16(4) was conceived in the interest of the backward classes, the guarantee of equality enshrined in clause (1) of Article 16 was a guarantee held out to every citizen and to the entire society and as such has to be given due consideration. The court also held that "adequate representation" under clause (4) does not speak of "proportionate representation" and hence the percentage of the total backward class population to the total population of the country need not be the sole decisive factor in fixing the size of reservation. Clause (4) was meant to be a special provision by way of exception to the main Constitutional provision of "equality of opportunity." Attention was also drawn to Dr. Ambedkar's views that the "exception should not be so large that it left no room for the rule to operate." Obviously exception was not intended to overshadow or eclipse the main rule of – 'equality of opportunity'. In October 2006 another Bench of the apex court had ordered a 50 per cent ceiling on quota saying "a numerical benchmark is the surest immunity against charges of discrimination. If the extent of reservation goes beyond the cutoff point then it results in reverse discrimination.

The court also held that reservation under Article 16(4) was not to operate like a communal reservation and accordingly it decided that if "some members belonging to, say the Scheduled Castes get selected in the open competition on the basis of their own merit, they will be treated as open competition candidates" and not as reserved category candidates. The 'creamy layer' concept (which will be discussed later) was also introduced to dilute the importance of caste in the classification of backward class as also to confine reservation for the genuinely backwards. According to this concept every member of a 'caste' listed as backward would not *ipso facto* become eligible for reservation. The forwards among them termed as "creamy layer" will have to be excluded from reservation benefits. Thus "caste" of an individual alone was not to be the sole criteria for being eligible for reservation benefits. Only the backward members of any backward caste were made eligible for reservation and not the "forwards" among them.

To limit reservation to 50 per cent the court also decided that the three per cent reservation allowed to physically handicapped persons–termed as 'horizontal' reservation as distinct from 'vertical' reservation so far as the SC/ST/OBC handicapped are concerned would have to be adjusted against their respective shares of reservation within the upper limit of 50 per cent of total reservation.

With regard to Scheduled Castes/Scheduled Tribes reservation, there was the practice of 'carry forward' of unfilled reserved vacancies of one year to the next year. At times it so happened that the 'carry forward' vacancies of previous years when added to the reserved vacancies of the recruitment year exceeded 50 per cent of the total vacancies of that year. Thus the accumulated size of the unfilled reserved vacancies to the extent it exceeded 50 per cent, deprived the general category candidates of their 50 per cent share. There were instances when the open competition vacancies for the general category candidates came down to less than 25 per cent, the rest being treated as reserved due to the "carry forward" provisions. The court therefore decided that the 50 per cent upper limit for reservation of vacancies should apply to both normal plus the "carry forward." In simple terms, the apex court wanted that the shares of vacancies in a year for both the categories should remain within their respective 50 per cent limits, in order to do substantive justice to both categories, i.e., reserved and general categories. The apex court was strongly of the view that "requirement of efficiency of administration is an overriding mandate of the Constitution." An inefficient administration, it held, "betrays the present as well as the future of the nation." To comply with this reasoning, the court decided that reservation is not to apply to promotion as that would be an "unacceptable inroad into the rule of equality of opportunity" apart from adversely affecting efficiency of administration.

In some earlier judgments, starting with the *General Manager Southern Railway* vs. *Rangachari* case of 1962 (2 SCR 586: AIR 1962 SC 36), the apex court had upheld reservation both for initial recruitment as also for promotion. The justification given for this at that time was that the word 'adequate' representation in clause (4) of Article 16 meant both 'quantitative' as well as 'qualitative' adequacy. The court accordingly was of the view that the advancement of the backward classes required not only adequate representation in the lower rungs of the services to which initial recruitments were made but at higher promotional levels as well, to which appointments were made through selections. In overruling this earlier judgment (with regard to reservation in promotion) the apex court, in the *Indra Sawhney* case, held that while at the initial recruitment stage reservation can be made for the backward class citizens, but once they enter the service, efficiency of administration demands that they too compete with others and earn promotion on their merit. The court had also observed "crutches cannot be provided throughout one's career. That would not be in the interest of efficiency of administration nor in the larger interest of the nation." The court accordingly overruled its own earlier decision in *Rangachari* case which had permitted reservation in the matter of promotion since 1962. This ruling as decided was to operate only prospectively and existing provisions relating to reservation in promotion in Central and state services were allowed to continue to be operative for a period of five years more, i.e. till mid-November 1997 and to cease only thereafter. This much time was allowed for smooth transition to the new situation, as it would have been unfair to take away a long-standing benefit of promotion in reservation too suddenly.

The judicial interpretations of the Constitution in limiting the size and scope of backward class reservation was obviously intended to ensure that while the genuinely backwards were helped to improve their conditions, the rest of the citizens did not find the extent of reservations unduly excessive, invidious and amounting to reverse discrimination. The reservation provisions of the Constitution were meant to help the backwards and not inflict any punishment on the rest of the citizens for any historical wrongs suffered by the weaker sections. While the victims of past discrimination had to be specially cared for, the generality of citizens striving to progress on their own merits were not to suffer to an unbearable extent. In caring for the interests of the backwards the Court had not overlooked the interests of others nor the need for the maintenance of efficiency of administration. Thus the verdict of the Court ensured that justice was done to both categories of the citizen i.e. the backwards and the general category keeping in mind the real intentions of the Constitution makers.

Justice Thomen a member of the nine-judge bench was of the view that "reservation by reason of its exclusion of the generality of candidates competing solely on merits must be narrowly tailored and strictly construed so as not to create hateful caste-prejudices and divisions between classes of people." Indeed that would be injurious to promotion of fraternity among all classes of people and assuring dignity of the individual.

The apex court in its various judgments relating to reservation had also held that the intention behind the special protection guaranteed by Articles 15(4) and 16(4) was to improve the lot of only those classes of backward citizens whose backwardness was due to historical discrimination and who were unable to join the mainstream of upward mobility because of their social and educational backwardness. The crux of allowing reservation benefits therefore lay in proper identification of those backward class of citizens who deserved special considerations. The expression 'backward class' not being properly and adequately defined in the Constitution posed as stated by the Apex Court in the Mandal Judgment "the single most difficult question" to be decided. This provision being loosely worded had allowed governments of different political parties to liberally interpret it to build up their own vote banks. The Court had therefore to rationally define the provisions in order to fulfil the main purpose of reservation to uplift the conditions of the genuinely backwards.

After lengthy and comprehensive discussions the majority view in the *Indra Sawhney* case that emerged was that the 'backwardness' contemplated by Article 16(4) is mainly social backwardness and not any other kind of backwardness. Under Article 15(4), backward classes (as mentioned in the clause itself) are those who are both "socially and educationally" backward. The Scheduled Caste/Scheduled Tribes have been specifically mentioned under this clause for purpose of special treatment for their advancement. Economic backwardness or poverty by itself was not found to be an acceptable criteria in the identification of backward class of citizens both under Articles 15(4) and 16(4). Similarly educational backwardness alone would not entitle any reservation benefits under these Articles. The Court held that caste being an identifiable social class could be taken as a starting point for 'backward class' identification. Reservation benefits are however meant for only the socially low ranking castes under Article 16(4). Social standing or, social status again depends in no small way on the occupation traditionally followed by the members of the caste. Lower the occupation, lower will be the social standing of the class in the graded social hierarchy. Even Dr. Ambedkar had stated that "caste is an enclosed class." In spite of urbanisation, the caste-occupation nexus still continues to a great extent. Lower occupations due to low incomes also result in poverty. Thus caste-occupation–poverty cycle is the ever present ground reality. All these factors have to be focused in deciding which of the socially backward classes should qualify for reservation under Article 16(4). There has to be no sole reliance on the caste factor alone.

Again constitutionally reservation benefit is admissible only to those backward citizens who are "not adequately represented" in the services of the state. The fact of adequacy or otherwise has, however, to be determined by the government as stated by Dr. Ambedkar in a fair and reasonable manner. This decision would also be subject to judicial scrutiny and verdict. Further, since the concept of 'class' denotes a number of persons having certain common traits which distinguish them from the others in a backward class the connecting link being social backwardness, it has to be broadly the same for all members. If, however, some members of this class are far too advanced socially, the connecting thread between them and the remaining class snaps. They would be misfit in the class and their exclusion alone would make the class compact. In fact that would alone benefit the truly backwards. The basis of identifying the socially advanced families or the 'creamy layer' could be the nature of posts or positions in public services, occupation and income, etc., of the persons of such families. As an example, the court mentioned that "if a member of a designated backward class becomes a member of IAS or IPS or any other All-India Service, his status in society (social status) rises; he is no longer socially disadvantaged." Exclusion of such socially advanced members will make the 'class' a truly backward class. The Court directed that reservation under clause (4) of Article 16 for the OBCs will be operative only after identification and exclusion of the members of the creamy layer from the OBC list. This 'creamy layer' concept was, however, not applied to the Scheduled Castes/Scheduled Tribes as their backwardness was not entirely due to social backwardness. They generally were historically far more disadvantaged groups than the OBCs and deserved separate reservation quotas and separate programmes for their upliftment. Moreover since SCs/STs were notified by Presidential notifications under Articles 341 and 342 of the Constitution there was no further need for their identification or listing.

The apex court had also, on rational considerations, suggested that government should specify certain services and posts like technical posts in research and development organizations, in specialties and super-specialties in medicine and engineering, in areas of nuclear and space applications, in the field of aviation, etc., where reservation may not be advisable because of the highly technical nature of the jobs and limited opportunities. The government, however, has not yet taken any action on this rational advice. In its judgment in *Kartar Singh* vs. the *State of Madhya Pradesh* (1999), the Supreme Court had also disallowed lowering of qualifications for admission to super-speciality medical courses in favour of the reserved category candidates. It had ruled that candidates for such courses were expected to possess 'exceptional competence and skill' in their chosen fields as these were required 'for absorbing highly-specialised knowledge'. Moreover, opportunities for such training being few 'it would be in the national interest that these were made available to those who could profit from them the most, viz., the best brains in the country, irrespective of the class to which they belong'. The Court had no doubt that even among the reserved category there would be a fair number of candidates who on their own individual merits could qualify through open competition for admission into the super-speciality courses without any lowering of admission criteria for them.

If the basic philosophy of the Constitution to ensure justice to all the people is to be followed the doors of reservations should not be thrown wide open so as to include the politically powerful groups of citizens within the definition of 'backward class'. That would go against the criteria of social justice and would also violate the right of "equality" in its true sense. Indiscriminate use of reservation provisions would belie the hope of Dr. Ambedkar that the qualifying phrase 'backward' in clause (4) of Article 16 would limit reservation to a 'minority of seats'. Any irrational and large-scale inclusion of numerous castes in the backward class list will deprive the genuinely backward and the poorer sections of them from the reservation benefits as the forwards among them would eat up all the reserved vacancies. In the opinion of the author, if any constitutional amendment is required with regard to reservation it should be to completely do away with 'caste' in determining backwardness for the OBC category. For them economic criteria only need to be made the basis for making reservation. Attempt should also be made to fix the upper limit of reservation for all categories of backwards (including SC/ST) to around 30 per cent or say one-third (rather than 50%) of the total vacancies in any recruitment year. Religion, race, sex or caste-based reservation for any unduly long period will be against the constitutional objective of making India a technologically advanced, egalitarian and secular republic. Like 'untouchability' which has been abolished under Article 17 of the Constitution, reservation on social or caste considerations too should end as early as possible. Casteism unfortunately not only got a fresh lease of life after the acceptance of Mandal Report but also got strengthened by adding more castes in the list of OBC. Now every caste wants and agitates to be classified as backward. This trend needs to be stopped by introducing economic criteria for reservation. As soon as possible merit–and not birth–should become the real basis for an individual's progress and advancement in life. Apart from introduction of the creamy layer concept for OBC identification, the Apex Court was fair in disallowing reservation in promotion. It also limited the size of reservation to 50 per cent of all vacancies inclusive of "carry forward" for recruitment in a year. Some of these judicial verdicts to make reservation more rational and equitable were however reversed by the government by resorting to constitutional amendments. Two new clauses (4A) and (4B) were added to Article 16 which allowed reservation in promotion and also allowed carry forward of old vacancies outside the 50 per cent upper limit for the SCs/STs. These amended clauses are as below:

> "(4A) Nothing in this article i.e.16(4) shall prevent the State from making provision for reservation in matters of promotion, with consequential seniority, to any class or classes of posts in the services under the State in favour of the Scheduled Castes and the Scheduled Tribes which, in the opinion of the State, are not adequately represented in the services under the State.
>
> (4B) Nothing in this article shall prevent the State from considering any unfilled vacancies of a year which are reserved for being filled up in that year in accordance with any provision for reservation made under clause (4) or clause (4A) as a separate class of vacancies to be filled up in any succeeding year or years and such class of vacancies shall not be considered together with the vacancies of the year in which they are being filled up for determining the ceiling of fifty per cent reservation on total number of vacancies of that year.

Thus for SCs/STs reservation in promotion will continue as before. OBCs, however, have been kept outside the scope of this amendment. Similarly, "carry forward" vacancies for the SCs/STs of any year will not be treated as part of the vacancy of the year of recruitment. These will be filled separately and would not count against the 50 per cent limit of reservation in the year of recruitment. As a result the judiciary's attempt to rationalize reservations has been nullified by the Executive by amending the Constitution to discard the judicial verdict.

RESERVATION OF SEATS FOR OBCs IN HIGHER EDUCATIONAL INSTITUTIONS

A Five Judge Bench of the Apex Court headed by the Chief Justice of India K.G. Balakrishnan in a Writ Petition (Civil) No. 265 of 2006 had considered several important issues relating to reservation of seats for the students belonging to the SCs/STs and the socially and educationally backward class of citizens (OBCs) in the higher central educational institutions. The judgement in this case—*Ashok Kumar Thakur* vs. *The Union of India* was delivered on 10.4.08.

The first issue considered was regarding the constitutional validity of the 93rd constitutional amendment which inserted clause (5) in Article 15 of the Constitution empowering the State to make any special legal provision for the educational advancement of any socially and educationally backward classes of people. The amendment reads as under:

> "Nothing in this article or in sub-clause (g) of clause (1) of Article 19 shall prevent the State from making any special provision, by law, for the advancement of any socially and educationally backward classes of citizens or for the Scheduled Castes or the Scheduled Tribes in so far as such special provisions related to their admission to the educational institutions including private educational institutions, whether aided or unaided by the State, other than the minority educational institutions referred to in clause (1) of Article 30."

Some parties had raised objection to this constitutional amendment on the ground that it is violative of the basic structure of the Constitution for being discriminatory between citizens of different classes for admission into educational institutions. Another related issue challenged was the validity of the law. "The Central Educational Institutions (Reservation in Admission) Act of 2007 passed by Parliament based on the 93rd constitutional amendment. Section 3 of this Act of 2007 provided for reservation of 15 per cent seats for SCs, 7½ per cent for STs and 27 per cent for the OBCs in central educational institutions. For this purpose OBCs were defined in Section 2(g) of the Act to mean "the class or classes of citizens who are socially and educationally backward and are so determined by the Central Government" The "Central Educational Institution" was defined under Section 2(d) of the Act to mean and include universities and other institutions of higher learning, technical as also non-technical like Medical and Engineering colleges, IIMs, IITs, etc. Minority educational institutions established and administered by the minorities under clause (1) of Article 30 of the Constitution were however excluded from the purview of the Act. Similarly some other institutions of excellence and research enumerated in the schedule to the Act were also excluded from the scope of reservation under the Act. Few such institutions listed are Homi Bhabha National Institute, Mumbai, Tata Institute of Fundamental Research, Mumbai, Indian Institute of Remote Sensing, Dehradun, etc. etc. Government is, however, empowered to make additions and omissions as and when required to the list of excluded institutions.

The main objectives of the above legislation were highlighted in the "Statement of Objects and Reasons" at the time of its introduction as a Bill in Parliament. These stated:

> "Part IV of the Constitution containing the Directive Principles of State Policy, in Article 46, laid down that the State shall promote with special care the educational and economic interests of the weaker sections of the people, and, in particular, of the Scheduled Castes and the Scheduled Tribes, and shall protect them from social injustice. Access to education is of utmost importance in insuring advancement of persons belonging to the Scheduled Castes, the Scheduled Tribes and the socially and educationally backward classes of citizens, who are referred to as the Other Backward Classes (OBCs).
>
> The Constitution (93rd Amendment) Act, 2005, inserted clause (5) in Article 15 of the Constitution, with a view to promote the educational advancement of the socially and educationally backward classes of citizens, the Scheduled Castes and the Scheduled Tribes through special provisions relating to admission of students belonging to these categories in all educational institutions, including private educational institutions, whether aided or un-aided by the State. In terms of this provision, Parliament as well as the State Legislatures are empowered to make appropriate laws for the educational advancement of the weaker sections of the people.
>
> With a view to give effect to the constitutional provisions, it is expedient and necessary to make statutory provisions in the proposed Bill for reservation in matters of admissions for the students belonging to the Scheduled Castes (SCs), the Scheduled Tribes (STs) and the educationally backward classes of citizens (OBCs) in the Educational Institutions, including institutions deemed to be Universities established, maintained or aided by the Central Government."

These aims and objects of the law are undoubtedly unquestionable being in tune with the constitutional directives.

The judicial verdict accordingly, as in the earlier Mandal case was, that since the State has the constitutional responsibility to remove inequalities and backwardness from society it can legally empower itself to take suitable actions to fulfil this obligation. Therefore to make any special provisions for uplifting people who are factually unequal in their wealth, social status and education is in conformity with the constitutional objectives of bringing about equality, fraternity and human dignity among the citizens.

The Directive Principles of State Policy also imposed an obligation on the state to take positive action for creating socio-economic conditions in which poverty, ill-health, lack of education and unemployment etc. do not allow large disparity among citizens. While Fundamental Rights protect individual liberty, Directive Principles of the State Policy are meant to ensure social and economic justice among all classes of citizens. Fundamental Rights which guarantee "equality"/"equal opportunity" are no doubt valuable in a democracy but so also are the Directive Principles which nourish the roots of our democracy as these direct and therefore enable the state to take care of large masses of the poor and deprived people so as to bring them to enjoy the fruits of equality and freedom.

For those who do not have the bare necessities of life liberty has really no meaning. They cannot stand on equal footing with the rich and socially advanced citizens. They being in a disadvantaged position need special care of the state and its institutions. This basic constitutional objective accordingly would justify the making of any special legal provisions for the advancement of the weaker sections of society. The Apex Court in its verdict therefore held that the 93rd Constitutional Amendment Act, 2005 and the Central Educational Institutions (Reservation) Act, 2007 were in conformity with the Constitution and legally valid in all respects.

The Court, however, did not accept the plea that the analogy of creamy layer applied in the case of OBCs for reservation of jobs may not be applied for reservation of seats in educational institutions. It held that the "Creamy Layer" concept, as decided in the Mandal Judgment has to be applied for reservation of seats in educational institutions also. Exclusion of the "creamy layer" is essential for proper and correct identification of OBCs for eligibility of reservation.

Para 150 of the judgment of the Five-Judge Bench which justified the exclusion of the creamy layer for OBC identification is reproduced below for clarity:

> "It may be noted that the "creamy layer" principle is applied not as a general principle of reservation. It is applied for the purpose of identifying the socially and educationally backward class. One of the main criteria for determining the SEBC is poverty. If that be so, the principle of exclusion of "creamy layer" is necessary. Moreover, the majority in *Indra Sawhney's* case i.e., Mandal Judgement upheld the exclusion of "creamy layer" for the purpose of reservation under Article 16(4). Therefore, we are bound by the larger Bench i.e. Nine-Judge Bench decision of this Court in *Indra Sawhney's* case, and it cannot be said that the "creamy layer" principle cannot be applied for identifying SEBCs. Moreover, Articles 15(4) and 15(5) are designed to provide opportunities in education thereby raising educational, social and economic levels of those who are lagging behind and once this progress is achieved by this section, any legislation passed thereunder should be deemed to have served its purpose. By excluding those who have already attained economic well-being or educational advancement, the special benefits provided under these clauses cannot be further extended to them and, if done so, it would be unreasonable, discriminatory or arbitrary, resulting in reverse discrimination."

This judgement, thus, could be said to mean that reservation should last only for so long as is necessary to remove backwardness. Reservation is not meant to be available to those who have moved ahead from backward to forward category of citizens. No backward class of citizens is to be treated as permanently backward because of his caste alone. That would defeat the very purpose of reservation to remove backwardness.

Another important issue specially clarified in the judgement of the five-judge Bench was regarding the non-application of the "creamy layer" principle to the SCs/STs. In the Mandal Judgement (*Indra Sawhney* case) it was specifically stated that the "creamy layer" principle will not apply to SCs/STs. The five-judge Bench in para 163 of their judgement upheld and clarified this further as below:

> "Right from the beginning, the Scheduled Castes and the Scheduled Tribes were treated as a separate category and

nobody ever disputed the identification of such classes. So long as the "creamy layer" concept is not applied as one of the principles of equality, it cannot be applied to Scheduled Castes and Scheduled Tribes. Accordingly the court held that for the purpose of reservation, the principle of "creamy layer" is not applicable to Scheduled Castes and Scheduled Tribes."

One more troubling question dealt with in the five judge Bench judgement related to devising a rational exit policy for ending reservation i.e. to fix a time limit for the continuance of reservation.

The Judges in this case though felt that any special provision like reservation for the benefit of weaker sections cannot continue indefinitely—they left the matter (of discontinuing reservation) to be decided by Parliament at an appropriate time. The relevant portion of the judgement is as below:

"This compensatory state action (i.e. reservation) can be continued only for a period till that inequality is wiped off. Therefore, the petitioners have contended that unless the period is prescribed, this affirmative action will continue for an indefinite period and would ultimately result in reverse discrimination. It is true that there is some force in the contention advanced by the learned counsel for the petitioners but that may happen in future if the reservation policy as contemplated under the Act is successfully implemented. But, at the outset, it may not be possible to fix a time limit or a period of time."

The court expected that depending upon the positive results of the affirmative measures taken by Government and the extent of advancement of the socially and educationally backward classes of citizens, Parliament would at a future time review the need for continuance or otherwise of reservation. The judgement further mentioned about the existence of the safeguard of judicial review for the continuance of reservation. It specifically stated that "the court can exercise its powers of judicial review and say that the affirmative action has carried out its mission and that reservation is no longer required."

The Court thus accepted that reservation should necessarily end at a future date to ensure equal opportunity and equality in all respects i.e. legal, social, political and economic to all citizens. While it is accepted that the genuinely poor, deprived, and "backward" classes of people irrespective of their caste or creed should be taken care of by the State, by way of allowing reservation benefits to them, the advanced groups of people must not enjoy the fruits of reservation. The judiciary is doing its best to bring about rationality in the matters of reservation. The concept of "creamy layer" and its exclusion from reservation benefits by the judiciary has undoubtedly dented and diluted the caste factor in reservation. Presently the attempt of the "forwards" among the "backwards" (or the creamy layer) is to make the income yardstick for measuring "creamy layer" excessively high. However, since this matter is justiciable, it would come within the purview of the Judiciary which would no doubt fix a realistic income yardstick to determine the "creamy layer".

On the whole it is seen that while the constitutional provision of social justice is being duly kept in view by the judiciary for the betterment and advancement of the genuinely backwards in their judicial verdicts, the politically influential sections are also being prevented to promote vote-bank politics by making irrational reservation claims. As a result there are now demands from some political class of people for reservation in the higher judicial appointments also. They hope that judges appointed on the reservation quota will be favourably inclined to extend the scope and duration of reservation for larger groups of politically influential castes. The emergence of such a trend is unfortunate and may endanger secular India to get over its caste and communal based politics in the near future. The dream of the freedom fighters and our Constitution makers to make India a classless, casteless and egalitarian society with equality of treatment for all its citizens may also remain unfulfilled. It has to be noted that one fundamental drawback halting the speedier progress of India is its age-old social division of the people into a multitude of castes and sub-castes. Lack of social harmony and cohesion among the people is giving rise to narrow caste-based identities and factionalism in different spheres. Power loving politicians are exploiting the "backward class" provision for reservation in the Constitution to promote vote bank politics. Thus instead of eliminating caste, it is being nourished and strengthened in the name of social justice. Communalism too is being pampered now for swelling vote banks. For example, in the pursuit of this Vote Bank Politics some states (like Andhra and West Bengal) have recently (February 2010) tried to provide reservation for Muslims on the ground that some sections of them are "backwards." A seven-judge bench of the Andhra High Court however held (February 2010) such religion-based reservation to be unconstitutional. By an ordinance the Andhra Pradesh Government had provided four per cent reservation to certain "Muslim Groups" terming them as "backwards." Chief Justice Anil Dave of the Andhra High Court held in the above judgement that such religion-specific "backward" class reservation has the risk of providing incentive for conversion to Islam and would thus be "subversive of the spirit of secularism" of India. This Muslim specific reservation was accordingly held to be unconstitutional. The judgement was not against backward class reservation as such but against their religion-based identification. On the same ground the announcement by the West Bengal Government of 10 per cent job quotas for Muslim "backwards" in West Bengal (in February 2010) may not withstand judicial scrutiny when challenged. In all likelihood such religion-based reservation policy (e.g. of West Bengal and Andhra Pradesh Governments) may again reach the Apex Court for its final verdict. Thus instead of devising an exit policy to end reservation all possible attempts are being made by the Executive in various states on political calculations not only to continue reservation but also to expand its reach and size. Fortunately, despite all the politically motivated pleadings of the Executive, the Judiciary has so far been able to keep reservation within its rational scope and limit as visualized in the Constitution.

An article written by me earlier and published in the Hindustan Times on 18th July 2003 to highlight how more and more castes and communities are claiming reservation benefits supported by different political parties for their electoral gains is reproduced below.

More Equal Than Others

"One would have imagined that reservation issues would cease to trouble the country after the historic November 1992 Supreme Court judgement in the *Indra Sawhney* vs. *Union of India* case—or the 'Mandal case', as it is popularly known. This special nine-member bench was constituted to "finally settle the legal position relating to reservation."

Unfortunately, unmerited reservation claims are still being made by people enjoying well-entrenched political advantages. Such claims are also being supported and encouraged by different political parties as part of their vote bank politics. Jats, Rajputs and even Brahmins have become claimants of reservation on some ground or the other. Political leaders in Rajasthan and Madhya Pradesh seem to be the leading players in this and have increased reservation percentages for their state services to above 60 per cent.

The two most basic questions addressed in the 1992 judgement were:

> One, who are the 'backward class of citizens' referred to in clause (4) of Article 16 of the Constitution eligible for reservation; and two, what should the extent of such reservation be so as to be fair to the 'backward', the 'general' category of citizens, as well as be "consistent with the maintenance of efficiency of administration" as laid down in Article 335 of the Constitution?

The judgement recognized that the "single most difficult question that tormented this nation related to the definition and identification of the 'backward class of citizens.'"[3] Article 16 merely stated that "nothing in this article shall prevent the State from making any provision for the reservation of appointments or posts in favour of any backward class of citizens which, in the opinion of the State, is not adequately represented in the services under the State." It neither defined who are to be treated as 'backward class' nor mentioned about the extent of reservation for them.

That the scheduled castes and tribes were part of the 'backward class' has never been in dispute. The real problem faced by the Constitution bench was who were the 'other backward class' (OBC) of clause 4 of Article 16. Are they to be identified on the basis of caste – as had been done by the Mandal Commission – or economic conditions, as the word used was 'class' and not 'caste' in Article 16.

The majority judgement in this case concluded that "a caste can be, and quite often is, a social class in India" and if it is 'backward socially ' it would be a 'backward class' for purpose of Article 16(4). The accent in the clause, it was ruled, was on social backwardness."— i.e. people of castes that are lower down in the social hierarchy. The court further stated that the word 'class' had been used "in the sense of social class—and not in the sense it is understood in the Marxist jargon." Thus, economic backwardness, unrelated to social backwardness, could not be the basis of reservation. So, according to this decision, Jats, Rajputs and Brahmins would be ineligible for reservation as they ranked high in the social hierarchy.

With regard to the size of reservation, the court decided that it should not exceed 50 per cent for all categories – i.e. SCs/STs and OBCs. The judgement stated that "clause (4) of Article 16 was conceived in the interests of certain sections of society" (the backward classes) which need to be balanced against the guarantee of equality under clause (1) of the same Article which is "a guarantee held out to every citizen and the entire society." This clause (1) of Article 16 reads "There shall be equality of opportunity for all citizens in matters relating to employment or appointment to any office under the State."

Accordingly, clause (4) being a special provision, can't overshadow the main provision in clause (1). The judgement also referred to B.R. Ambedkar's speech in the Constituent Assembly with regard to this provision where he had stated that reservation should be confined to "a minority of seats" so as to "allow the main provision of equality" to have primacy. He had also clarified that if 70 per cent of the posts are reserved and only 30 per cent are left open for general competition, "that would not be satisfactory in giving effect to the first principle, namely, that there shall be equality of opportunity." The court also opined that while the genuinely backward deserve reasonable reservation for their advancement, the rest of the citizenry should not find the extent of reservation "unduly excessive, invidious and amount to reserve discrimination."

The judgement held that 'adequate' representation under clause (4) did not mean proportionate representation for the backward classes in terms of their population. It also observed that "just as every power must be exercised reasonably and fairly, the power of reservation should also be exercised in a fair manner and within reasonable limits."

Affirmative action and special treatment of the 'backward classes' is a legal and constitutional requirement. Through its judgements, the Supreme Court has fixed the outer limit of reservation not to exceed 50 per cent of the vacancies filled at any time. This has been done to balance the interests of the 'backward classes' and the general citizenry. Any excessive reservation would amount to denial of justice to the latter. It would not also be "consistent with the maintenance of efficiency of administration" as required under Article 335.

Instead of increasing the scope and size of reservations, it may be desirable to adopt a sound long-term 'exit policy' that aims at reducing reservation by half or 1 per cent annually for various classes. That would, of course, require the minimizing of inequalities through greater economic progress of the weaker sections. Sectarian approaches like reservations for disadvantaged sections for long periods of time may stand in the way of social harmony and speedy economic development of the country."

If the present reservation policy for the OBCs is continued indefinitely there may be justified demand for similar special treatment by way of reservation and other affirmative action in favour of the Economically Backward Classes (ECBs) belonging to the upper classes. Poverty pinches them as much as to the other socially and educationally backward classes or the OBCs. Economic criteria would therefore be quite relevant for being introduced in the reservation policy for doing justice to all classes of people similarly placed. In fact the National Commission for the ECBs has recently (2010) recommended such a course of action in its report. People below the poverty line irrespective of their castes and creeds should be equally entitled to state help in areas like employment, education, health and subsidized items of food.

11

PROTECTING INDEPENDENCE OF THE ELECTION COMMISSION

"Free and fair" elections are the pre-requisite of a true democracy known to be "government of the people by the people and for the people." A democratic government is run by the people's representatives elected through periodical elections. These elections have therefore to be free and fair in all respects to make their results credible. These must ensure freedom of voting for all eligible voters and their names must figure in the list of voters of their electoral constituencies updated at regular intervals. Neither fictitious names should find place in them nor names of genuine voters omitted. Preparation of complete and accurate voters' lists are vital and important for holding free and fair elections. The results of such polls alone can be said to reflect the true choices of their representatives by the people.

Accordingly Article 324 of the Constitution has vested the power of "superintendence, direction and control of the preparation of the electoral rolls and the conduct of all elections to Parliament and to the legislatures of every state and elections to the offices of the President and Vice-President of India" to an "independent" body designated as the Election Commission.

Presently the Election Commission is a three member body comprising of the Chief Election Commissioner (CEC) and two other Election Commissioners (ECs). They are all appointed by the President and their tenures of offices and other service conditions are determined by law passed by Parliament. According to the existing provisions of law the tenures of offices are for six years subject to the upper age limit of 65 years for all the members of the Election Commission i.e. the CEC and the ECs.

To ensure the "independence" of the Election Commission Article 324(5) of the Constitution provides that the CEC once appointed cannot be removed from his office "except in the manner and on the like grounds as a judge of the Supreme Court." The other ECs also cannot be removed from their offices "except on the recommendation of the CEC." Their other conditions of service too cannot be varied to their disadvantage while holding their offices.

The removal of a Supreme Court judge from his office in the manner as laid down under Article 124(4) of the Constitution is very difficult, if not an impossible proposition. This is one of the main reasons for which no judge of the apex court has so far (2009) been removed from his office on grounds of any misconduct. In one case even where the Supreme Court itself had recommended the removal of a judge on grounds of lack of integrity he could not be so removed due to want of Parliamentary approval of the required number of members of the two Houses. The grounds of "proved misbehaviour or incapacity" for removal of a judge of the Supreme Court under the above Article requires an address to the President by the Parliament supported by a majority of the total membership of each House and 2/3rd majority of the members of each House of Parliament present and voting. The intention of the Constitution makers in laying down this stiff condition for removal of a judge was obviously to make the judiciary fully independent and fearless in discharging its important constitutional functions. These include to uphold the constitutional rights of the citizens and to prevent excesses, if any, of the Legislature or the Executive by not adhering to the constitutional limits of their powers. Healthy governance in a democracy requires that the three organs of the state i.e. the legislature, the executive and the judiciary between whom the state powers have been distributed abide by the constitutional provisions. To ensure this a legal system of checks and balances has been provided. All the three organs of the state have to observe the constitutional "Laxman Rekha" of their jurisdictions and powers. The judiciary of course plays the most vital role in safeguarding the rule of law. While the legislature enacts laws and the executive enforces them it is the judiciary which interprets and decides on their constitutional validity. If it decides any law passed by the Parliament or any state legislature to be unconstitutional the same becomes invalid and cannot be enforced. Thus the judiciary is the umpire to decide on governance being in accordance with the rule of law. The judiciary is therefore, constitutionally insulated from any kind of interference by the other two state organs in discharging its functions. That explains why a judge of the Supreme Court cannot be so easily removed from his office.

Some other constitutional institutions, e.g. the Election Commission and the Comptroller & Auditor General of India also enjoy "independence" or freedom from interference in the performance of their important constitutional duties. The C&AG is required to function as a watchdog over public expenditure incurred by the executive. All public expenditure (save some specified ones termed as "charged") have to be voted by the legislature. All public expenditure proposals have therefore to be included in the annual Budget placed for approval by the legislatures (i.e. Parliament at the Centre and state assemblies in the states). Any deviations from the same e.g. excess of expenditure or unapproved expenditure, are to be taken note of as "audit objections" by the C&AG while auditing the government accounts. Where necessary any such unauthorized expenditure is reported by him to the respective legislatures who may in turn summon the Executive to explain the causes for the same to its Public Accounts Committee (PAC). The executive is accountable to the legislature in financial matters and for this purpose the C&AG works as the watchdog on behalf of the legislature. Hence he is designated as the "Comptroller" of government's financial transactions. To make him fearless in performance of this important duty, the C&AG like the CEC once appointed cannot be removed from his office under Article 148 of the Constitution "except in the like manner as a judge of the Supreme Court." His conditions of service too cannot be varied to his disadvantage during his tenure of office. To further ensure his "independence" clause (4) of Article 148 of the Constitution lays down that the C&AG "shall not be eligible for further office under the Government of India or under the Government of any State" after he ceases to hold his office. Thus the C&AG is not only free from any harm while holding his office but he is also made temptation free after retirement so as not to look for any favour from government by way of appointment to another high office. Being made ineligible for any office after retirement he would not be tempted to oblige the executive by ignoring and not reporting any of its financial wrong doings.

In the case of the Central Vigilance Commissioner another "independent" institution dealing with corruption charges against public officials, temptation of securing any post retirement office has similarly been removed under Section 6 of the Central Vigilance Commission Act, 2003 which provides:

> "On ceasing to hold office, the Central Vigilance Commissioner and every other Vigilance Commissioner shall be ineligible for:
>
> *(a)* any diplomatic assignment, appointment as administrator of a Union territory and such other assignment or appointment which is required by law to be made by the President by warrant under his hand and seal.
>
> *(b)* Further employment to any office of profit under the Government of India or the Government of a State."

This debarment provision is more elaborate and un-ambiguous.

Unfortunately, no such constitutional provision exists at present to debar the CEC and other ECs from being appointed to any government or public offices after their retirements. Compared to the C&AG and the CVC, the CEC and the ECs have far greater interactions with political parties and political leaders as the Election Commission's main function is to conduct elections fought by political parties and their members. The CEC and ECs have several election related functions where they deal with political parties more closely e.g., delimitation of electoral constituencies, recognition of national and regional level political parties, fixing of election schedules, observance of the model code of conduct on the eve of elections by the candidates and political parties, dealing with various kinds of election disputes, complaints of non-observance of the upper limits of election expenses, etc. etc. The Election Commissioners have to act as impartial and neutral umpires in their several such election related functions. Some of these functions are also of a quasi-judicial nature and the members of the Election Commission must not only be fair and impartial but also appear to be so. Their political neutrality and impartiality must be above suspicion. They must not only be, but also appear to be true umpires in the conduct of elections.

Fortunately, the Election Commission of India had so far enjoyed an excellent image not only in India but also abroad for its political neutrality, fairness and competence in conducting free and fair elections. There were no talk or even whispers against the Commission's impartiality in playing its role of a true election umpire.

Unfortunately, certain unseemly developments have taken place recently which, if not properly addressed, could adversely affect the credibility of the Election Commission as an impartial umpire. One example of this worrisome development is that the CEC Mr. M.S. Gill shortly after his retirement joined a national level political party and was soon thereafter appointed as a central minister by the party being in power. The individual concerned may have been a man of integrity and above board; his appointment as a minister may also have been with the bona fide intention of benefiting the country because of his special expertise and knowledge. But irrespective of all these, Mr. Gill's appointment as a minister shortly after his retirement did invite criticism of the public and the media for being harmful to the independence of the Election Commission. Such political appointment of any Election Commissioner soon after his retirement has the risk of politicisation of the members of the Election Commission. Any kind of greed or temptation to get post retirement favours by a member of the Election Commission by obliging a political party in power ought to be curbed to protect the Commission's independence, political impartiality and public confidence in it.

In another recent case the CEC N. Gopalaswami wrote to the President of India (in January 2009) recommending the removal of his fellow Election Commissioner Navin Chawla allegedly for being partial to a political party in some cases handled by the Commission. Shri N. Gopalaswami's recommendation to remove Shri Navin Chawla was, however, not accepted by the President and he continued to be the Election Commissioner. In fact Shri Chawla was appointed as the Chief Election Commissioner after Shri Gopalaswami's retirement. However, this incident also raised doubts about the clean image of the Election Commission. As a remedial measure therefore like the C&AG and the CVC, the CEC and the ECs should be made ineligible for any post retirement public offices. In addition, the CEC and the ECs because of the political nature of their jobs should also be debarred from joining or becoming members of any recognised political party or to contest any election to the Parliament or state legislatures or to offices of the President, Vice-President for some reasonable period of time which may be at least for 5 years after retirement. Five years of debarment appears to be a reasonably long enough time interval to prevent any temptation of reward as a motive to show partiality to any political party. This debarment period is also not too long for a talented person to refuse to accept appointment to offices like the

Election Commission for the fear of later being deprived of his right to stand for elections or to join a political party or even to get other prestigious public office like that of a governor, etc. The present upper age limit for holders of offices like the C&AG, CVC, the CEC and ECs is 65 years. Accordingly after retirement and after a further gap of the debarment period of 5 years for the holders of all those offices they will still be of about 70 years of age. This age may not present a serious problem for them, if otherwise healthy, to pursue political or other official activities—if any of them so desire. Permanent or a very long debarment period may not only be unfair to the individuals concerned but may also deprive the society of their experiences and knowledge if any of them are considered suitable for any public office.

Strangely there is no constitutional provision at present for the debarment of retired High Court or Supreme Court judges for being appointed to public offices even where such appointments though made by the President are really by the executive governments. To make the higher judiciary temptation free, the judges should also be made ineligible for posts of President, Vice-President, Governors, Ambassadors, etc for a period of 5 years after their retirements. They could however continue to be appointed to quasi-judicial offices or to the offices of various enquiry commissions as at present. In such cases their appointments should, however, be with the approval of the serving Chief Justice of India.

12

THE CONSTITUTION AND CITIZENSHIP VALUES

India was fortunate in having a galaxy of great leaders at the dawn of its independence. They as members of the Constituent Assembly also framed the Constitution of the new democratic republic.

The basic goals and objectives embodied in the Constitution are "to secure to all its citizens justice—social, economic and political; liberty of thought, expression, belief, faith and worship, equality of status and of opportunity; and to promote among them all fraternity assuring the dignity of the individual and [the unity and integrity of the nation."] The bracketed portion as also the words "secular" and "socialist" were added in 1976 to the Preamble. The "Preamble" mentions the resolve of the people of India "to constitute India into a sovereign socialist, secular, democratic republic." These undoubtedly are lofty and noble goals. The Preamble in brief reflects the gist of the constitutional goals and ideals. It also makes amply clear that "sovereignty" or the ultimate power and authority of the State is derived from the people of India. "We the people of India" have been recognized to be the creators of the Republic. There is no question of any "divine right" theory of sovereignty or rulership on hereditary basis. The common people or "citizens" in political language are the real source of sovereignty. Power flows from them to all the institutions and instruments of governance under various provisions of the Constitution. The residents of the old Greek city states with political rights were known as "citizens" as distinguished from slaves and foreigners who had no such political rights. The word "citizen" with its political connotation is now of common use in the Constitution of every country. Article 5 of the Indian Constitution conferred "citizenship" on every person who was a domicile of India for not less than five years immediately preceding the commencement of the Constitution in 1950. "We the People of India" or the citizens adopted the new Constitution to regulate the affairs of the state and its governance. The citizens in sum are the creators of the republic and its rulers. They are its body and its soul. They have bound themselves and the state to abide by the provisions of the Constitution in the governance of the country. The constitution is thus the fundamental rule book or the political holy book which must be respected by all the organs and institutions of the State.

The power of the state in its totality is distributed between its three main organs, i.e., the legislative, the executive and the judiciary. Such rational distribution of state power commonly known as "separation of powers" was devised by eminent political scientists and thinkers to ensure the "rule of law" and is in vogue in all genuinely democratic countries. Framers of our Constitution also adopted this well devised system of separation of power for good governance and to follow the "rule of law". Concentration of power in any single hand or authority has the risk of giving rise to dictatorship, arbitrariness and high handedness in governance. The three independent organs of the State (i.e. the legislature, the executive and the judiciary) constitute the "Trimurty" of the State. These organs with their respective shares of powers are intended to exercise checks and balances on each other to safeguard the rule of law. Since power tends to corrupt and absolute power corrupts absolutely, it is prudent to distribute power between different agencies. An independent judiciary is vital to safeguard the fundamental rights of the people and to uphold the rule of law. It exercises the required checks on the legislature and the executive with regard to enactment of laws and their enforcement in conformity with the constitutional provisions.

The Legislature or Parliament at the national level is elected by the citizens—of the age of 18 and above having one vote each. Parliament as the representatives of the citizens elected through "free and fair" elections periodically, enacts laws to fulfil the constitutional goals and purposes. The political executive comprising of the "Council of Ministers" is also a part of the Legislature under our constitutional scheme. The ministers as representatives of the citizens are thus citizens first and ministers afterwards. They as citizen ministers have to implement the laws passed by the Legislature. They are also to control, guide and supervise the functioning of the permanent civil servants who run the administration of the country and execute the programmes and policies of the elected governments. The word "permanent" implies that the civil servants are not changed with change of political executives after every general elections. Thus they provide continuity to governance and administration. They however work under the political executives and implement their programmes and policies. They belong to a variety of civil services—technical and non-technical. They are recruited by the UPSC at the Centre and State Public Service Commissions in the states. These commissions are independent bodies to ensure fairness and impartiality in the recruitment of all categories of civil servants.

The Legislatures at the State levels and the Parliament at the national level elect the head of the republic, i.e. "the *Rashtrapati*" or the President of India. He too has to be a citizen of India – popularly known as the "first citizen." The President in his turn appoints legally qualified citizens as members of the judiciary, i.e., of the Supreme Court of India and of the High Courts. Though appointed by the President, and not elected by the citizens, the members of the judiciary are independent of the executive and the legislature as mentioned earlier. Their judicial powers are derived from the Constitution which safeguards judicial independence in conformity with the theory of "separation of powers" of the three State organs. The judiciary has been empowered to protect the fundamental rights of the citizens as laid down in the Constitution from being encroached upon by the executive or the legislature. The higher judiciary enjoys vast writ jurisdictions under Articles 32 and 226 of the Constitution for this purpose. Appointments to a few other institutions vested with constitutional powers e.g. Comptroller and Auditor General of India, the Election Commission of India, Union Public Service Commission, etc. are also made by the President of India but their independence is ensured by the constitutional scheme in order that they discharge their responsibilities in a free and fair manner without any political bias. All persons appointed to these institutions are also to be citizens of India.

In substance, all public functionaries from *Rashtrapati* downwards are "citizens" themselves. Without being citizens of the country they cannot be elected or appointed to their respective offices and positions. Thus the quality of governance and the realization of the constitutional goals and ideals depend on the citizens themselves. Since citizen is a political term as mentioned earlier "citizenship values" would relate to the interest and public spirit of the citizens in the proper functioning of the "polity" or the republic. They are expected to take active and healthy interest in the affairs of the state and its institutions and in the realization of the constitutional goals. Quality of governance will largely depend on the quality of good citizenship values shown by the people.

Before we discuss the nature and quality of the "citizenship values" required, it may be useful to have an idea of the socio-economic goals and objectives set by the Constitution in the realization of which the citizens in their public or private capacities have to show interest, initiative and commitment. It is necessary to examine not only the kind of values required of the citizens in fulfilling these constitutional objectives but also to see how they have behaved so far and the extent to which the various socio-economic goals remain unfulfilled. We have also to look into the causes of our failings and short-comings and the steps that need to be taken to improve the citizenship values so that the dreams and visions of the framers of the Constitution are realized as fully as possible.

The Constitution has in several of its articles emphasized on "equality" of all the citizens. They are equal before the law and enjoy equal protection of law (Article 14). There are no high or low, rich or poor, high caste or low caste citizens in the eyes of law. "Untouchability" has been specifically abolished (Article 17) to satisfy provisions of equality in the social sphere. Discrimination of any kind between citizens is prohibited "on grounds only of religion, race, caste, sex, place of birth or any of them (Article 15). Similarly, all citizens have "equality of opportunity in matters relating to employment or appointment to any office under the State (Article 16). All citizens have also the freedom of speech and expression; right to form associations; right of movement and residence throughout the country (Article 19). All citizens enjoy the right of protection of life and liberty (Article 21) and freedom of conscience and to freely profess, practice and propagate religion (Article 25). The aim of the Constitution is thus to free the citizens of India from some of its age old vices like casteism, communalism, regionalism and feudalism etc. and to modernize the country by bringing about egalitarianism, secularism and socialism through legal means and arrangements.

The Fundamental Rights incorporated in Part III and the Directive Principles of State Policy in Part IV of the Constitution reflect some of the dreams and visions that our great leaders had for the freedom and well-being of the people of India.

When India awoke to freedom at the stroke of the midnight hour on 15th August 1947, Pandit Jawahar Lal Nehru in his famous "tryst with destiny" speech had cautioned the people that "freedom and power bring responsibility" and that "the future is not one of ease and resting but of incessant striving" in the service of India. That "service" he said meant "the ending of poverty and ignorance and disease and inequality." He also mentioned about the dream of Mahatma Gandhi–"to wipe every tear from every eye " in free India.

Speaking on this occasion Dr. Rajendra Prasad, President of the Constituent Assembly said "let us resolve to create conditions in this country when every individual will be free and provided with the wherewithal to develop and rise to his fullest stature, when poverty and squalor and ignorance and ill-health will have been vanished." In his lucid speech Dr. Rajendra Prasad also focused on the major challenges that free India would face and the way to resolve them for the common good of all the people.

To achieve the various objectives, Dr. Rajendra Prasad indicated what the citizens themselves have to do and the type of citizenship values that would be required of them in the service of India. He said "all must realize, that what is needed most today is a great constructive effort–not strife, but hard solid work, let us hope that all will be prepared to make their contributions." He also explained further that "we want the peasants to grow more food, we want the workers to produce more goods, we want our industrialists to use their intelligence, tact and resourcefulness for the common good." He also added that:

> "not only have the people to dedicate themselves to this great task that lies ahead but those who have so far been playing the role of rulers and regulators of the life of our men and women have to assume the role of servants."

He thus wanted the civil servants in various departments of Government to shed their role as rulers and become true servants of the people.

Dr. Radhakrishnan gave his wise advice and warning to the citizens of free India in the following words:

> "Our opportunities are great but let me warn you that when power outstrips ability, we will fall on evil days. We should

develop competence and ability which would help us to utilize the opportunities which are now open to us. From tomorrow morning—from midnight today—we cannot throw the blame on the Britishers. We have to assume the responsibility ourselves for what we do. A free India will be judged by the way in which it will serve the interests of the common man in matter of food, clothing, shelter and the social services. Unless we destroy corruption in high places, root out every trace of nepotism, love of power, profiteering and black marketing which have spoiled the good name of this great country in recent times, we will not be able to raise the standards of efficiency in administration as well as in the production and distribution of the necessary goods of life."

As far back as 1931, Gandhiji had written: "I shall work for an India where the poorest shall feel that it is their country in whose making they have an effective voice; an India in which all communities shall live in perfect harmony... . This is the India of my dreams. I shall be satisfied with nothing less."

The dreams and visions of our great leaders not only pictured the kind of India they wished to see but also the extent of hard work that would be expected from the citizens whether farmers, workers, industrialists, political leaders or civil servants in the making of such an India. All of them as citizens of free India have to put their best efforts for the common good of all. They can no longer pass on the blame to any one else for their failures or non-achievements. India could be as great as its citizens would make it through dedication and commitments to their duties and by following high norms and values in the service of the country.

The framers of our Constitution were not only men of great vision but many of them were well aware of the country's strength and weaknesses viewed from its history and social realities. They knew very well how and where things may go wrong in a multi-ethnic, multi-religion and multi-caste or a pluralist Indian society. It was accordingly considered necessary as mentioned earlier to make constitutional provisions of "non-discrimination" between citizens on grounds only of religion, race, caste, etc. It can be said of the Indian Constitution to some extent what the great American jurist Joseph Story had written about the American Constitution in his celebrated book "Commentaries on the Constitution of the United States of

America." He had written—"let the American youth never forget, that they possess (in their constitution) a noble inheritance, bought by the toils, and sufferings, and blood of their ancestors; and capable, if wisely improved, and faithfully guarded of transmitting, to their latest posterity all the substantial blessings of life, the peaceful enjoyment of liberty, property, religion and independence. It may, nevertheless, perish in an hour by the folly, or corruption, or negligence of its only keepers, THE PEOPLE. Republics are created by the virtue, public spirit, and intelligence of the citizens. They fall, when the wise are banished from the public councils, because they dare to be honest, and the profligate are rewarded, because they flatter the people in order to betray them". Wise words indeed. Recent Indian experience has shown that the country is failing to achieve its great potential as sycophants who lack talent and merit are being rewarded while men of merit and honesty who are dedicated to serve India are being largely ignored. Such good persons do not indulge in flattery of any kind and do not hesitate to call a spade a spade. Good of India matters more to them than their own good. Fortunately, such people are still there though their number may not be large.

Since ultimately it is the people or the citizens who have to work out our democratic Constitution, realization of its ideals, and vision for securing a just social order and good governance depend on their citizenship values. Any Constitution, however, good and matchless can become a scrap of paper in unworthy hands. Presenting the final draft of the Indian Constitution for approval of the Constituent Assembly, Dr. Ambedkar, Chairman of the Drafting Committee, expressed some apprehensions about the future course of free India's history. He said, "what perturbs me greatly is the fact that not only India has once before lost her independence, but she lost it by the infidelity and treachery of some of her own people". He elaborated this by recalling how at the time of invasion of Sindh by Mohammed-Bin-Kasim the military commanders of King Dahar accepted bribes from the agents of Mohammed-Bin-Kasim and refused to fight on the side of their king. He also stated: "It was Jaichand who invited Mohammad Ghauri to invade India and fight against Prithvi Raj and promised him the help of himself and Solanki kings. When Shivaji was fighting for the liberation of Hindus, the other Maratha noblemen and the Rajput kings were fighting the battle on the side of Moghul Emperor." He gave more such examples of betrayal and treachery and then reflected "Will history repeat itself? It is this thought which fills me with anxiety. This anxiety is deepened by the realization of the fact that in addition to our old enemies in the form of castes and creeds, we are going to have many political parties with diverse and opposing political creeds. Will Indians place the country above their creed or will they place creed above country? I do not know."

Viewed in the context of few decades of post-independence developments in India, one has to sadly admit that Dr. Ambedkar had good reasons to be worried about its future. Alas! his apprehensions are coming to be true rather too soon. The old enemies in the form of "caste and creeds" as also the many political parties "with diverse and opposing political creeds" as apprehended by Dr. Ambedkar are already working as great divisive forces to slow down India's growth and development. They are also proving to be great obstacles in the path of national integration. Their divisive hands are visible in provoking social and communal discords between citizens of different classes.

Dr. Ambedkar and other illustrious founding fathers of our Constitution had great foresight indeed in visualizing the possible emergence of negative forces in various fields i.e. social, economic and political. In spite of an excellent Constitution framed by them to be able to withstand such divisive forces, unfortunately, the country has already started to face serious problems damaging national unity, integrity and social cohesion. Several state and national level political parties have started to adopt policies that encourage casteism, regionalism and communalism with the malafide motives of electoral gains through "vote-bank politics." These policies are dividing citizens on caste and communal lines. Citizenship values to unite India are not being promoted but greater emphasising is laid on caste and communal divides. Common Indian identity of all citizens of the country is no longer talked about or felt to be a matter of pride. Narrow caste identity of one being a Rajput, a Jat, a Yadav, or a Dalit etc. carry more weight.

The greatest damage has been done to social harmony by the pernicious vote-bank politics. The founding fathers of our Constitution had given the pride of place to ideals like justice, liberty, equality and fraternity, among all the people of India. But the growing practice of vote-bank politics has, by now, divided the people or citizens into various groups and classes based on castes and creeds. The dying institution of caste has not only been revived but revitalized by accepting and implementing the Mandal Commission Report on reservation in government jobs on caste basis. It has enabled caste leaders claiming closer affinity to citizens of their own castes to claim their votes in preference to candidates of other castes. This is being practiced despite the fact that several Articles of the Indian Constitution dealing with fundamental rights have provided that no citizen shall, on grounds only of religion, race, caste, sex, place of birth or any of them, be subjected to any disability liability, restrictions, etc. Dignity of the individual, equality for all and the unity and integrity of India are the cherished ideals of the Indian Constitution. Accordingly, the form of oath prescribed for a Central or a State Minister lays down that the minister will faithfully and conscientiously discharge his duties and will "do right to all manner of people in accordance with the Constitution and the law without fear or favour, affection or ill-will." These provisions were deliberately made to keep in check what Ambedkar described as "our old enemies in the form of castes and creeds."

The Constitution also begins with the words, *"We the People of India"* meaning members of a large Indian joint family—a big 'fraternity'. Unfortunately, the vision and goal of building a socially integrated and united India without any feeling of separateness of castes and creeds has been greatly damaged by the practice and propagation of vote-bank politics. In fact, to swell their vote bank, even millions of foreign infiltrators mostly from Bangladesh are being clandestinely helped to come over and settle in India by some interested political parties and individuals. Such captive vote-banks of foreigners are solely intended to improve their political fortunes at the cost of national security. Are such parties and individuals not playing the role of Jaichand as referred to by Dr. Ambedkar? Instead of taking pride in one common Indian identity, we are now championing our separate caste and communal identities. Unfortunately, very few leaders now talk in terms of India. They instead like to identify themselves with different States and castes. Power and politics have been communalized and regionalised. Lust for power has to a great extent eroded all our value systems of public spirit, humanistic and selfless service for common good for all the *aam aadmi* of India. The public functionaries, who as mentioned earlier are all citizens themselves, are striving to grab power and positions only for their own personal aggrandizement and pompous living at public expense. They seldom subordinate their greed for money and power to the more desirable task of helping their poor and deprived fellow citizens. For acquiring seats of power they have criminalized politics. Large numbers of criminal history sheeters, with crime records like that of murder, rape, smuggling, dacoity etc. are now standing for and winning Assembly and Parliamentary elections. It is generally seen that they use their money and muscle powers to seek and get votes. Rigging, booth capturing and unfair electoral practices too are beginning to impair "free and fair" elections. Unfortunately, most political parties have developed some kind of unholy alliances with one or more mafia gangs. There are official reports of nexus between the under-world dons and goons and political leaders of different parties.

From the mid-seventies it had become quite obvious that the country was losing track of its many lofty constitutional goals. Strikes, dharnas, gheraos, burning of public properties like trains, buses, and office building etc. have become quite common to express anger on the slightest excuse. Citizens indulging in such activities hardly think that the public properties they are destroying are their own. While there may be justification to raise one's voice against corrupt officials, destruction of public properties should not become the target of public anger and protest. Good citizenship values lie in safeguarding public properties.

To curb popular unrest against the corrupt governments of the time, at the state and central levels, "emergency" was imposed in 1976 by Mrs. Indira Gandhi. The immediate cause for this was of course to safeguard her own political survival as the Allahabad High Court in its judgement in a case against her had declared her election to Parliament invalid on the ground of illegal use of official machinery in her election campaign. However, one good outcome of this was the constitutional amendment which added Article 51A to the Constitution laying down the following fundamental duties for the citizens:

- To abide by the Constitution and respect its ideals and institutions, the National Flag and National Anthem;
- To cherish and follow the noble ideals which inspired our national struggle for freedom;
- To uphold and protect the sovereignty, unity and integrity of India;
- To defend the country and render national service when called upon to do so;
- To promote harmony and the spirit of common brotherhood

amongst all the people of India transcending religious, linguistic and regional or sectional diversities;

- To renounce practices derogatory to the dignity of women;
- To value and preserve the rich heritage of our composite culture;
- To protect and improve the natural environment including forests, lakes, rivers and wildlife and to have compassion for living creatures;
- To develop the scientific tamper, humanism and the spirit of inquiry and reform';
- To safeguard public property and to abjure violence; and
- To strive towards excellence in all spheres of individual and collective activity so that the nation constantly rises to higher levels of endeavour and achievement.

While the fundamental rights of the citizens are legally binding and enforceable their duties under Article 51A are only morally binding on them as part of good citizenship values. These are advisory and persuasive in nature but not legally enforceable. Breaches of any of these duties could, however, become punishable where any existing law is violated e.g. causing insult to the National Flag or if rioting causes injury to any individual and becomes a punishable offence under the IPC.

The important duties laid down in the Constitution under Article 51A broadly highlight the kind of citizenship values that are expected from every citizen of India to fulfil the constitutional goals and ideals. These goals aim to make India a great nation with visible economic strength, political stability, social harmony and security of life and property of the people. The intention of the founding fathers ***inter alia*** was to make India occupy a high international status through significant progress in scientific, educational, cultural and in various other technological fields. With India's vast human and natural resources these goals are attainable if "we the people" or the citizens of the country develop and display the requisite character, values and dedication for the good of the country. The Indian citizens have to put the interest of the nation first and everything else afterwards. They have to love India to make it loveable and great. The Constitution only provides the basic legal framework for the attainment of the goals and objectives incorporated in it. The driving force for realizing these goals has to come from the citizens themselves.

The Constitution visualizes and expects every adult citizen to be an active participant in its proper working. Basically there is nothing very much wanting or missing in the constitutional scheme to achieve its lofty goals. However with experience of its working so far (i.e. more than 60 years) some aspects of it appear to need a fresh look . There have also been, according to experts, distortions and narrow interpretations of some of the constitutional provisions. One such gross distortion relates to the "secular" aspect of the state. Narrow and myopic interpretation of the word "secularism" is coming in the way of inculcating basic moral and ethical values to our younger generations through the educational system.

For the proper understanding and appreciation of the constitutional values like liberty, equality, fraternity and other fundamental rights and duties conferred on the citizens our educational system need to be suitably designed. The moral character of the citizens has to be appropriately moulded and nourished through imaginative value-based textbooks. The educational syllabuses for students at all levels must be sound and impart true moral values in addition to knowledge of new technological developments. Our children should lack neither new knowledge nor old values of right and wrong. Some fundamental human and social values like love, compassion, truthfulness, friendship, gratitude, respect for parents, teachers, and the aged; love of nature in all its splendour, love for the motherland etc. need to be taught for character building of our children from the primary and secondary stages of education. For effective teaching of these values and to make them part of their character and mental make-up these need to be taught through interesting stories and episodes derived from our holy books, classics and epics like *Ramayan, Mahabharat, Gita, Upnishads,* etc. Sacred books of all religions could be rich sources of character building by including stories and lessons from them in the text books. However, the wrong criteria used to describe or interpret "secularism" virtually excludes educational lessons derived from our ancient scriptures and epics like *Ramayan* and *Mahabharat*. In fact the very mention of the word "Aryan" or "Hindu" raises suspicious eye-brows among the so-called "secularists." They have politicized the word "Hindu" and "Hinduism." Some "secular" fanatics or mindless "secular' turks are proving to be more injurious and harmful to genuine secularism, national unity and integration than the smaller groups of religious fundamentalists. Fundamentalism in any sphere is harmful and our citizens have to be taught to develop liberal attitudes of mind and heart in their social, political and economic thinking and relationships. Some aspects of spiritualism and divinity derived from the religious classics of all faiths may be made part of our educational courses at different levels for the sake of inculcating the right type of moral values and norms among our children. They have first to be made good human beings for making them good economists, good technocrats, good administrators and good soldiers. Good human beings alone could be good citizens. The penal laws of a state and their effective enforcements alone will not suffice to ensure an orderly, united and harmonious civil society. For citizens to show fraternity towards each other and tolerance for each other's faith and belief, these values need to be ingrained in their character from the school stage itself. "Secularism" should be taught to be accommodative and tolerant towards persons of all faiths. It should stand for showing respect to all religions rather than to keep away from all of them. The concept of God and His divine force guiding and regulating human societies, should not be allowed to be frowned upon or belittled by the false "secularist" and other such mindless "progressive" elements. Through experience it was found necessary even by the Western political thinkers long back to "discover" God even if one did not really exist. Such a "discovery" was considered to be absolutely necessary for the smooth and peaceful existence of human societies. The communist states perished after their very brief Godless existence as they ignored the divine force by calling God and religion to be the "opium of the poor." These communist states lacking spiritual values neither served the poor nor spared the rich. They perished because they turned human societies into "Animal Farms." For them the State was everything, it was all rolled into one and all citizens were meant to work for it like slaves. The state was not for the people but the people were to be for the state, according to the communists. There was no dignity for any individual citizen in a communist state. In simple terms the state was the demon or the "Leviathan" whom citizens must feed and please in all possible ways to prevent being devoured by it. The communist states and societies lacked human values, feelings and sentiments, and regard for the dignity of citizens. They accordingly perished after a few decades of existence. They were full of "sound and fury" of their being pro-poor but only indulged in violence and killings of millions of their citizens to assert their dictatorships. They did not realize the importance of religious teachings in making "man" out of animal. They devalued human civilization developed over centuries of efforts. Even Pandit Nehru in his book "Discovery of India" has admitted the great role that the stories from our religious epics-*Ramayan* and *Mahabharat* played in the making of his personality. We should derive appropriate lessons from them and do not allow our citizens to be propelled by animal instincts or guided by materialistic considerations alone. Need for moral and ethical values in life should be given importance in the education and character building of the citizens. That would make them give due importance to performance of their citizenship duties with dedication and "*shraddha*" (or heart felt love). Our citizens have also to be taught from their childhood about India being a large joint family of people of diverse faiths and castes so that we respect and love each other irrespective of our caste or religious divisions. These diversities of caste, religion, language, dress and food habits, etc. should be taught to be minor compared to our common identity of being Indians. Our Bharatiya or Indian identity need to be stressed more to promote fraternity among us all. Faith in the oneness of India, in its unity and integrity has to be awakened and strengthened through proper educational courses and by exemplary conduct of top leaders. Oneness of India and its integrity should overshadow all other diversities of the citizens, mentioned earlier i.e. faith, belief, dress, food habits, language, caste or customs etc.

The front ranking leaders have to set good examples of moral and ethical behaviour. They have to talk in terms of "our India" and not "my state", "my caste" and "my religion." Unfortunately, contrary to our constitutional values focusing on national unity and integrity, narrow "caste" identities are becoming more important for political alignments and casting of votes. A candidate of one's own caste even if otherwise unsuitable is generally preferred to a better candidate of another caste in electoral contests. This is leading to the feeling of "we" and "they" based on caste and community identities of different groups of people. "Fraternity" of all Indians on national basis is not being emphasised. Some top ranking caste leaders had been seen to be publicly hurling abuses on people of other so called higher castes for the alleged historical wrong doings of their forefathers against the lower castes. Now that we have started afresh our social and political journey on the termination of centuries of foreign rule, the best way to correct the past social wrongs and mistakes should be to practice new citizenship values of total equality in conformity with free India's constitutional ideals and goals. The Constitution of our

Sovereign Democratic Republic has taken due care to ensure that the previously wronged groups or classes of citizens i.e. the SCs/STs/OBCs are now adequately compensated by allowing special treatments to them in various ways. Though the new value system is based on complete "equality" of all citizens irrespective of their caste or creed, language or dress, colour of skin or even gender still some special treatment has been accepted to be legally permissible in the case of the weaker or backward sections of people. Every Indian citizen is otherwise an equal member of the larger Indian family, society and state. The citizens have to maintain peace and harmony by suitably adjusting to each other's genuine needs and requirements particularly of those who were victims of past social discrimination. It is imperative that their human potential is fully developed through special care as visualized under the Constitution. Articles 14, 15 and 16 of the Constitution are meant to achieve this goal. The concept of "social justice" inherent in these Articles is meant to strengthen true 'equality' of all citizens and to promote 'fraternity' among them all. This requires a spirit of public service, rising above personal interests, specially on the part of the leading citizens of the country both in public and the private sectors.

Prominent public figures occupying important posts and positions as leading citizens ought to follow such codes of conduct as are ethical from every angle and set high norms of social and professional behaviour for others to follow. The public servants as important groups of citizens need to be more public service oriented and not mere wielders of power. Unfortunately, their value system has become quite the opposite. They are seen to care more for their pay, perks and perquisites and less for the quality of their public services. The people in general have a poor opinion of this class of citizens who they feel ought to be more public spirited than the ordinary citizens. Similarly the professional classes of citizens, i.e., doctors, lawyers, engineers, financial experts, etc. barring exceptions are found wanting in their spirit of public service and citizenship values. They too give primacy to money making for their own enrichment rather than for doing good to the people whole-heartedly. Professional ethics and high citizenship values seem to occupy secondary place in performance of their duties. As a result public credibility of the soundness of a doctor's treatment or of a lawyer's handling of a case entrusted to him has gone down considerably. Undue greed for money making is now more prominently visible in them and others all round. There are complaints that teachers no longer take adequate interest in teaching their students in the schools but instead spend time for their private tuitions. They are supposed to be character builders of our future citizens through good teachings in the schools. The teachers in government schools allegedly take many private tuitions to make money. Similarly, doctors in government hospitals spend more time in their private clinics than in public hospitals to make extra money. Public duties for all classes of public servants barring exceptions are becoming secondary or casual affairs. While they keep demanding higher wages as public servants they also keep making extra incomes from side businesses at the cost of official duties. Money making culture seems to have overshadowed all other good norms and values of our citizens. This is causing various social ills like ostentatious marriage parties, birthday parties, lavish and vulgar display of wealth in other ways. All these lead to the feelings of rich and poor, high and low among the citizens. Caste and communal angles also come into display.

Swami Ranganathananda in one of his lectures on "social responsibilities of public administrators" stated that the current mode of callousness and unconcern, the utter lack of a sense of duty and spirit of service and rampant corruption cannot and should not be allowed to continue longer among public servants, if the nation is to succeed in its chosen path of peaceful and democratic revolutionary progress for its immense population. He also found wanting among public servants "the sense of duty, of punctuality, of social responsibility and human responsiveness, the attitude of being helpful to the people."

As citizens of free India it is necessary for us to be guided by higher thoughts and motives than motives of personal monetary gains alone. Mentality of a job-holder of doing one's work to earn a living may not bring the kind of quality and excellence to the work as would come from the feeling that it is also being done in the larger interest of serving the country and for the good of other fellow citizens. Again in the words of Swami Ranganathananda "the carpenter, the stone-cutter, the shoe-maker, the student, the teacher, the administrator, the industrial executive, the house-wife—each and all of them can become more energized by the one thought that I am primarily a citizen of free India and that the work that I do has got a tremendous human and national reference."

Herein lies the true quality of citizenship values that could make us citizens of a great country and enable us to achieve the lofty ideals of our Constitution. Swami Vivekananda had advocated for "man-making education" and "nation building" resolve to energize and awaken the citizens of free India. This requires great national leaders of high moral character to inspire and guide the citizens. Winning freedom from foreign rule, particularly from a civilized colonial power like Great Britain was comparatively an easier task, than building a new and prosperous India of over 1000 million population with years of accumulated social, educational and economic ills afflicting them. We had great leaders to lead and guide us during the freedom struggle. But now when the country needs many more such great leaders it hardly has any. The present day leaders prefer to talk in terms of their states e.g. Maharashtra for Marathis; Tamil Nadu for Tamilians etc. They also talk of their respective castes and creeds, i.e. Lingayats, Vokaligas, Jats, Meenas, Gujjars, Rajputs, Muslims, Sikhs, etc. They also want special treatment and privileges for their castes and communities on one ground or the other. Hardly any leader is bold enough or tall enough to talk in terms of India as a whole in preference to his narrow caste, creed, communal or regional interests. The present leaders do not "lead" but are being "led" by vote bank political motives. The feeling of belonging to the larger Indian fraternity fortunately does make its appearance among the people whenever any big tragedy afflicts any part of the country e.g. havoc of Gujarat earthquake, super cyclone of Orissa; Sunami devastation of Tamil Nadu and other coastal areas; killing acts of terrorism in Mumbai, Jaipur, Bangalore, Hyderabad, etc. On all such occasions of "national" calamity people from all over India do respond quickly to help their suffering fellow citizens. This is quite heartening and should give us hope that our citizens can rise above their local horizons and narrow caste outlooks whenever required in the larger interest of the country and its people. To promote such national outlook India needs great national leaders, world reputed intellectuals and literary giants like Gurudev Rabindra Nath Tagore. They would inspire and guide the nation in all spheres to achieve its great potentials. Great citizenship values are required in making India great as depicted in the following words of Rabindra Nath Tagore:

"where the mind is without fear and the head is held high;
where the knowledge is free; where the world has not been

broken up into fragments by narrow domestic walls...
into that heaven of freedom, my father, let my country awake"

As mentioned earlier since leaders of All-India outlook and vision have now become scarce, every citizen or *aam aadmi* should show greater citizenship values and sense of national responsibility. They can no longer live in the comfortable feeling that they have great and reliable leaders like Pandit Jawaharlal Nehru, Sardar Patel, Dr. Rajendra Prasad and Maulana Azad etc. to take care of national interests and take the country forward. Every citizen of India has now to rise to the occasion individually and follow the constitutional path and values set by those great leaders. If we as citizens could observe the norms and ideals practiced during the freedom struggle we could tide over with ease our current social, political and economic difficulties and bring smiles on the faces of millions of our suffering brethren. The ultimate aim should continue to be "to wipe every tear from every eye" as desired by Mahatma Gandhi the father of the Nation. This requires the spirit of true social service and sincere dedication to achieve the constitutional goals. For this not only politics has to be rescued from the evil grip of criminals but the administration too has to be made more people friendly, responsive, transparent and accountable. The entire educational system has to be revamped with emphasis on the teaching of ethical and moral values. There have to be moral codes of conduct for all sections of the citizens, i.e., public servants, professionals, businessmen, industrialists and politicians etc. to highlight their social responsibilities. Honesty and probity are as important for the private sector as for the public functionaries. Adulteration of food items or selling of inferior drugs is as reprehensible as corruption among public servants. India's image in international trade gets tarnished when our exported items are found to be of inferior quality and in breach of the agreed terms. Our business honesty should take due care of national prestige involved in the "Made in India" brand.

Broadly speaking, our farmers and workers with comparatively less education but more Indianness in them have fared much better than the so-called "modern" and educated categories of citizens in performing their duties. The farmers through their hard work and application of higher agricultural technology and farming methods have succeeded in making the country self-sufficient in its foodgrain requirements. They have done real service to India as in spite of our population having increased nearly three-fold since independence, the foodgrains production has been increased by them more than four-folds. Similar results could not be achieved in the industrial and manufacturing sectors due to lack of good governance and faulty economic policies of different political parties. Additionally the same segments of citizens engaged in industry attached greater importance to easy and unscrupulous ways of money making rather than creating true wealth through better research and innovation. They believed in "making" money rather than in "earning" money. Quality aspects did not get due attention in manufacturing of goods instead monopolistic environment was contrived to market inferior goods and make easy money. This did not allow competition to improve the quality of our products. In spite of these shortcomings, India is still being counted to be an emerging economic super power. The apprehensions however are that some negative aspects of citizenship values and lack of good governance may become serious bottlenecks to delay India's progress. There is therefore need to rise above our narrow identities and undue greed for money to be able to take the country forward.

The country is also now trying to come out of the past economic mistakes by following the path of liberalization. But here also the industrial class should keep national interests in mind. Hiding incomes and avoiding payment of justified taxes to government need to be avoided for the larger good of society. Significant growth of black money shows that we lack proper citizenship values in not paying the state its legitimate tax revenues. It may be true that money in the hands of government is not always well spent. There are according to the audit reports of the C&AG increasing amount of wasteful, and infructuous expenditure in many Government departments in the states and at the central level too. Only a few days back a minister in Bihar was arrested by the CBI for fraudulent expenditure in the purchase of coal tar worth Rs. 100 crore for road work. The money allegedly was not fully spent for this purpose but was partly misappropriated. Earlier a former Chief Minister of Bihar and a number of Bihar officials were chargesheeted for large scale corruption involving around Rs. 900 crore for purchase of fodder for the Animal Husbandry Department. One Chief Minister is allegedly spending several crores of public money for self-advertisement through building marble statues in dozens of self and party political leaders. The Apex Court while hearing a writ petition before it against such a wasteful expenditure of around Rs.

2,600 crores on memorials wanted to know from the UP State Government "as to how such a colossal expenditure can be incurred" when the state has a meagre GDP growth of around 2 per cent annually? (media report of September 9, 2009). Obviously the apex court hinted that such a large amount could have been better spent for the benefit of the poor people, i.e. on providing education, health and drinking water facilities for them rather than building stone statues of political leaders.

At the central level too thousands of crores of rupees in several defence purchase deals were allegedly taken as bribes by some political persons and public officials in the recent past. This kind of corruption and wasteful expenditure may discourage tax-payers to pay taxes to the public exchequer. They may consider that paying taxes would only increase corruption and waste. This is a vicious circle and needs correction. However, we have to accept the fact that Government cannot function without adequate tax revenues and therefore legitimate taxes have to be paid as part of our citizenship duties and responsibilities.

In conclusion, the sum and substance of good citizenship values lie in doing everything possible by the citizens to make India strong and stable. Since the world has become a global village and there are frequent interactions with foreigners, every Indian citizen must make sure that India's prestige is held high by them in their dealings with the foreign nationals. Our endeavour has to be to make India the largest democracy, to be qualitatively the greatest democracy as well by adopting higher ethical norms and values. This requires adherence to the ideals of the Constitution by the citizens. The last verse of the *Geeta* may be relevant to quote to emphasize the higher quality of citizenship values we need in our various actions. It says:

Yatra yegesvarah Krisna
Yatra Partho dhanur-dharah;
Tata srih, vijayo bhutih,
Dhruva nitih matir mama-

'Wherever (there is the spirit) of Krishna, the master of yoga (the master of vision), (and) where (there is the spirit of) Arjuna, the wielder of the bow (the hero of action), there, I am convinced, wealth, victory, welfare, and unshakable justice (shall prevail).'

All our actions as citizens have to be morally and ethically justifiable. Good ends have to be achieved through good means. All the citizens have to be made fully aware of this for promoting good citizenship values.

13

MEANING AND SIGNIFICANCE OF HINDUISM TO MAKE INDIA A SECULAR STATE

The ancient "Arya dharma" in course of several thousand years of history came to be known as Hindu Dharma or "Hinduism" even though no such word was mentioned in any of our ancient holy books like the Vedas, Upnisads, Puranas. Smritis, the two great epics, *Ramayana* and *Mahabharat*, or the *Bhagvad Gita* the main sources of *Arya Dharma*.

Pandit Jawaharlal Nehru, in his famous book "The Discovery of India" also wrote (page 76) that the word "Hindu" does not occur at all in our ancient literature. The word he explained was used for thousands of years by the people of Western and Central Asia for India or rather for the people living on the east of river "Sindhu." They pronounced "S" as "H" and hence they called "Sindhu" as "Hindu." Later the Greeks during Alexander's invasion of India towards the end of 4th Century B.C. pronounced "Sindhu" as "Indus" and the country beyond it was named as India.

The famous Chinese pilgrim I-Tsing who came to India in the 7th Century A.D. wrote in his travel records that the people of Central Asia called India "Hindu" (Hsin-tu) and that it was not at all the name in common use. According to him the name of the country was "Aryadesha" (noble country) or the land of the Aryans.

The land of the Aryans of that time according to historians stretched from the river Sindhu in the west to Brahmputra in the east and from the Himalayas in the north to Vindhya mountains in the south. It was then known as Arya Varta. In course of time but still many thousand years back, the Aryans with their growing population spread over to the south of the Vindhyas. This enlarged territory of the Aryans which also included the Dravidians of Southern parts was named as *Bharat Varsha* after King Bharat the legendary founder of Arya Varta. The *Vishnu Purana* gave the geographical boundary of the country as below:

> *"uttaram yat samudrasya,*
> *Himadraishcha dakshisnam*
> *Varsham tad Bharatam naam*
> *Bharati yatra Santiti."*

(The land north of the sea and south of the Himalayas bears the name Bharat Varsha.)

However, since the Europeans and the British knew India through the Greeks, the name "India" originally given by them to the Arya Varta or Bharat Varsha came in common use by the Europeans. The Britishers continued this name officially during their rule over India. After attaining independence the new Constitution of the Indian Republic in its first Article names the country "India that is Bharat." This Article reads: "India that is Bharat shall be a union of States". Independent India's Constitution has thus officially recognised both the old and the new names of this ancient land. Accordingly "Government of India" in English is *"Bharat Sarkar"* in Hindi. The emotional attachment of the people, however, is more with its ancient name Bharat Varsha. This name is more intimately connected and associated with the country's centuries old history, faith, culture, civilization, myths and mythologies. The name Bharat is more dear to the people following the Arya Dharma or Hinduism as it is now commonly known. Historically that period of Indian history when the Aryan ruled it, is now known as the "Hindu period."

Even though the words "Hindu" and "Hindustan" came to be applied to India long back, these had originally no religious connotations. In course of time, however, *"Aryans"* and "Hindus" came to be identified to be one and the same people and *"Arya dharma"* also came to be known as Hindu Dharma or "Hinduism." Some also call it *"Sanatan Dharma"* or universal religion because its moral and ethical values are of a universal nature. It is also called Vedic Dharma as its primary sources are the four Vedas i.e., The Rig Veda, the Yajurveda, the Samveda and the Atharva Veda.

Several Upnishadas, forming part of the Vedas, Puranas, Smritis like the Manu Samriti, the two great epics *Ramayan* and *Mahabharat* and the *Bhagvad Gita* are the other important sources of Arya Dharma or "Hinduism" of the present. Thus Hinduism is not a one book religion like Christianity with its single holy book the Bible, and Islam with its one holy book—the Koran.

The common Hindu masses, however, know about the essence and ethics of Hinduism more from the *Ramayan* and the *Mahabharat*. The various stories and episodes in these two great epics reflect the beliefs, faith, ideals, practices and philosophy of Arya Dharma. To a great extent these precious epics have guided and influenced the social relationships and lives of Hindus for centuries. Pandit Jawaharlal Nehru wrote in his book The Discovery of India how the two great epics have promoted cultural unity and social stability among the Indian people for centuries. His words are:

> "I do not know of any books anywhere which have exercised such a continuous and pervasive influence on the mass mind as these two. Dating back to a remote antiquity they are still a living force in the life of the Indian people.
>
> They make us understand somewhat the secret of the old Indians in holding together a variegated society divided up in many ways and graded in castes, in harmonizing their discords, and giving them a common background of heroic tradition and ethical living. Deliberately they tried to build up a unity of outlook among the people, which was to survive and overshadow all diversity." He also mentions that:
>
> "Among the earliest memories of my childhood are the stories from these epics told to me by my mother or the older ladies of the house."

Like Pandit Nehru, other Indian children too since time immemorial have been told the absorbing stories of *Ramayan* and *Mahabharat* by their elders. These inculcate in them the culture and ethical values of Arya Dharma. The stories in the epics specially impress upon the young minds the virtues of adhering to ones pledged words. The great virtue according to *Ramayan* is *"pran jaye per bachan na jaye"* (one should keep one's pledged words even at the cost of his life). Another great lesson is to uphold truth and justice under all odds and circumstances. Truth and justice are the essence of "Dharma" and according to *Mahabharat* God is on the side of "Dharma" and it always prevails over Adharma. The popularity of these epics is so vast , deep and enduring that much of India's literature, its cultural outpourings like dances, music, paintings etc. to a large extent veer around important characters and episodes in the two epics. People in many parts of the country also claim and try to prove the visits of Rama and Sita and the five Pandavas to their places during their *Vanbas* periods. Accordingly hundreds of human habitations–towns and villages, hills and mountains, streams and rivers in all parts of India bear the names of Rama, Sita, Lord Krishna, Arjuna or of other great figures in the two epics. Stories and episodes from these epics are also enacted in drama forms or recited in musical folklores in most villages all over India—specially during festive occasions. Even now millions watch with rapt attention the *Ramayan* and *Mahabharat* serials over the TV. When these were shown for the first time on TV, road traffics came to a halt during the TV timings of the serials. These epics thus constantly keep reminding us of the divine law of victory of truth over falsehood and of right over wrong *(Satya-meva Jayate)*. The basic values of Hinduism are thus always inculcated into the minds of our people. Even those belonging to other faiths witnessing such performances get no less influenced by the moral values conveyed by the epics. This greatly helps in establishing moral and cultural bonds between Hindus and non-Hindus in India.

The Hindu Dharma and its culture are strongly woven into the thought processes and social life of the Indian people. We may say that India's heart and soul rhythm in tune with the philosophy and core values of Hinduism and some kind of filial attachment has developed between them. Bharat or India is lovingly called Bharat Mata by people in general and like Rama in *Ramayan* they regard their motherland to be greater than the heaven as in the following words of Shri Rama:

Janani Janama bhumi—Swargadapi Gariyasi
(The motherland is greater than heaven)

For India's freedom struggle Mahatma Gandhi to inspire and unite the masses appropriately chose the slogan *"Vande Matram."* He knew the enormous love and reverence people in India have for "Bharat mata" and they will be prepared for any sacrifice for its freedom.

The word "Dharma" in Hinduism is a much wider concept than what is commonly understood by the word "religion" in its limited spiritual sense of God and his worship. According to Hindu scriptures dharma essentially means practice of righteous conduct in every sphere of life. Dharma means that which holds together. It is derived from the root word "Dhar" in Sanskrit, i.e. that which holds or we may say lack of which may lead to downfall. The few words Sadachar (righteous conduct), Satvichar (right thinking) and Satvachan (good words) are the core of Hindu Dharma.

In *Mahabharat* on being asked by Yudhistira to explain the meaning and scope of *DHARMA*, Bhishma Pitamaha replied:

> "It is most difficult to define Dharma. Dharma has been explained to be that which helps the upliftment of living beings. Therefore, that which ensures the welfare of living beings is surely Dharma. The learned rishis have declared that which sustains is Dharma."

Madhavacharya, a renowned scholar, in his commentary on Parashara Samriti, explained the meaning of Dharma as follows:

> "Dharma is that which sustains and ensures progress and welfare of all in this world and eternal bliss in the other world. Dharma is promulgated in the form of commands. (Positive and negative vidhi and nishedha)"

We may therefore say that Dharma comprises of righteous conduct or *sadachar* in every sphere of life. The faithful practice of Dharma enables a believer in God and heaven to attain his ultimate objective of life i.e. to attain *moksha* (eternal bliss) or Nirvan or freedom from the cycle of birth and death. Blessings of Hindu Dharma cover all mankind; these are not restricted to followers of any one religion or to the inhabitants of any one country. Hindu Dharma is indeed "Manav Dharma" or universal religion with focus on all mankind. In *Gita* also the message is for all mankind and its approach is universal. For example the Lord in *Gita* says "All paths lead to Me" which means people may reach God by following any faith and spiritual practices if only truth and justice are adhered to. Arjun in *Gita* is the symbol of the tortured spirit of man torn by conflicting thoughts, and moralities. The Lord solves his dilemma by bringing in the concept of Dharma and how to uphold it and whenever necessary to fight for it. To drive home the point to Arjuna, Lord Krishna says that to uphold and restore Dharma whenever it is violated beyond a point *(Dharmasya Glanir Bhawati)*. God himself takes birth in the world for the deliverance of the good people *(Paritranaya Sadhunam)* and for the destruction of the evil doers *(Binasaya cha duskrutam)* and to restore Dharma or justice *(Dharma Sansgasthapanaya)*.

The Lord thus emphatically says that one could fight against his near and dear ones also to uphold Dharma if so required. To stand for truth, and justice is Dharma. No relationship is considered to be above Dharma. Arjuna was accordingly advised to fight against his elders as also against his Guru to uphold Dharma. To fight for Dharma was explained to be a Godly act for peace and harmony in society.

The Supreme Court of India in a judgement defined Dharma as below:

> "Dharma" is that which upholds, nourishes or supports the stability of the society, maintains social order and secures the general well-being and progress of mankind."

The judgement thus to a good extent reflects the Hindu view of *Dharma*.

Adherence to Dharma or righteous conduct in word and deed for an individual requires effective control over certain common human weaknesses like *Kama* (Desire), *Krodh* (Anger), *Lobha* (Greed), *Moha* (attachment), *Mada* (infatuation) and *Matshrya* (enmity). The code of conduct dear to the Lord as stated in *Gita* (Chapter XII) is as below:

> "The person who hates none, who is friendly and has compassion for all, who has no selfishness and ego, who maintains balance of mind in pain and pleasure, who has contentment, is steady in meditation, self-controlled and firm in his decision, who is dedicated to me and who is my devotee is dear to me."
>
> In one word such an accomplished individual is known as "*Stitha Pragnya*." To be a good Hindu accordingly one must try to abide by the above righteous conduct or Dharma.

An essential part of Dharma according to Vedas and other holy scriptures is to acknowledge and discharge the following four debts or obligations that each man owes to God, his Parents, his Guru and the Society at large. The nature of these debts and the manner of their discharge as laid down in the holy books bring out the essence of Hinduism i.e. its liberal approach, tolerance and sense of deep gratitude to the benefactor. It may therefore be relevant to briefly explain the nature of these "debts" to understand the moral and social values of Hinduism.

The four debts are:

1. Deva Rina (debt to God)
2. Pitru Rina (debt to parents)
3. Rishi or Guru Rina (debt to the teacher)
4. Manav Rina (debt to society at large).

Hindu Dharma highly values the expression of gratitude and discharge of obligations of a benefactor. According to Hinduism man firstly owes obligations or debt to God for his birth in the highest Yoni i.e. the *Manva yoni.* Man should therefore devotedly worship God to acknowledge the divine debt. Secondly, man owes gratitude to his parents for his birth and upbringing by them. Hence they need to be humbly, reverentially and lovingly looked after in their old-age. Thirdly, man is obliged to his Guru or the teacher for the knowledge imparted by him and thus making him man out of animal. Education *(Vidya)* is considered to be greater than other worldly riches as stated below in the Hitopadesha:

Vidya Rajsu Pujitah
Natu dhanam
Vidya vihinah Pashuha.

(Vidya is respected by the King and not wealth.
A man without vidya is like an animal.)

Accordingly a Guru deserves respect and high status in society. A sacred prayer in our holy book is: "*Guruar Brahma, Guruar Vishnu, Guruar Deva Maheswarha.*".

Fourthly, man also owes gratitude to society and the humanity at large for his survival, overall development, material gains and happiness. Hindu Dharma thus recognises the importance of society and interdependence of the mankind as a whole. Man is accepted to be a social being and his living in a good and civilised society enables him to develop his divinely endowed potentials better. Unhealthy social environment on the other hand may turn a man to be uncultured, anti-social and brutish. He would also be deprived of the light of knowledge and the accumulated wisdom of a good human society. We may say that "terrorists" and "terrorism" are the ultimate products of undeveloped societies. A man brought up in such less cultured and less humane society would have little inclination towards "Dharma" or good conduct. Violence and brutality would make life less liveable in such social environment. Hinduism because of its liberal and humane approach treats the entire world as one family. Its emphasis is on righteous conduct and to be tolerant and friendly towards all. It is the well-wisher of all mankind as stated in the following Hitopadesha verse:

Udar charitesu
Vasudheya kutumbakam

(Those who are large hearted regard the world as one family.)

Hinduism stands for large heartedness as it regards all human beings to be members of one universal family. Hinduism has a global approach in uplifting human societies.

In the following daily prayer of a Hindu the entire humanity is kept in mind. It says:

Sarvepi Sukhinah Santu,
Sarvesantu Niramayah,
Sarve Bhadrani Pashyantu,
Ma Kaschit dukhabhag Bhavet.

(Let all be happy, let all be healthy, let all see auspicious things and let nobody suffer from grief.)

Another similar prayer is:

Lokaa Samastaa
Sukhino Bhavantu

(Let all people be happy.)

The manner of discharge of Deva Runa brings out the liberal values of Hinduism concerning God and his worship. According to the Vedas "Truth is one (though) the wise call it by various names. *(Ekam Sat, Vipra bahuda vadanti)*. It simply means that God is one but He is called by different names and worshipped in different ways by different people. According to the Hindu scriptures God is Infinite *(Anant)*, with no Beginning *(Anadi)*, no End *(Amar)* and no Form (*Nirakara*). Hence one is free to worship the Infinite God in infinite ways and forms. No one can say that any particular form is the true form of God. Jesus and Allah were prophets of known historical times and were actually seen in their sacred human bodies by people of their times. Therefore, the Christians and Muslims worship and pray more or less in uniform ways and manners as laid down in their respective holy books i.e.—the Bible and the Koran. There is no such single way of worshipping the God among Hindus as God is formless *(Nirakar)* and infinite *(Ananta)* and as such cannot be seen or visualized for uniform ways to worship Him. The Vedas did not mention of any temples or images (Idols) for the worship of God. He is *Sarva Vyapi* (all pervasive). God was taken to be present everywhere in his creation including in all the living beings. God the creator according to Hinduism is one with his creation. Thus man too was treated to be himself divine and his soul *(Atma)* is regarded to be part of the *Paramatma* (super soul) or God. This was known as the philosophy of *"Advaita"* or oneness of God and His creation. Individuals themselves being part of the divine were free to worship the Supreme being *(Paramatma)* in their own diverse ways. About this freedom of approach in spiritual matters Pandit Jawahar Lal Nehru wrote in The Discovery of India as follows:

> "It is interesting to compare and contrast the intense individualism and exclusiveness of the Indo-Aryans with this all-embracing approach, which overrides all barriers of caste and class and every other external and internal difference. This latter is a kind of metaphysical democracy. He who sees the one spirit in all, and all in the one spirit, henceforth can look with contempt on no creature. Though this was theory only, there can be no doubt that it must have affected life and produced that atmosphere of tolerance and reasonableness, that acceptance of free thought in matters of faith, that desire and capacity to live and let live, which are dominant features of Indian culture, as they are of the Chinese. There was no totalitarianism in religion or culture, and they indicate an old and wise civilization with inexhaustible mental reserves."

After the Vedic period however to enable the common devotees to worship God, as a practical way out, Idols or images of the one God with many names and forms came to be worshipped. The common man wanted to see God in some human form and hence worshipping some Saguna version of God, (i.e. with some specific divine powers) became the practice. Thus the one God with many names and forms of Devis and Devtas with special divine attributes (or divine powers) came to be worshipped. Thus the infinite and invisible one God was in a way domesticated in idol forms of many devis and devtas for purposes of worship. For the idols of each Devi and Devta temples were built. For each of them special prayers, and rituals were prescribed. Many of the ancient temples are now places of great pilgrimages on different religious occasions connected with different Devi and Devta. They attract lakhs of pilgrims from all parts of the country and thus play a unifying role among Hindus of all parts of India.

Saints and sages of the past gave three principal names to one God i.e. Brahma, Vishnu and Mahesh attributing separate divine qualities to each of them. These three (Trimurti) constituted the one God or Parameswar. Of the three—Brahma is worshiped as the Creator of the Universe, Vishnu as the one who maintains it by enforcing Dharma and Shiva, as the destroyer of all evils. As stated in *Gita*, Vishnu incarnates in human form from time to time to restore Dharma whenever it is seen to be in serious decline. He thus maintains the divine balance and prevents chaos and upheavals in human societies. Vishnu is said to have so far incarnated in ten Avtars (Das Avtars). Better known of these are Ram Avtar of *Ramayana* period and Sri Krishna Avtar of the *Mahabharata* period. Thus one God (Parameswar) with three names each with special attributes (i.e. divine powers) came to be worshipped in course of time by the Hindus. Their consorts and offsprings too are worshipped for special divine powers assigned to them i.e. Lakshmi wife of Vishnu for wealth, Saraswati wife of Brahma for learning, Durga or Kali wife of Mahesh or Shiva for Shakti or strength. Other Devis and Devtas with specific divine powers assigned to them too came to be worshipped. For example, Surya (sun), Agni (fire), Vayu (wind), Varun (water) were worshipped for providing the most basic human needs of life. Thus Hindus by praying them show gratitude to them as their benefactors. Ganesh is worshipped for removal of obstacles and difficulties before commencement of any important work. Accordingly Ganesh is also called Bighnaraj. Worshipping a reputed Bhakta or a great devotee of God also amounted to worshipping God himself. Hence Hanuman the great Bhakta of Sri Rama is worshipped to gain strength, and self-confidence. Hanuman is known to be "*Sankat mochan*" or one who provides relief at times of great hardships.

Since God is thus worshipped in several forms and names, foreigners mistakenly think that Hinduism is polytheistic with multiple

Gods. The fact, however, is as stated earlier, Hinduism is monotheistic and believes God to be one and one only. He is however, worshipped in several forms and names as appropriate for his different powers and attributes. Human mind being fickle and weak is somewhat incapable of comprehending one all powerful *(Sarva Shaktiman)* and *Nirakar* (formless) God. Hence worshipping Him for His different attributes in different names and forms came into practice. The harmful results of worshipping God in such numerous forms, names and ways has been the emergence of multitude of priests and priest craft, rigid rituals, ceremonies and all kinds of religious superstitions. Worshipping God in such diverse forms requires the help of special priests who know the special prayers and rituals for the worship of different Devis and Devtas. For the ways and rituals to worship Laxmi, Saraswati, Durga, Ganesh, Hanuman etc. are different. Thus specialisation has come for worshipping one God in His diverse forms and names. There are also separate temples for the idols of different Devtas and Devis. Thousands of Pujaris, Pandas and Sewaks make their living as middlemen for facilitating access to these deities by the common worshippers. This is undermining to some extent the sanctity and popularity of Hinduism particularly among the younger generations. Temples in course of time have virtually been turned into commercial establishments by the priests and temple managers. They have in courses of time acquired legal rights to manage the religious affairs of many of the ancient temples. Unfortunately, Idols of Devis and Devtas are mute witnesses to various abuses practised in their names by many of the priestly classes.

The one relieving aspect of Hinduism however is that a Hindu continues to be a Hindu even if he is an atheist and does not believe in God, does not pray to God, or does not go to any temple. Visiting a temple for prayer is not at all obligatory for a Hindu. As mentioned earlier temples were not even visualized during the Vedic period. In fact most Hindu households set apart a separate room or place in their houses for worshipping their chosen Devis and Devtas whose idols or Murtis are kept there for the daily puja. Further one can be a true Hindu by following the Hindu code of righteous conduct in different spheres of life discussed earlier. Gratitude to God too can be expressed by serving the poor and the needy as they too bear the name "Daridra narayan". A good Hindu believes that God is best pleased when He sees a helpless and destitute is helped.

Swami Vivekananda also supports this way of worshiping God by saying:

> "Where should you go to see for God? Are not all the poor, miserable, the weak, God?"

Therefore for many Hindus serving the poor, the helpless and the needy individuals is the best way to discharge their Deva Runa or gratitude to God.

In the words of our late Philosopher President Dr. S. Radhkrishnan, "Hinduism is more a way of life than a form of thought. While it gives absolute liberty in the world of thought, it enjoins a strict code of practice. The theist and atheist, the specific and the agnostic may all be Hindus if they accept the Hindu system of culture and life. Hinduism insists not on religious conformity but a spiritual and ethical outlook in life.... Hinduism insists on a moral life and draws into fellowship of all who feel themselves bound to the claims which the moral law makes upon them. Hinduism is not a sect but a fellowship of all who accept the law of right and earnestly seek for the truth."

The core values of Hinduism stated above clearly show that it accepts all religions as diverse paths to the one Absolute Truth or the God. Lord Krishna's sermon in the *Bhagvad Gita* is "whosoever comes to Me, through whatever form, I reach him; all men are struggling through paths which in the end lead to Me." Hinduism thus accepts the sanctity and legitimacy of all religions in the worship of God and in the way they worship Him. According to Hinduism there is divinity in the hearts of all men irrespective of their caste, creed, race, colour, or country of residence. Hence it is a truly universal religion *(Manav Dharma)*. It stands for the happiness of all human beings. There is no bar to call God by any name. Hence Gandhiji's daily prayer was *"Ishwar Allah Tere nam"* thus equating "Ishwar" of Hindus to "Allah" of Muslims. Gandhiji as all know was a devout Hindu and hence he spontaneously uttered the words "Hey Ram" when dying after being shot from close range by a fanatic Hindu. To him Allah and Ishwar were no different. Swami Vivekananda whom the Americans described as "Cyclonic Hindu" in his famous speech in the Parliament of Religions in Chicago in 1893 said:

> "Sisters and Brothers of America
>
> I am proud to belong to a religion which has taught the world both tolerance and universal acceptance. We believe

not only in universal toleration, but we accept all religions as true."

Vivekananda's addressing the audience as "Sisters and Brothers" won the hearts of the Americans. It evoked favourable sentiments for Hinduism which regarded all human beings to be members of one human family.

Since Hinduism sees divinity in all beings there is no place for conversion of a non-Hindu into Hinduism. No one is a "*Kafir*" in Hinduism as all human beings carry the divine spark in them. Every individual's soul or Atma is part of the supreme soul or Parmatma. There is no question therefore of harming or hurting let alone killing any one for his being a non-Hindu. Hinduism stands for universal love and tolerance. Thus ideas of secularism are in-built in HIinduism. We may say, secularism is the soul of Hinduism.

The Vedic concept of "Sarva Dharma Sambhav" (Equal respect for all religions) is writ large in Hindu culture. Such liberalism and humanism enabled Hinduism in its many centuries of history to welcome and accommodate hordes of refugees of other religions who came to India from time to time to escape religious persecutions in their own countries–like the Jews, the Zorostrians (Persians), the Syrian Christians, etc. About this liberalism of Hinduism and its culture Swami Vivekananda stated in his speech in the Parliament of Religions in Chicago as follows:

> "I am proud to belong to a nation which has sheltered the persecuted and the refugees of all religions and all nations of the earth. I am proud to tell you that we have gathered in our bosom the purest remnant of the Israelites, who came to Southern India and took refuge with us in the very year in which their holy temple was shattered to pieces by Roman tyranny. I am proud to belong to a religion which has sheltered and is still fostering the remnant of the grand Zorastrian nation."

The Greeks, Sakas, Kushans, and Huns initially came as invaders but were absorbed and assimilated in the course of time in the vast ocean of Hindu society and its culture of humanism. Such cultural assimilation at different times also had the beneficial effect of invigorating and rejuvenating the old culture of the land. New blood each time gave it new strength. Thus the Indian culture gradually became a composite culture of many races and creeds but with pronounced visibility of the ancient Vedic culture of human brotherhood. The foreign elements with elapse of time became largely indistinguishable from the earlier inhabitants. Each new wave was a thin layer on the colossal body of Vedic religion and the culture of Aryans or Hindus.

The Arab invasion of India and later the long period of Muslim rule, however, put great stress and strain on the assimilating and uniting spirit of the ancient Hindu culture. The Vedic ideas of "live and let live" suffered severe jolts due to gross brutalities and fanaticism in the name of religion by some Muslim rulers like Aurangzeb. According to religious fanatics like him converting non-Muslims to Islam was the best way to please Allah. Similarly, destroying Hindu temples and building mosques in their places too was considered to be part of serving Islam. This is despite the fact that earlier during Akbar's rule good amount of brotherly understanding had started developing between the Hindus and the Muslims. Such spirit of mutual understanding could not however go sufficiently deep or become lasting due to a variety of reasons. To cut short a long story of religious violence and hatred short, India got partitioned at the end of the British rule in 1947. This was mainly due to the Muslim leader Mohammad Ali Jinnah's rigid communal attitude and his theory that Hindus and Muslims were "two nations" and that they could not live together peacefully and harmoniously on the termination of the British rule. "Mr. Jinnah's family, it is interesting to note, was originally Hindu" writes Pandit Nehru in The Discovery of India (p. 414). Strangely the two nation theory of Mr. Jinnah had the mass support of those Muslims who themselves largely had Hindu backgrounds. The Muslims of North-West Frontier Province, the Pathans who had Islamic origin *ab initio* on the other hand were till the end of British Rule pro-Congress and Anti-Muslim League which wanted partition of India on communal lines. Pandit Nehru seems to have stated this though somewhat indirectly in the following words:

> The idea of partition was "least in evidence in the North-West Frontier Province (95% Muslims) where the Pathans are brave and self-reliant and have no fear complex. Oddly enough, the Moslem League's proposal to partition India finds less response in the Moslem areas sought to be partitioned than in the Moslem minority areas which are unaffected by

it. (He meant perhaps U.P. and Bihar.) Yet the fact remains that considerable numbers of Moslems have become sentimentally attached to this idea of separation without giving thought to its consequences."

As apprehended the consequences of partition have been very much damaging to both India and Pakistan, The hostility between the two gets aggravated from time to time on one ground or the other. Three wars have already been fought between the two. Both countries are spending huge amounts of money on defence forces and military weapons at the cost of social and economic developments. Pakistan unfortunately is following a policy of "Jihad" against India through brutal terrorist acts from time to time causing serious loss of life and property. These are also aimed to disturb peace and communal harmony among Indian Muslims and Hindus. The pre-partition mind-set of the Pakistan state does not appear to have very much changed even though people in general in both countries want their brotherly ties to be restored and strengthened.

After partition for sometime Hindu-Muslim divide in India had somewhat eased. But in recent years due to acts of terrorism by the Islamic Jehadi elements of Pakistan the fraternal understanding of Hindus and Muslims in India is being disturbed. Fortunately, however, it is still intact due to the liberal attitude of Hindus derived from their religion Hinduism. The short-sighted "politics of vote bank" is another factor feeding communal ideas and separatist mentality among the Indian Muslims.

It may be mentioned that even after partition India has more Muslim population than Pakistan (presently around 150 millions). A large percentage of Muslims are in the states of U.P. and Bihar who though had stood for partition yet chose to stay in India. In many constituencies of U.P. and Bihar Muslim votes are a decisive factor for electoral victory of candidates. Some political parties accordingly try to placate the Muslims by promising special benefits for them to get their votes. This kind of approach is termed as "minority appeasement" or "minorityism" by some other political parties. There is some kind of political warfare between groups who call themselves "secularists" or in reality Muslim supporters and others who are termed by their opponents as "communalists" or the Hindu supporters. Unfortunately, the words "Hindu" and "Hinduism" are now indiscriminately being labelled as symbols of communalism. This is unfair and hurts Hindu sentiments as generally Hindus (barring some fanatical groups) continue to be secular minded in keeping with the philosophy of Arya Dharma or Hinduism with its culture of tolerance and human brotherhood. India after partition has remained a secular state despite Pakistan having become an Islamic state and continuing its hostile attitude towards India. This is because Hinduism provides strong foundation for India's secularism. Hindus believe in the theory of 'forgive and forget'. That enabled them to reconcile with the tragic events of partition and also the post partition terrorist activities supported by Pakistan. It is regrettable that to praise India's ancient culture and heritage at times invites wrong comments of the same by "pseudo secularists." For example, the release of an Indian Council of Historical Research volume by the eminent historian Irfan Habib sometime back was adversely commented by a prominent national daily for glorification of the Vedic period not on account of any historical inaccuracy but simply on the plea that "such praises in the past have played pivotal role in the formation of Hindu nationalism." Does it imply that the Hindu children should no longer be told the stories of *Ramayana* and *Mahabharata* and these epics should not be allowed to be reading materials in schools/colleges? Stretched a little more there may be demands by such fake secularists to change the national moto *"Satya meva Jayate"* as it is an Upnishadic verse. It will be unfortunate to ignore our glorious past in the name of false secularism. This was also in a way the wise advice of Pandit Nehru who wrote in The Discovery of India (p. 541) –

> "We can never forget the ideas that have moved our race, the dreams of the Indian people through the ages, the wisdom of the ancients, the buoyant energy and love of life and nature of our forefathers, their spirit of curiosity and mental adventure, the daring of their thought, their splendid achievements in literature, art and culture, their love of truth and beauty and freedom, the basic values that they set up their understanding of life's mysterious ways, their toleration of other ways than theirs, their capacity to absorb other peoples and their cultural accomplishments, to synthesize them and develop a varied and mixed culture; nor can we forget the myriad experiences which have built up our ancient race and lie embedded in our sub-conscious minds. We will never forget them or cease to take pride in that noble heritage of ours. If

India forgets them she will no longer remain India and much that has made her our joy and pride will cease to be."

Since the Communists claim to be the present day flag bearers of secularism and disdain Hinduism, I looked for Pandit Nehru's views on them. He wrote about the communist in The Discovery of India (p. 549) as below:

> "I know that in India the Communist Party is completely divorced from, and is ignorant of, the national traditions that fill the minds of the people. It believes that communism necessarily implies a contempt for the past. So far as it is concerned, the history of the world began in November, 1917, and everything that preceded this was preparatory and leading up to it. Normally speaking, in a country like India with numbers of people on the verge of starvation and the economic structure cracking up, communism should have a wide appeal. In a sense there is that vague appeal, but the Communist Party cannot take advantage of it because it has cut itself off from the springs of national sentiment and speaks in a language which finds no echo in the hearts of the people. It remains an energetic but small group, with no real roots."

Thus communists in India are far removed from the feelings and sentiments of the people. They are not one with them as normal human beings. One wonders how proud they feel to call Bharat Mata as "janani" and it to be greater than heaven. In any case for the communists there is no concept of heaven. They have accordingly little idea of Dharma that has bonded and safeguarded the Indian people during periods of adversities in their long history of thousands of years.

About the others who like to ignore India's ancient Dharma and culture i.e. the Westernised fake "secularists" Panditji wrote in The Discovery of India–

> "There are others who talk glibly of modernism and modern spirit and the essence of western culture, and are at the same time ignorant of their own culture. Unlike the communists, they have no ideal that moves them and no driving force that carries them forward. They take the external forms and outer trappings of the west (and often some of the less desirable features), and imagine that they are in the vanguard of an advancing civilization. Naive and shallow and yet full of their

own conceits, they live, chiefly in a few large cities, an artificial life which has no living contacts with the culture of the east or of the west."

Such persons plainly speaking may be described as cultural refugees. They have little love for Bharat Janani their motherland. For them the word "Bharat" is a symbol of backwardness and the word "Hindu" is the symbol of communalism. It is doubtful if many of them had the joy and privilege of hearing stories of *Ramayan* and *Mahabharat*. Lack of Indianness or Bhartiyata in its true sense can be said to be their basic inadequacy in following and promoting real secularism. India as stated earlier is a secular republic mainly because of its dominant religion Hinduism which stands for the well being of all human beings and is tolerant of all religions.

Caste system is one of the weakest feature of Hinduism. Whatever its rationale may have been in the long historical past, in its present degenerated form caste division among Hindus is proving to be a great liability in nation building. It is proving to be a serious handicap for the country's unity, solidarity and progress. Unfortunately, many so-called secularists whole-heartedly indulge in caste-based politics to grab political power for their own gains. They have little sense of "social justice." They are also devoid of the ideas of "Rajdharma" which essentially means to look after the welfare of all the people irrespective of their caste, creed or race. *Praja Sukhe, Sukham Rajah* is a holy verse meant to be followed by the rulers in India. The word "praja" stands for all people irrespective of their caste or creed. Only our ancient Arya Dharma or Hinduism and its culture had laid down such ideals for all inclusive justice.

If the tenets of Hinduism are followed in their true spirit it would be far more easier for the country to attain social cohesion, political unity, national integration and economic progress. The one major reform required however is to eradicate the caste system as early as possible and not to abuse it for vote bank politics. For this purpose the policy of reservation in public services and educational institutions need to be rationalized in keeping with the true spirit of social justice and the basic goals of our Constitution as laid down in its Preamble. Reservation should not be allowed to continue for too long as it promotes and strengthens casteism and caste prejudices. A sound exit policy need to be devised.

To conclude, Hinduism briefly means *Sadachar* (righteous conduct) and *Sarva Dharma Sambhav* (or showing equal respect for all religions). In political terms it would mean true secularism. Hinduism is the root from which India derives its cultural and civilisational sustenance of tolerance and human brotherhood. Let not fanatics among Hindus and Muslims and above all the "fake secularists" be allowed to create disharmony in the large joint family of people of all faiths of this great nation. Pakistan our neighbour an Islamic republic too should be persuaded and prevented from creating rifts between Indian Muslims and Hindus. India a secular republic has bountiful material resources and a massive billion plus population to make it a great power politically and economically in the world. For this it is important that we rise above petty discords of castes and creeds by following the liberal values of our ancient *Arya Dharma* or Hinduism. Since this religion alone holds all other religions to be equally sacred, different paths to reach the Supreme being it promotes and accepts secularism for governance of the country. It is therefore the strongest pillar for preserving and promoting national unity, peace and prosperity.

14

JUSTICE SACHAR COMMITTEE REPORT ON MUSLIM BACKWARDNESS

Justice Sachar Committee Report (November 2006) on the Economic and Educational status of the Muslim Community of India has recommended several measures for their special treatment and progress in areas like education, employment, housing, political empowerment, etc. Similar problems of backwardness of the castes classified as OBCs were dealt with by the Mandal Commission Report of 1980. It had recommended various measures including reservation in higher educational institutions and Government jobs for the castes classified as "OBCs" for their upliftment. Thus the Sachar Committee Report appears to have followed the footsteps of the Mandal Report in recommending various remedial measures including reservation for the removal of backwardness of the Muslims even though the Constitution does not allow any religion based reservation.

While Mandal Report identified "backwardness" on the basis of "caste" the Sachar Committee Report took "religion" as the criteria in categorizing all Muslims as backwards. It suggested reservation and other special measures specifically and exclusively for all Muslims to ameliorate their backwardness.

The Sachar Committee Report appears to have accepted (p. 240) the Muslim minority "feeling" of discrimination against them in justification of Muslim specific schemes and welfare measures for their upliftment. Without going deeper into the validity or otherwise for such feelings of alleged discrimination the Committee has somewhat casually mentioned that "the fact of belonging to a minority community has, it cannot be denied an in-built sensitivity to discrimination". If that be so why the other minorities like the Sikhs, Christians, Jains,

Parsees and Buddhist etc. do not have any such "feelings" of discrimination? And if they have, should not special provisions like reservation be made for them also as in the case of Muslims recommended by the Sachar Committee? There is no discussion on this aspect in the Report. The Report further elaborates the need for special treatment of Muslims by saying:

> "Democratic process founded on universal adult franchise often fails to provide opportunities to ethnic, linguistic and religious minorities from getting elected and becoming part of the governance structure because of their low population shares." The Report also says: "over the last sixty years minorities have scarcely occupied adequate public spaces. The participation of Muslims in nearly all political spaces is low which can have an adverse impact on the Indian society and polity in the long run. The marginalized either have inadequate numbers that comes in the way of making their presence felt in the normal course of governance or they are not politically empowered. Given the power of numbers in a democratic polity, based on universal franchise, minorities in India lack effective agency and political importance. They do not have the necessary influence or the opportunity to either change or even influence events which enables their meaningful and effective participation in development process."

Therefore, the Committee has emphasized that "there is a strong case to put mechanisms in place that enable them to engage in democratic processes at various levels of polity and governance." (p. 241)

The above understanding and assessment of the Sachar Committee on the disadvantages allegedly suffered by the Muslim minority in India appears to be based more on wrong assumptions and questionable conjectures. It is likely that some sections of the Muslims may be having such unfortunate grievances which need to be properly verified and appropriate action taken for their removal. Some sections of Muslims as mentioned on page 12 of the Report also allegedly say that "the burqa, the purdah, the beard and the topi – while adding to the distinctiveness of Indian Muslims have been a cause of concern for them in the public realm. These markers have very often been a target for ridiculing the community as well as of looking upon them with suspicion. Muslim men donning a beard and topi are often picked up for interrogation from public spaces like parks, railway stations and markets."

Such feelings and apprehensions of discrimination appear to have no rational basis. The Report does not quote specific instances or figures of any such suspicion based false criminal cases against innocent Muslims. Undoubtedly isolated instances if any of anti-Muslim thinking must be condemned. But it may be unwise for this purpose to treat all Muslims separately from the rest of the Indian people. To prepare and implement only Muslim specific socio-economic development programmes and projects would isolate the Muslims from the mainstream of the Indian people. Muslims in India even though treated as a "minority" community have a very large population of nearly 150 millions. Unfortunately, the Sachar Committee Report has not done sufficient justice in considering all these aspects before making recommendations for Muslim-specific policies and programmes for their upliftment in various sectors. These faults of the Report which have the risk of communalizing India are discussed below:

India is a pluralistic society and world over it is held in high esteem for being truly secular and treating all its citizens on equal footing irrespective of their caste, creed or religion. In support of their admiration for secular India, it was highlighted by many eminent Western political observers that India had a Sikh Prime Minister (Dr. Manmohan Singh), a Muslim President (Dr. A.P.J. Abdul Kalam) and a Christian lady as the Chairperson of the ruling political party i.e. the All-India Congress Party (Smt. Sonia Gandhi) at that time i.e. 2006. A Sikh was also the Chief of the Indian Army during the same period. In view of this liberal and high secular rating of India by most countries of the world including the USA, UK, Germany, and France etc. there could be no justification for any "feeling" of discrimination, against any minority community including Muslims in India. Muslims may be seen occupying important political positions in regional and national level political parties including BJP the main opposition party. A prominent Muslim is also presently (2006) the political advisor of the Congress President – Mrs. Sonia Gandhi. Muslims have effective and visible presence in the media–as editors, reporters, political analysts, etc. There are several Muslim judges in the High Courts and in the Supreme Court. Yet accepting the validity of the imaginary and unjustified feelings of discrimination against the Muslims without any serious examination the Sachar Committee has recommended not only special treatment for them in the socio-economic sectors but also in the political spheres. It has recommended "nomination" of Muslim minority representatives proportionate to their population – to various elected public bodies. The Committee does not appear to have given thought that any special treatment by way of "nomination" to elected bodies or allocation of funds for Muslim specific development purposes may generate feelings of separateness between the Muslims and the non-Muslims of this pluralist and secular country. It may create and activate a separatist mindset among Muslims again as in the pre-independence and pre-partition years and endanger national unity. The fear is that any Muslim specific approach in socio-economic and political spheres may lead to demands of separate electorate and reservation of seats in the legislatures for Muslims. Top Muslim leaders in the Constituent Assembly at the time of framing of the Constitution of independent India had realized the harm of isolating Muslims from the mainstream of Indian society by way of making any special provisions for their progress and well-being. That kind of separatist thinking in the pre-independence years gave birth to the "two-nation" theory leading to the partition of the country. They had accordingly opposed any kind of Muslim specific measures like reservation in legislatures or employment for Muslims. For example during debates in the Constituent Assembly Begum Aizas Rasul had said that "reservation is a self-destructive weapon which separates the minority from the majority for all time." Naziruddin Ahmad had said: "reservation is a kind of protection which always has a crippling effect upon the object protected. I shall strongly oppose any reservation for Muslims." Muhammad Ismail Khan had stated: "this reservation of seats (i.e. in legislatures and employment) would only keep alive communalism and would be ineffectual as a safeguard for the Muslim minorities…" Pandit Jawaharlal Nehru also advised against any special safeguards for Muslims saying—"we decided sometime ago in another connection that we should have no truck with communalism or separatism. Where you are up against a full-blooded democracy, if you seek to give safeguards to minority, and a relatively small minority, you isolate it. May be you protect it to a slight extent, but at what cost? At the cost of isolating it and keeping it away from the main current in which the majority is going…." The Sachar Committee Report does not appear to have given sufficient thought to these views of our illustrious Constitution makers.

Some instances quoted below also prove the non-existence of any discrimination against Muslims in recruitment to various Government jobs. In mid-1970, Dr. A.R. Kidwai (now 2008) Governor of Haryana was the Chairman of the UPSC—a post he held for nearly 6 years. During those years Shri Saiyed Hamid, IAS (a member of the Sachar Committee) was also the Chairman of the Central Staff Selection Commission (CSSC). While the UPSC recruited officers to the IAS and other Central Class 'A' services and posts, the CSSC recruited all other gazetted, and non-gazetted officers (classes 'B' & 'C') of Government of India including teachers for Government schools. In sum the two Commissions between them and both headed by two eminent Muslims made recruitments to all the Central Government posts and services. Both Dr. Kidwai and Shri Hamid had been the vice-chancellor of the Aligarh Muslim University at one time or the other and had good knowledge of Muslim students and their competitive abilities. They were appointed to their respective posts of Chairman on their own merit and suitability and not because they were Muslims. Such high level posts of Chairman of the UPSC and CSSC are held by persons of known eminence, integrity and honesty. As the then Establishment Officer (EO) to the Government of India and Secretary to the Appointments Committee of the Union Cabinet (1973-78) I had the privilege of knowing and also officially dealing with both Dr. Kidwai and Shri Hamid intimately. Obviously Muslim candidates appearing for recruitment to various Central Government services and posts during those years could not have faced any kind of discrimination against them. Yet the average number or size of their recruitment in those years was, more or less, of the same order as in the previous years. There was no noticeable change in the percentage of entry of Muslim candidates into Central Government services and posts. Lower recruitment of Muslims compared to their population in the country as mentioned in the Sachar Report could be on account of some other causes like deficit in their educational standards, or their lack of aptitude for Government jobs, etc. Among the majority community also there are some castes and communities who do not show keenness for Government jobs but prefer hereditary family occupations like agriculture, industry, trade and business, etc. For example even well educated Gujaratis prefer industrial or trading activities of their own rather than Government services. Similarly, students of agricultural families of jats etc. prefer agriculture to government jobs. Additionally large number of educated and government service minded Muslims could have migrated to Pakistan at the time of partition and those who chose to remain in India were more of the self-employment categories e.g. masons, carpenters, blacksmiths, mechanics, etc. Hence any feeling of discrimination against Muslim recruitment to government jobs appears to be unreasonable and unjustified. The Sachar Committee could have examined this aspect more thoroughly and devised better solutions to remove Muslims' backwardness. The remedy for higher representation of Muslims in Government jobs lies more in improving their educational opportunities and standards and not in job reservation for them. Even now many Muslim candidates, products of good educational institutions, do come out with flying colours in competitions for top Central Government jobs each year. Some of them also hold high ranks among the successful candidates. Muslim backwardness could be overcome with better educational exposure for them particularly of the women. The Sachar Committee could have more objectively and critically examined this short coming and suggested some positive steps. Competitive abilities of Muslim students need to be developed rather than thinking and prescribing the separatist approach of reservation for them.

It needs hardly to be emphasized that many talented Muslim citizens of India, of whom the country has reason to be proud have contributed immensely to brighten the image of the country in diverse fields. For example, many Muslim players have been in the forefront of the Indian cricket teams. They included Zaheer Khan, Irfan Pathan, Mohammed Kaif, Munaf Patel, etc. In earlier years Nawab of Pataudi and Md. Azrudeen, (who is now a M.P.) were reputed captains of the Indian cricket teams each for several years. Sania Mirza a young Muslim girl of India has become a world ranking tennis player. In the film world Shah Rukh Khan, Amir Khan, Salman Khan, and many others have been among the top Indian film stars. Muslim actresses like Nargis, Madhubala, Meena Kumari were also once house-hold names in India. Shri A.R. Rehman is among the top film musician. He has recently made India proud for winning two Oscar awards for his musical talents in the film "Slumdog Millionaire" (2009). Shri Bismilla Khan of Shehnai fame was a Bharat Ratna indeed. There have been many other illustrious Muslim citizens of India to be proud of for having brought glories to India. There has been no discrimination in recognizing their talents and according them the respect and honour they deserved. There has been no suppression or casual treatment of any talented Muslim in any field. In fact they are honoured as talented Indian citizens and not because they are Muslims.

As explained earlier it may not also be correct to say that Muslims have no effective political voice or space in India. One cannot overlook the fact that several eminent Muslim personalities both men and women had occupied high public offices like the President of India, the Chief Justice of India, Central Cabinet Ministers, (including Home), State Chief Ministers and State Governors, etc. There have been many eminent Muslim IAS/IFS officers some of whom had held the posts of Union Cabinet Secretary, Home Secretary, Secretary External Affairs and ambassadors to important countries including Muslim countries. In the Defence Services also many Muslim officers had held posts of Commanders with distinction. More recently an eminent scientist, Bharat Ratna awardee and nationally respected Dr. A.P.J. Abdul Kalam was the President of India. He was lovingly termed as the "peoples' President" and continues to be a house-hold name ever after his retirement. Mr. S.Y. Quraishi has now become the Chief Election Commissioner of India.

Thanks to their sizeable number in many states and electoral constituencies (of U.P., Bihar, Andhra Pradesh, Tamil Nadu, Maharashtra and Kerala, etc.) Muslims enjoy well deserved political weight. In fact there are accusations that several All-India and regional political parties vie with each other to woo Muslim voters and when in power shower various favours on the Muslim community for their electoral support. Muslims reportedly being around 13.4 per cent of the Indian population carry sufficient political weight. No political party desirous of coming to power at the Centre and in some other states can ignore the massive political weight and electoral strength of the Muslims. Realistically speaking Muslims in India need no other safeguards or legal backing for their upliftment considering their heavy political weight. No Government can ignore their legitimate interests. The 15th Lok Sabha election results (2009) are a proof that the Congress Party came out victorious on account of sizeable Muslim vote support for it. The appointment of the high level Sachar Committee to look into their social, educational and economic problems and to make recommendations for their special treatment itself shows the effective Muslim voice in the affairs of governance of the country. Is not the much publicized statement of the Prime Minister, Dr. Manmohan Singh (2008), that "minorities, especially the Muslims must have the first claim on the country's resources" sufficient proof of the caring attitude of Government for the Muslims? To look after Muslims' interest there is also a Ministry of Minority Affairs and a National Commission for Minorities in addition to the National Human Rights Commission. In the midst of all these will constitution of an Equal Opportunities Commission recommended by the Sachar Committee to safeguard Muslim interests serve any useful purpose? Too many cooks may spoil the meal. The attempts of these Muslim oriented organisations should be more to integrate the Muslims with the mainstream of Indian population rather than create feelings of separateness among them. To provide special benefits for Muslims alone in different spheres would be isolating them and create separatist mindset among them. All such measures may turn out to be counter productive by dividing Muslims and non-Muslims. Good governance lies in integrating the country rather than dividing it on caste and communal lines.

Since in our democracy every adult irrespective of caste, creed or religion has one vote each and equal political rights in all respects including the right to stand for elections the idea of "nominating" Muslims to elected bodies like the state Assemblies, Parliament or any of the PRIs recommended by the Sachar Committee appears to be ill-conceived, ill-advised, unconstitutional and undemocratic. In a democracy direct election is the legitimate way to be members of elected bodies. In a secular democracy like India candidates who wish to get elected should cultivate the support of voters of all castes, creeds and religions of the constituency concerned. Muslims like non-Muslims should get elected with the vote support of all fellow citizens irrespective of their castes or religion. That is the way to promote fraternity among them all, as is the objective of our Constitution. That would also promote secularism. In fact large number of Muslims do get elected in this manner to Parliament and the State legislatures without any provision of reservation for them. Most political parties nominate fair number of Muslims as their candidates for elections to legislatures. Reservation of jobs for Muslims or their nomination to elected bodies will sow seeds of communal division and give rise to feelings of separateness. We must not facilitate or promote the rebirth of the pernicious "two nation" theory in our democracy. That is why any proposal of reservation for Muslims was decried in the Constituent Assembly even by top Muslim leaders who chose to stay in India and not to migrate to Pakistan. Britishers had followed the policy of "divide and rule" which ultimately led to the partition of the country on religious basis. Should we sow the seeds of partition again? That kind of thinking of separateness must be nipped in the bud in the long-term interest of the country and its Muslim community as well.

Many other Muslim specific developmental measures suggested by the Sachar Committee appear to be shortsighted as these may lead to thinking on communal lines in government functioning. Some of these harmful suggestions of communal nature made by the Sachar Committee include the following:

- examination of contents of all school text books "keeping in mind the sentiments and feelings of Muslims;"
- opening of Muslim minority schools and minority managed professional institutions in Muslim "areas with reservation for Muslims;"
- application of relaxed norms and standards for admission of students of backward social religious categories (SRC) "particularly Muslims;"
- recognition of the degrees of Madarsas for eligibility in competitive examinations;
- promoting and enhancing access to Muslims in priority sector bank loans and advances by fixing certain percentages for them;
- improve the participation and share of the minorities "particularly Muslims" in business of regular commercial banks and fix certain percentages of total lending for Muslims;
- Muslim experts to be included in the recruitment panels and Boards.;
- Central Government should introduce a few schemes with large outlays for the welfare of minorities with an equitable provision for Muslims;
- location of ITIs and Polytechnics in Muslim concentration areas "with reservation for Muslims;" and
- increase the employment share of Muslims among the teaching community, health workers, police personnel, bank employees and so on. For this purpose job advertisements should be in Urdu and vernacular newspapers and other media containing a message like "women minority and backward classes candidates are encouraged to apply." (This appears to imply that candidates of these categories will be given preferential treatment.)

The Report also suggests that "it may be useful to have at least one Muslim inspector/sub-inspector in the Muslim concentrated Thanas, Muslim health personnel in health units, Muslim teachers in schools located in such areas of Muslim concentration.

A superficial reading of some of the above proposals appears to make these to be harmless and unobjectionable. In fact in actual practice some of these suggestions may be already in vogue as part of good administration. But there may be trouble if such suggestions and recommendations become part of any law or rule with their inherent legal rigidity and compulsion of applicability. Any kind of compulsion or rigidity may make them matters of right and give rise to disputes and litigations. That may also communalise administration and create feelings of separateness among Muslims and non-Muslims. There should not be separate procedures of recruitment, postings and promotions for Muslim and non-Muslim employees. Muslim appointees in public dealing organizations, on the lines suggested by Sachar Committee may rightly or wrongly be viewed to be pro-Muslim by contending parties of Muslims and non-Muslims. It may be wise to avoid creation of such impressions by introducing any rigid communal system of postings and placements. Personnel of all castes, creed and religion should be posted to public offices and posts on the basis of their individual merit and suitability. The appointing and placement authorities should not be bound by any communal quotas or considerations. They should be trusted and be free to find the right persons for the right jobs, keeping in mind the circumstances, time and places of postings. Undoubtedly as mentioned earlier some of the suggested posting plans may already be in operation for the sake of fair and impartial administration. For example as a matter of administrative convenience and practice the Collector and District Magistrate of Puri in Orissa is generally a Hindu Officer as he has to visit the temple often for various purposes. As an illustration, Dr. Rajendra Prasad the President of India stayed for a few days in Puri during his visit to Orissa. As the then collector of the District (1959) I had necessarily to accompany him during his visit to the famous Lord Jagannath's Temple. Life of the common man in Puri also generally revolves around the religious activities of this historic temple. The collector of Puri also literally plays a leading role at the time of the famous annual Jaggannath Rathyatra as he generally leads the team pulling Lord Jaggannath's chariot. This was also my experience as collector of Puri. There is however no law or rule that a Hindu officer alone is to be the collector of the District. In fact there were occasions, though very few, when non-Hindu officers too were appointed to this post. Certain obvious things in administration should best be left to the common sense and judgement of the relevant authorities. Legal rigidity may come in the way of good and practical administration. There should be room for flexibility. Therefore, posting of Muslim personnel where necessary for good reasons should be left to the concerned authorities to decide and should not be made legally binding. Moreover in our secular administration there should be no legal compulsion of caste, creed or community etc. in placement of public officials.

Another recommendation of the Sachar Committee Report which appears to be a retrograde step is with regard to collection of data of participation of different Social and Religious Categories (SRC) specially Muslims in government jobs and programmes both at the Central and state levels. Such religion-based communal data will be undesirable. So far the government policy has been not to keep any statistical information on caste and communal basis except with regard to the SCs/STs. Reply to questions in Parliament seeking information regarding number of Muslims posted in the Central Secretariat etc. were therefore truthfully and correctly replied by saying that such religion-based placement figures or communal data are not kept. I remember of an instance when one honourable M.P. asked a question in the Parliament (Lok Sabha) addressed to the Home Minister as to how many Muslim Joint Secretaries were there in the Central Secretariat. The reply given by the Home Minister was that such communal statistics are not kept. The M.P. who had asked the question knew me personally and since I was the Secretary of the Department of Personnel in the Home Ministry at that time he came to see me to find out why the information of the number of Jt. Secretary level Muslim officers could not be collected. I explained to him the rational of the policy of government to avoid keeping or collecting information on caste or communal lines. The whole idea was to eliminate the importance of caste or religion in the functioning of our secular state and its administration.

It was accordingly correct for the Indian Army authorities to have declined to furnish any statistical information to the Sachar Committee regarding the number of army personnel of different castes and religion in the Army (as mentioned in the Sachar Report). It was unfortunate for the high level Sachar Committee to have asked for caste or religion-based information from the army of a secular state like ours. This itself discloses the negative and narrow approach of the Committee in finding more positive and constructive solutions to Muslims backwardness in keeping with the language and spirit of our Constitution.

Many of the suggestions and recommendations of Justice Sachar Committee Report outwardly may appear to be innocuous and helpful in the advancement of Muslims. However, a closer reading of the report and its likely long-term harmful impact brings home the danger that the Muslim specific social, educational, employment and other developmental programmes may set an undesirable separatist trend in motion. India may be back to the pre-partition days when there were arrangements for "Muslim water" and "Hindu water" on the Railway Platforms. The risk of other castes and religious groups making similar separate demands for development expenditure proportionate to their population sizes cannot be ignored. That may undo the labour of our freedom fighters and the eminent framers of our Constitution who gave us an excellent Constitution to make India a truly secular republic. Their primary objective was to bring about unity in diversity. India a pluralistic society had to be kept united and integrated by making provisions of equality for all citizens. All were to be "equal" in the eyes of law without any discrimination based on caste, creed, sex or region. Oneness of all Indians is implicit in the constitutional words of "we the people of India."

The basic fault of Justice Sachar Committee Report is that it has wrongly and without any rational basis accepted Muslims' feelings of discrimination against them to be the real cause of their backwardness. Therefore the remedial measures of Muslim specific programmes of development and reservation recommended by the Committee are faulty.

In this connection the following question of Shri Khushwant Singh (a well-known intellectual and journalist of India) to Ms Asma Jehangir (a reputed human rights activist of Pakistan) and her reply deserves to be quoted. These appeared in Khushwant Singh's WEEKLY column in the Hindustan Times of 20th June 2009.

The question was "why do Muslims the world over, including Pakistan, suffer from a feeling of hurt and discrimination?"

Asma Jehangir's reply was:

"the decline of Muslim Power of the cultural and scientific supremacy it once had and looking for scapegoats as excuse".

Not only Muslims but other groups of people also allege "discrimination" as an excuse in case of lack of success in any sphere. It is common human fault to attribute the blame for one's failure to some external causes rather than do any introspection to find out own faults if any and how to set them right. For example some state governments in India ascribe their lack of progress due to centre's discrimination in allocation of less funds to them. Allocation of funds to the states is normally governed by policies as approved in consultation with the National Development Council. The state chief ministers along with the central ministers and other eminent persons are its members. Therefore, in allocation of funds there may not be much scope for discrimination between different states. Yet the non-performing states plead Central "discrimination" as the cause for their low performance.

Reservation in government jobs or seats in educational institutions for Muslims or allotting funds for Muslim specific development activities would be inappropriate and unconstitutional. There are several millions of Muslims and non-Muslims in India who suffer from the same problems of poverty, unemployment, lack of supply of drinking water, electricity, etc. These problems need to be taken care of commonly for all the similarly placed persons and not separately for different categories of them based on their caste or religion. All the poor and disadvantaged sections of "we the people of India" should have equal claim on the resources of the country without their being split into Hindus, Muslims, Sikhs, Christians, etc. Not to do so would amount to discarding our present Constitution which treats all citizens to be equal in all respects and in every sphere. Hopefully, our present day political leaders would also give some thought to the following quoted portion of a letter of advice by Pandit Jawaharlal Nehru, the first Prime Minister of India addressed to the State Chief Ministers in June 1961 as to why he disliked reservation.

> "I dislike any kind of reservation, more particularly in services. I react strongly against anything which leads to inefficiency and second-rate standards. I want my country to be a first

> class country in everything. The moment we encourage the second-rate we are lost. The only real way to help the backward group is to give opportunities of good education, this includes technical education which is becoming more and more important. Everything else is provision of some kind of crutches which do not add to the strength or health of the body ...if we go in for reservations on communal and caste basis, we swamp the bright and able people and remain second-rate or third rate. I am grieved to learn how far this business of reservation has gone based on communal considerations. This way lays not only folly, but disaster."

In the light of the above wise advice of Pandit Nehru, the implementation of the Sachar Committee Report requires careful thinking. Nothing should be done which divides people and make them think on caste or communal lines. In a globalized world of today narrow caste and communal approach in solving problems of backwardness of any class of citizens may not be correct or appropriate. Attempts should be to unite the people in fighting and solving their social and economic problems. All the backward people including backward Muslims should be placed on the same footing in the removal of their backwardness.

15

ROLE OF PUBLIC ADMINISTRATION IN NATIONAL INTEGRATION

India is a vast country in terms of area as well as population; it is indeed a sub-continent. India is also a great country with its many centuries old civilization and culture nourished and enriched by many generations of our forefathers. In the long past when most of the world was steeped in darkness, India was wide awake and far advanced in art, architecture, science, philosophy, medicine and literature. Because of India's large size and ancientness of its social and religious practices some differences and variety have arisen in these among the people living in different parts of the country. In addition important historical forces and events made India a multi-lingual, multi-racial, multi-religious or a pluralist country. People speak many languages, profess diverse faiths with differences in forms and ways of prayer and religious rituals. Even within the same religion like Hindusim, people belong to diverse sects emphasizing the worship of one God (*Ekam Sat*) in several ways and forms. They observe different religious fasts, feasts and festivals. They worship different Devis and Devtas There are numerous castes, sub-castes and creeds with differences in social and religious customs and practices. Again, because of climatic variations between different regions due to India's vastness, there are regional differences in food habits, dress, social etiquettes and behaviour among the people. In spite of all these outer diversities, and variations, there is inner unity of culture, civilization, ethical norms and values which bind the people of India together. This unity of thoughts, ideas, and ideals has been strengthened further through centuries of living together and sharing of common joys and sorrows in facing historical ups and downs. Our saints, sages and spiritual leaders had also preached about the basic unity of all mankind. They regarded the whole world as one family *(Vasudheya Kutumbakam)*. Various sub-cultures and sub-social systems of our people in course of time got interwoven into one composite Indian culture and civilization which has come to be known as Indianness or "*Bhaartiyata.*" People have imbibed a sense of fellow-feeling, and camaraderie. One may say that they have become members of one large Indian joint family. This idea of one composite India needs to be nourished, strengthened and propagated for the inheritance of all future generations of Indians. There have been of course times and occasions when differences of language, religion or caste were adversely highlighted to set people against each other. Various interest groups did disturb the family peace on such occasions. At times social and religious differences were aggravated by the anti-social and criminal elements who liked to fish in the troubled waters to serve their own evil designs of loot and arson. Prolonged communal convulsions for decades between Muslims and Hindus on one wrong pretext or the other, and the ill-conceived "two nation" theory propagated by some communal minded Muslim leaders like Mohammad Ali Jinnah led to large scale violence and finally the partition of the country in 1947. Yet we do not appear to have derived sufficient lessons from this recent history of sorrow, shame and tragedy. Some divisive forces of communalism, regionalism, casteism are again showing their ugly heads aided and abetted by practitioners of vote bank politics. These divisive forces should cause serious worry and concern as these may again become threats to national unity and integration.

After independence when the founding fathers framed our basic law–the Constitution of India, they gave primacy to the need of equality of treatment to all the citizens, irrespective of their religion, race, caste, sex, descent, place of birth or residence, etc. They were eminent people, illustrious sons and daughters of India who were well conversant with the long history of the country. They were aware of the country's social and religious diversities and large economic disparities among different classes of people. They accordingly made suitable provisions in the Constitution to take care of the social and economic diversities of the people in the interest of equity, social justice and national unity. The very preamble of our Constitution therefore starts with the solemn statement that the people of India have resolved to constitute India into a sovereign, socialist and secular republic and that this democratic State will secure to all its citizens "justice–social, economic and political" and that it will promote among them all unity and fraternity. The Fundamental Rights enumerated in the Constitution *inter-alia* guarantee to all citizens equality before law and equal opportunities in the matter of public employment. All citizens enjoy the right to freely move throughout the country and are free to reside and settle anywhere in India. The framers of our Constitution rightly felt that there should be no walls of separation and all Indians must feel at home in every part of India. Special care was taken to protect the interests of the minorities whether based on language or religion. They are free to establish and maintain their own religious, charitable and educational institutions and are free to profess, practice and propagate their religion. Those having distinct languages or culture of their own have been bestowed the right to conserve the same. The Constitution also allows some special treatment to the socially and educationally backward classes of citizens as also to the weaker sections of society like the SC/ST/OBCs, keeping in view their past sufferings, social disadvantages and handicaps. It was realized that they needed special treatment as they were not in a position to compete with others on equal footings because of their backwardness. Such special treatment was necessary and wisely provided in the Constitution in the interest of social justice and national integration. To make the Indian state equal protector of all its citizens and to secure to them all the fruits of independence and economic development, it was of paramount importance that some special considerations for the weaker and backward classes of citizens were allowed to satisfy the constitutional provision of equality for all. However, such special considerations were not meant to be permanent features and should hopefully become unnecessary once the disadvantaged classes of citizens attain the educational and social levels of the general category of people. To expedite this process, one of the Directive Principles of the State Policy enjoins upon the State to promote with special care the educational and economic interests of the weaker sections of the people in particular of the SCs/STs. We may notice that the two important basic features of our political system enshrined in the Constitution are "secularism" and "socialism". These were adopted as one can visualize in order to strengthen national unity and harmony. Apart from any theoretical consideration, "secularism" is a pragmatic policy to follow in a multi-religious and pluralist country like India. Similarly, the importance attached to "socialism" was probably viewed not only from an ideological angle but in the context of widespread poverty and large economic disparities among the people. Overwhelming majority of them had no property, lacked sufficient food, clothing and even roof over their heads. Their poor economic conditions required to be specially improved by the new democratic state by undertaking special programmes of social and economic upliftment for them. India could not be strong and remain united unless the concept of equality was properly understood and implemented so as to benefit the weaker sections of the people. Hence socialism, like secularism had to be a key factor for promoting national unity and integration. To realize the socialistic aims of our state a specific provision in the Directive Principles of the Constitution [Article 38(2)] requires that the State should endeavour "to minimize the inequalities in income and eliminate inequalities in status, facilities and opportunities" not only among individuals but also among groups of people residing in different areas or engaged in different vocations.

We may thus see that the founding fathers of our Constitution who were fully aware of the diversities of the Indian society, its strong and weak points, gave it a legal framework which, if properly implemented, by the public services would ensure peace, harmony and fraternity among all sections of its population.

To achieve these necessary and desirable goals, the political leaders holding ministerial offices and the public servants engaged in public administration have to play vital roles in implementing the policies and programmes of the state based on the constitutional directives in a just and fair manner. The administration however can be as good, as effective and as efficient in realizing the constitutional goals and ideals as the functionaries of government would like to make it. Ultimately, it is not the constitutional framework or detailed legislative enactments favouring secularism, socialism and national integration that could ensure the realization of these but the instruments of governance and the men behind the same who are to implement them. Good intentions and policies alone would not suffice but the implementation of policies in the right spirit is of vital importance. Hence the importance of the men who are in charge of public administration, i.e. the civil servants. The role of civil services as visualized by our great leaders and the framers of the Constitution therefore deserve to be briefly mentioned.

Dr. Rajendra Prasad the first President of India had in a speech (on 31 March 1959 in the Indian Institute of Public Administration) said that "Public Administration in a vast country like India has a deep bearing on the happiness and welfare of the people." He emphasized that "Administration, let it not be forgotten, is not an end in itself. It is essentially a means to an end which is promoting the welfare of the community. This can be achieved only if those entrusted with the task of administration undertake it in a spirit of public service. They must conduct themselves in a manner which inspires people's confidence and cooperation." He also wanted that apart from honesty and efficiency, the administration need to have human approach in dealing with all problems.

Dr. S. Radhakrishnan, Vice-President of India on the First Annual Day of the IIPA (on 20th November, 1959) stated that administration has to be above politics; "that ministers come and change, governments are established today and are altered the next day but administration is something which gives stability to the life of a country." He accordingly wanted administration to be fair to all manner of people and that "the administrators must feel that they are not there merely to lord over the people but they are essentially servants of the people." He desired that this new ethos should be imparted to the new class of administrators in the changed conditions of the country. He also stated that Administrators are not to regard themselves as a privileged class. They are not to grow into bureaucracy. He desired that the higher civil servants "must understand the needs and aspirations of the common man and woman and try to protect them from the petty officials who are inclined to harass them and show their authority." Above all he said, "it is my great anxiety that in this country we should have administrative integrity first, efficiency next, economy third—with these conditions we will be able to build a happier Indian society." He thus placed integrity in administration above all other requirements for better governance.

C. Rajagopalachari in a talk over the All-India Radio, in 1956 had emphasized that character is a fundamental requirement of a good administrator. This obviously meant many good qualities like honesty, integrity and commitment to public duties with a high sense of justice and fair play. He also stated that people are not so much interested in the 'form' of a Government, i.e., whether it is a parliamentary democracy or it is the American Presidential form of government but "they want honest, efficient, prompt, just and sympathetic officers; and they do not mind the form of government". He warned against the dangers of political or social groups functioning in the legislature or outside to influence recruitment or promotion in the services as that may affect political neutrality of public administration.

Shri Govind Ballabh Pant as Home Minister of India had (in his talk over the All-India Radio in 1955) said that "the administrators have to serve the people because that is the only purpose for which they can and they ought to exist. Every ounce of their energy, their intellect, their capacity has to be surrendered to the devoted service of their masters, the people. That has to be their all-consuming passion, and their guiding mission."

Sardar Vallabhbhai Patel, Dy. Prime Minister while speaking in the Constituent Assembly on the need for All-India Services in the new administrative set up said "I need hardly emphasize that an efficient, disciplined and contended service assured of its prospects as a result of diligent and honest work, is a *sine quo non* of sound administration under a democratic regime even more than under an authoritarian rule. The service must be above party and we should ensure that political considerations, either in recruitment or in its discipline and control, are reduced to the minimum, if not eliminated altogether."

In his famous tryst with destiny speech (of 14th August 1947 at midnight hour) Pandit Jawaharlal Nehru had pledged that "service of India" will be the mission of free India's administration. What the "service of India" means, he explained, "it means the ending of poverty and ignorance and disease and inequality of opportunity. The ambition of the greatest man of our generation has been to wipe every tear from every eye. That may be beyond us but as long as there are tears and suffering, so long our work will not be over."

The essence of the observations and expectations of our great leaders quoted above was that the Indian Public administration and the personnel engaged in it should make sure that they function as servants of the people. In their day-to-day dealings with them none should feel that there is any discrimination against any one on grounds of race, religion, caste or community. Administration should be above any communal, political, caste, or regional bias. Much of this will depend on the outlook, character and conduct of the top level administrators and, the soundness of the institutional procedures and arrangements for transaction of government business.

Soon after independence as is well known the State's involvement in social, and economic activities increased tremendously. The role of administration and its contact with the public widened and deepened. In addition to maintenance of law and order, the government machinery also got engaged in agricultural, rural and industrial developmental activities, and in the provision of host of other social services like education, health, housing, water supply, etc. There was hardly any area in a citizen's life where he did not come in contact with the public administration and the public officials at the Central, State or local body levels. Large investments of public funds were made to achieve the economic objectives of self-reliance, modernization, and poverty elimination. In realizing these economic goals the public services were required to ensure that there is no discrimination between different classes of citizens. They were to feel confident of being equal in the eyes of the administration. For example, an agriculturist, irrespective of his religion, caste or creed or place of residence should be sure of getting whatever assistance is provided by the Government to the agricultural sector like supply of fertilizers, credit, irrigation water or HYV seeds etc. Similarly, administration should have no discriminatory approach in dealing with any industrialist, trader or a member of any business community because of his caste, religion, or place of birth. Administration was not to distinguish between Gujaratees, Maharashtrians, Telgus and Tamils, etc. Social services like education, health, housing, and water supply should also be equally available to all citizens according to their needs. There should be no privileged groups or second class citizens in the eyes of public administration. All have to be treated as the "sons of the soil" in every part of India. There would be dissatisfaction if admissions to educational institutions are based on caste, communal or regional considerations save for what has been constitutionally permitted for the weaker sections of the society. For plan investments the aim should be to achieve balanced regional growth. No area should feel neglected or discriminated. Growth potential of every state and region must receive due consideration. In brief public administration and the personnel engaged in it have to be truly "national" minded. They should inspire confidence of all sections of the society by being just, fair and impartial.

The institutional arrangements to carry out the tasks of public administration should also be free from any narrow caste or communal considerations. There should be no publicly financed institution specially or exclusively meant for any particular caste or community or religious groups. All citizens must have access on equal footing to all public institutions financed by the state. Persons manning public services and posts should also be truly secular and should accordingly be recruited entirely on their own individual merits and qualifications and not on any narrow considerations of their caste, creed or place of birth etc.

It may however be noted that public servants are part of the larger society in which they live. Their likes and dislikes, their attitudes and behaviour are therefore influenced in no small measure by their social environment. It is true that public servants themselves, particularly at higher levels contribute in the creation of the social environment. In addition in a democracy like ours the elected representatives of the people, front-ranking political leaders, eminent professionals, artists, educationists, intellectuals, journalists, mass media-men, and other elite groups of citizens also play vital roles in the making of the social environment. All such leading groups of citizens following different vocations and pursuits have to realize the importance of national integration for the common good and happiness of all the citizens. Healthy mindsets and good citizenship values have to be developed from the childhood, through our educational system. The school curricula and the text books have to be such that they emphasise the basic unity of India and the need for solidarity and unity in the midst of diversity. It has to be ensured that seeds of distrust, differences or prejudices of any kind are not sown among the school children belonging to different castes and communities. In this task not only policy makers are involved, but also many other engaged in various educational activities. The most important players in the educational field are, of course, the school teachers. Their own training and commitments have to be focused on larger national loyalty and identity in preference to any narrow caste, creed, or regional loyalty and identity. This requires special care and emphasis on the recruitment and training of school teachers. They are the key public functionaries who shape and mould the hearts and minds of the future citizens of India. They have, therefore, to be national minded and secular in their thinking and approach. They must be made to understand the real meaning of "India" of being the "home" of all Indians of diverse castes and creeds.

Public administration and public servants whether they are school teachers, grassroots level workers in the fields of agriculture, rural development or higher level officers including those dealing with trade and industries have to play important roles by ensuring impartiality of administration towards all sections of citizens. Importantly higher level public functionaries ought to have the required national vision to formulate policies and programmes that are in conformity with the basic goals of the Indian State and its ideals of secularism and socialism. Considering the all-pervasive nature of public services in India, its public servants are expected to play important roles in achieving the laid down constitutional goals of unity and national integration.

Because of the importance of the higher civil services for ensuring the unity of India the founding fathers of our Constitution retained the All-India Services like the IAS and IPS after independence even within the federal structure of the country. The State Governments also whole-heartedly agreed to this arrangement in the larger interest of the country. Members of these Services are recruited on an All-India basis through open competitive examinations conducted by the Union Public Service Commission. There is no quota or reservation for any State or community except for the SCs/STs. Constitutionally these Services are "common" between the Centre and the States and officers belonging to these services are posted for service at the Centre and in the States. Since they hold posts in key areas of administration both at the State and Central levels, they could be effective instruments in preserving national unity and integration through impartial implementation of policies and programmes of the concerned governments. The common All-India Services is a unique feature of our administrative set-up for Centre-State cooperation in a federal polity and greatly help the cause of national integration. Different political parties may hold power at the Centre and in the states but the "common" All-India Services provide administrative cooperation between them and facilitate good Centre-State relations in the governance of the country. As recruitment to these services is not based on regional, communal or caste considerations, members of these services are expected to have broader vision and national outlook while discharging their administrative responsibilities.

Apart from the All-India Services, members of the other higher Central Services i.e. Group A Services too are recruited on an All-India basis. These services are meant to work in specialized areas falling under the sphere of the Central Government like Railways, Posts and Telecommunication, Income-Tax, Custom and Excise, Audit and Defence Accounts, etc. They also play key roles in bringing about All-India outlook in their respective spheres of work. Members of these services too are recruited without any reservation on regional or communal lines. Since they are transferable throughout the country, they are expected to be above state or other local boundaries. It may be still more useful if members of these Services, as a matter of practice, are posted outside their own home States so that they could function with greater objectivity, impartiality and fairness on being free from local pulls, pressures and prejudices.

To sum up public administration and the civil servants engaged in it have to play very important roles in preserving the unity and integrity of India. All public servants should fully realize that "Public Service" means "national service" and that their first and foremost duty is to maintain complete allegiance to the Indian Constitution in fulfilling their public responsibilities.

16

SARDAR PATEL– "THE IRON MAN OF INDIA"

Sardar Vallabhbhai Patel's role in India's freedom struggle and in its political consolidation soon after freedom was truly historic. His birthday falling on 31st October is a day for every Indian to remember. Accordingly this has been written on his 125 Birthday to pay him the nation's grateful tributes. He was born on 31st October, 1875 and passed away on the 15th December, 1950.

In the concluding phases of India's freedom movement Mahatma Gandhi, Pandit Jawahar Lal Nehru and Sardar Patel were regarded as the "triumvirate" or the "trinity" of the movement. Gandhiji as the father figure was affectionately called "Bapu" (father) by all others. He was the philosopher and guide of the movement and had laid down "truth" and "non-violence" to be its guiding principles. He was a real "Mahatma"in the eyes of all others.

Pandit Nehru was an idealist and a visionary who had written extensively on India's history, its great civilization and cultural legacy. He was a great patriot and at the same time a universalist. He had visualised a socialistic pattern of society for free India. He was a true "Pandit" with his great intellectual depth and breadth of vision. Truly a "luminous personality" as stated by Smt. Indira Gandhi, his illustrious daughter in her "Foreword" to his famous book "The Discovery of India." He was a "Bharat Ratna" in the truest sense of the word.

Sardar Patel was another most shining "Bharat Ratna" of Indian History. He in contrast to Nehru was more of a pragmatist and a realist with his feet solidly on the ground. He gave practical shape to the visions and ideals of Gandhiji the spiritual and saintly leader in order to make the freedom struggle led by him a political success. Towards this end he mobilised the masses for many "satyagrahas" and "swadeshi" campaigns. The most successful of these was the Bardoli farmers satyagraha of 1928 against excessive increase in the assessment of land revenue by the British ruled provincial government. This satyagraha under Patel's leadership became a landmark event in India's freedom struggle. Its grand success brought Vallabhabhai Patel to national and international notice. As a mark of popular esteem Patel earned a life-long title of "Sardar" from the people. Gandhiji also observed that "Vallabhbhai found his Vallabh (God) in Bardoli. At the time of Patel's sad demise in 1950, N.V. Gadgil recalled that "without the active cooperation of Sardar Patel, Gandhi's experiment of non-violent satyagraha, for which he is remembered all over the world, would not have been feasible. In fact, from 1917 till 1947, over a period of 30 years, what Gandhiji conceived, Sardar concretised and carried out." He was a man of action and made the Gandhian concept of satyagraha a successful political weapon. He was indeed a great strategist, a man of foresight, skill and tact and could foresee events for taking appropriate timely action.

Patel was a great organiser and this capacity was displayed in activating the Congress Party all over the country to lead many satyagrahas and swadeshi movements in furtherance of the freedom struggle. This also helped Sardar Patel to acquire intimate knowledge of and a firm hold on the Congress Party and its active members. For the 1937 provincial elections under the 1935 Government of India Act, Sardar Patel accordingly was given a free hand to choose Party candidates and lead the election campaigns in every state. His dedicated and systematic work resulted in Congress victory in 11 out of the 14 states with overwhelming majority. He was thereafter chosen as the Chairman of the Congress Parliamentary Board. Because of his deep involvement in the work of the Party, he came to be regarded as the *de-facto* "Congress High Command." Because of his clear vision, and capacity to take unwavering and speedy decisions, he also came to be known as the "Iron Man of India." He very well visualized "what to do, when to do, and how to do."

In due course the freedom struggle came to a virtual end with the formation of the Interim Government on 2nd September 1946 comprising of the Congress and the Muslim League. The League however, showed little interest in the work of the Interim Government of undivided India. Instead it kept demanding Pakistan and put all kinds of obstructions and created deadlocks in the functioning of the interim government. Large-scale mutual killings and bloodshed continued unabated. The whole situation had become so disgusting and sickening that even though Gandhiji was opposed to partition of India at any cost, Sardar Patel showed his exceptional sense of political pragmatism and courage to be the first leader of the Congress High Command to accept the inevitability of partition in spite of it being very painful. He courageously persuaded other leaders to accept the demand for Pakistan so that the rest 80 per cent of India could remain united and progress peacefully. This was pragmatism at its best in the views of many historians. Sardar Patel enjoyed immense confidence and credibility of the vast masses of the Indian people and hence his opinion to accept partition, however, sad and tragic it might be, was seen to be appropriate under the prevailing circumstances.

Sardar's tenure in the governance of free India was very brief (about 4 years) as he passed away on 15th December 1950. But during this short spell he politically consolidated India by integrating about 560 princely states into the Indian union. This Herculean task was performed by him in less than two years' time. While the merger of Nizam's Hyderabad alone needed "Police Action" all other princely states were merged in the Indian union smoothly through talks and negotiations with their rulers. On this achievement the London Times wrote: "this will stand out as a great historic achievement by Sardar Patel on a level with Bismarck (of Germany), if not higher." This was indeed a bloodless revolution brought about by Sardar Patel, the nation builder. Unfortunately, since Kashmir did not fall within Sardar Patel's sphere of work (being under the External Affairs Ministry) it has remained a troubling "problem" for India to this day.

Sardar Patel also left his mark of statesmanship in the framing of the Constitution of free India. His views and advice counted most with regard to all important constitutional provisions relating to national unity, integrity, good governance and administration. In a vast country like India while Sardar Patel realised the need to decentralise power and functions between the Centre and the States he was also convinced that the Central authority has to be sufficiently strong to safeguard the unity and integrity of the country. Therefore to prevent fissiparous forces to raise their ugly heads certain constitutional provisions were made on Patel's advice to enable the Central authority to assert its power over the states in the larger national interest when so required. By way of institutional arrangements to preserve national solidarity and unity, constitutional provisions were made among others for a common higher judiciary, a common election commission and for two common All-India Services (IAS and IPS) between the Centre and the states. These provided for administrative unity and uniformity in the country. Emphasizing the need for a competent and good civil service, Sardar Patel as the then Home Minister and Deputy Prime Minister of India, stated in the Constituent Assembly:

> "It needs hardly to be emphasized that an efficient, disciplined and contended service assured of its prospects as a result of diligent and honest work, is a *sine qua non* of sound administration under democratic regime even more than under an authoritarian rule. The service must be above party and we should ensure that political considerations, either in its recruitment or in its discipline and control, are reduced to the minimum, if not eliminated altogether."

In the Constituent Assembly there were some voices of criticism and reservation in providing constitutional protection and safeguards in the matters of pay, leave and pension, etc. to the ICS officers (officers of the pre-independence Secretary of State's Services). There was not only criticism but bitter comment on the privileged status and position allowed to the ICS officers, who were said to be the virtual rulers of the country during the British Raj. Even a reputed and senior member like Sri Ananthasayanam Ayyanger said about such unwarranted protection "this guarantee means that they were the rulers under the old regime and that they will continue to be so in this regime. This guarantee asks us to forget that these persons who are still in service–400–of them committed excesses thinking that this was not their country." He was thus against their being "pampered" by way of protecting their earlier pay, pension etc. Large number of ICS officers who continued in service in post-independence India were however Indians, as most of the British officers had already left India.

Sardar Patel vigorously defended the constitutional provision of protecting their conditions of service on the ground that this was a condition agreed upon, a pledge given by them, in passing the Indian Independence Act by the British Parliament.

He said "learn to stand upon your pledged word, and, also, as a man of experience I tell upon you, do not quarrel with the instruments with which you want to work. It is a bad workman who quarrels with his instruments. Take work from them. Every man wants some sort of encouragement. Nobody wants to put in work when every day he is criticized and ridiculed in public. So once and for all decide whether you want this service or not. If you have done with it and decide not to have this service at all (i.e. the ICS and its successor service IAS) even in spite of my pledged word, I will take the services with me and go." A very strong statement indeed for continuing the All-India Services (i.e. the IAS and the IPS). Sardar Patel virtually threatened to resign if the constitutional protection was not allowed to All-India Services. No wonder that the relevant constitutional provision relating to the proposed safeguards to the ICS officers particularly was duly adopted and the new services of IAS and IPS were also allowed to continue. Sardar Patel took this opportunity for expressing his words of appreciation in the Constituent Assembly for the work done soon after independence by the higher civil servants because of the trust, confidence and freedom allowed to them. His words were:

> Today, my Secretary can write a note opposed to my viewpoint. I have given that freedom to all my secretaries. I have told them, "if you do not give your honest opinion for fear that it will displease your minister, please then you had better go. I will bring another secretary." I will never be displeased over a frank expression of opinion. He also stated:
>
> "Many of them with whom I have worked, I have no hesitation in saying that they are as patriotic, as loyal and as sincere as myself. Those who think that the leaders were mistaken in giving these guarantees, they do not know their mind. They do not know what happened. They do not even now know. Yet we have difficult time ahead. We are talking here under security kept in very difficult circumstances. These people are the instruments. Remove them and I see nothing but a picture of chaos all over the country."

This approach of allowing full freedom to the civil servants to express their views and freedom of speedy action when so required paid rich dividends in restoring administrative order. With an efficient and satisfied civil service Sardar Patel was able to handle the many post-partition problems like communal riots and killings, rehabilitation of millions of penniless migrants from Pakistan and integration of the princely states etc. with remarkable speed and efficiency. The services had full faith in his political leadership and he had full confidence in their sense of duty and loyalty to the country.

The Manchester Guardian wrote soon after Patel's death "Without Patel, Gandhi's ideas would have had less practical influence and Nehru's idealism less scope. Patel was not only the organiser of the fight for freedom but also the architect of the new State when the fight was over. The same man is seldom successful as rebel and statesman. Sardar Patel was the exception."

Though suffering from ill-health due to very heavy burden of work before his demise Sardar Patel said in 1950 in a public meeting at Bombay, "I have reached an age when it is my right to take rest, but heart is yearning to utilise the time that is still left to me in service of my country in these critical days. It is my earnest wish to see India stable, strong and prosperous and I wish to dedicate the rest of my life to that task".

Alas! That was not to be, as shortly thereafter on the 15th December 1950 the great "Sardar" passed away. The country had felt the loss of his bold and courageous leadership on several occasions of national crisis. Such great leaders are a rare gift of God to any country.

17

GOVERNANCE FOR DEVELOPMENT: CONSTITUTIONAL GOALS AND DIRECTIVES

"Governance", taken in its political sense (as in this chapter) means the exercise of legal power and authority vested in the government to carry out the avowed goals and purposes of the State. The primary aim of any good state particularly of a democratic republic like India, should be to protect the life, liberty and property of its people. Governance of such a state should also aim to promote the general well-being of the people through provision of proper health-care, educational facilities, access to basic needs and facilities like food, water, sanitation, electricity, road, and employment opportunities, etc. The former NDA finance minister Jaswant Sigh had emphasized these important aspects of governance in his budget speech of February 3, 2004 as below:

> This Government has consistently placed the citizens' well-being at the core of its responsibilities. Our adherence to *'Panch priorities'* remains. The objectives of the life-time concerns of our citizens: enhanced employment, and eradication of poverty; a second green revolution in agriculture; infrastructure development; fiscal consolidation and greater manufacturing sector efficiency, are our solemn commitments.

According to our ancient holy books (like the *Mahabharat* and the *Ramayana*) *"Raj Dharma"* or the duty of a 'king' (which could be taken to mean the "state" in a democracy) is to derive happiness in making his people happy and feel secure. Kautilya's *Arthshastra* (treatise on governance) also emphasised this in the following words:

"In the happiness of the subjects lies the king's happiness, in their welfare his welfare."

The fundamental goals and duties of the Indian state as laid down in the Constitution are in keeping with the above philosophy of *Raj Dharma*. The Preamble to the Indian Constitution which reflects its primary aims and objects lays down that the State shall strive to secure "JUSTICE—Social, Economic and Political" to all its citizens. The Directive Principles of State Policy (Part IV, Arts. 37-51) enumerate and elaborate some of these goals and principles of governance for the well-being of the people.

Arts. 38 and 39 being specially relevant are reproduced below for easy reference:

"38. State to secure a social order for the promotion of welfare of the people

(1) The State shall strive to promote the welfare of the people by securing and protecting as effectively as it may a social order in which justice, social, economic and political, shall inform all the institutions of the national life.

(2) The State shall, in particular, strive to minimize the inequalities in income, and endeavour to eliminate inequalities in status, facilities and opportunities, not only amongst individuals but also amongst groups of people residing in different areas or engaged in different vocations."

These principles of governance are obviously meant to promote social harmony among all the citizens by reducing among them the inequalities of wealth and income and giving them equal opportunities of progress and development. The need for balanced regional development has been highlighted so that there is no feeling of step-motherly treatment by the people residing in any area.

"39. Certain principles of policy to be followed by the State

The State shall, in particular, direct its policy towards securing:

(a) that the citizens, men and women equally, have the right to an adequate means to livelihood;

(b) that the ownership and control of the material resources of the community are so distributed as best to sub-serve the common good;

(c) that the operation of the economic system does not result in the concentration of wealth and means of production to the common detriment;

(d) that there is equal pay for equal work for both men and women;

(e) that the health and strength of workers, men and women, and tender age of children are not abused and that citizens are not forced by economic necessity to enter avocations unsuited to their age or strength; and

(f) that children are given opportunities and facilities to develop in a healthy manner and in conditions of freedom and dignity and that childhood and youth are protected against exploitation and against moral and material abandonment."

The above constitutional provisions have socialistic aims being based on the ideals of equality, equal opportunity and social justice. The interests of women, children and the working class are required to be given special care as any good state in its governance ought to ensure that the weaker sections of society do not become victims of exploitation of the well-placed individuals or groups. The "state" must ensure justice for all the citizens.

Since over 70 per cent of our people living in rural areas earn their livelihood from agriculture and allied activities like horticulture, animal husbandry, forests and fisheries, special emphasis has been given to the need for the development of the cattle wealth of the country in Arts. 48 and 48A quoted below:

"48. Organisation of agriculture and animal husbandry

The State shall endeavour to organise agriculture and animal husbandry on modern and scientific lines and shall, in particular, take steps for preserving and improving the breeds, and prohibiting the slaughter of cows and calves and other milch and draught cattle.

48A. Protection and improvement of environment and safeguarding of forests and wildlife

The State shall endeavour to protect and improve the environment and to safeguard the forests and wildlife of the country."

Apart from our centuries old philosophy of *Raj Dharma* the other important reasons for the above developmental approach was due to the fact that India gained freedom during the hey-days of socialism and the founding fathers of our Constitution like Pandit Jawaharlal Nehru were themselves persons of socialistic outlook. Their thinking was that free India's government should play a key and effective role in the socio-economic development of the country to ensure economic justice to all the people or what is called "inclusive growth." They had felt that the fruits of development were likely to be cornered by a few strong and powerful individuals if major economic activities were left in private hands and to the market forces alone. Accordingly it was visualised that bulk of the country's natural resources like land, water, forests and minerals were to be publicly managed so that "the commanding heights of the economy" are in public hands. The private sector of course was allowed to play its role in several other areas. Thus both the public and private sectors had been assigned specific roles for economic development of the country.

In pursuit of the socialistic goals many large-scale public sector undertakings (PSUs) were set up and assigned as intended major developmental roles in key economic sectors.

It may be noted that when India gained freedom communist and other leftist parties were in power in several other countries like Russia and the East European countries of the Soviet bloc. Even in some West European countries, left oriented political parties, like the Labour Party in the U.K. had come to occupy seats of power. Many newly independent countries of Asia and Africa in the 50s and 60s had also followed the communist or socialist models of governance and development. Capitalist countries like the USA with their free market economy did not enjoy much intellectual support globally at that time. Socialistic winds of development were blowing all over the world.

In the Communist ruled states all developmental activities were the monopolies of the governmental agencies. Private individuals in these countries owned no private properties nor had any private economic activities for their own financial incomes. Every individual had to work for the state with modest, if not low, living wages. The noble sounding communist moto of 'to each according to his needs and from each according to his capacity' was trumpeted of being followed. However, the ground realities were otherwise as living conditions were unbearably hard for the general masses. The communist philosophy of state ownership of all material resources of the country did not provide the necessary incentives to private individuals to work hard and to the best of their capacities so as to enjoy the fruits of their labour. As a result the productive activities of the state suffered with continuous decline in productivity and production year after year. The indifferent functioning of the economy in the communist countries largely remained hidden behind their "Iron Curtains." There was lack of transparency. There were periodic "purges" or mass killings to force the pace of development but with little long-term gains. The downhill journey of the economy continued until the bitter truth came to light on the assumption of power by Mikhail Gorbachev in Russia in 1985. His policy of "Glasnost" (openness or transparency) and attempts of "Parestroika" or restructuring of the communist state revealed the hollowness of their state run and state owned economy. The communist system with its above inherent shortcomings and weaknesses was found to be beyond reforms and repairs. It needed instead to be replaced by a more pragmatic system of growth and development with sufficient space for private initiative and participation by allowing them full benefits of their knowledge, skill and labour. This happened after the monolithic Communist state of Russia collapsed in 1992 disintegrating into 15 smaller states each of which adopted more liberal systems of economic growth with due place for the private sector in economic development. Rights of private ownership of property, private management of industries and private profit making were permitted as necessary incentives and motivations. State monopoly in development was thus terminated.

Fortunately, for India, as mentioned earlier its socialistic goals enshrined in the Constitution did not totally debar private ownership, initiative, enterprise and profit earning. It followed the path of 'mixed economy' with scope for both the public sector and the private sector for various economic activities. Indian planners had allowed the private sector to continue to operate as previously in certain areas. For example, agriculture and allied activities like horticulture, animal husbandry, fisheries, etc. were left as earlier in private hands for development with additional support and guidance of the state. The farmers and tillers of the land continued to be the land owners. The state only played a supportive role to facilitate speedy services and planned development. There were healthy private-public cooperative efforts in the development of this important sector. For example, large investments were made by the state in irrigation, in the research and production of high yielding varieties of seeds, in providing subsidized fertilizers, pesticides and low interest credit facilities to the farmers. Scientific and technological research results for higher agricultural productivity were passed on to the farmers through a countrywide network of government run National Agricultural Development Blocks. Programmes like rural electrification, rural roads, warehousing and cold storage facilities, establishment of regulated markets were some of the other important supportive developmental activities and services of the state. The state also guaranteed the purchase of farm produces on a pre-notified minimum support price (MSP). All these agricultural development policies and activities of the state gave the required incentives and support to the farmers for higher agricultural production. As tillers and land owners they could derive the benefits of higher production due to their hard work and labour.

This private-public joint effort made India not only self-sufficient but an exporter of surplus foodgrains, fruits, vegetables, fish and poultry products for some years. India had successfully overcome the earlier fears of food scarcity and famine. At the time of independence with its then population of around 363 millions, India had on the average foodgrains production of only about 50 million tons a year and was heavily dependent on imported foodgrains. Now with over 1000 million population and with annual foodgrains production of over 220 million tons, India is self-sufficient on the food front. In fact it also has presently (2008) a large buffer stock of nearly 45 million tons of foodgrains (of rice and wheat). Unfortunately, due to lack of adequate storage space lakhs of tons of foodgrains are kept in the open and go waste. Plentiful supply led to complacency and waste which is also undesirable. India has also emerged as the second largest producer of fruits and vegetables in the world. On the average, it produces 46 million tons of fruits per year which accounts for about 10 per cent of the total world production. India has also become the largest producer of milk in the world, production of which per year having risen from 17 million tons in 1950-51 to 84 million tons in 2001-02 (All the statistics quoted here are from the "Economic Survey of India 2002-03"—Section 8 dealing with Agriculture). These achievements are justifiably called as "green revolution" for higher foodgrains production and "white revolution" for the higher milk production. Thus the public-private participatory development strategy of India has paid off well.

With the attainment of self-sufficiency in the foodgrains production the state's developmental role in the agricultural and allied sectors cannot be said to have ended as problems on this account will still be there because of rising population and its larger volumes of food requirements. The available cultivable land having nearly been already put to use, greater reliance for higher production has now to be on higher productivity of crops per hectare of land. That would necessitate more cultivated areas to be brought under irrigation as currently hardly 40 per cent of it is irrigated. For this purpose large amounts of public funds have to be invested for construction of big sized water storage dams on major rivers, inter-basin linking of rivers, better maintenance of irrigation structures and canals etc. Since nearly 50 per cent of the irrigation is now ground water based, re-charging of ground water should also get more public funds. Water-harvesting, soil conservation, watershed management are other equally important aspects of development for obtaining higher agricultural production and require due attention of government and its agencies. Individual farmers or groups of them cannot by themselves tackle these tasks. Accordingly the Approach Paper to the Tenth Five Year Plan Para 3.17 had highlighted some of these issues as below:

> "...agricultural output increased in the 1990s because of higher output support price and input subsidies. Now it must come from higher investments in irrigation, seeds, power and roads. Therefore public investment in irrigation, power and roads should be sufficiently stepped up by reducing subsidies on fertilisers, water and power. Canal systems are in poor shape for lack of operations and maintenance outlay. These should be improved by stepping up plan allocations for maintenance, involving users' groups in management, and appropriate pricing of water to cover operation and maintenance costs. Minimum Support Prices for foodgrains and other commodities will be so adjusted as to promote diversification of agriculture, environmental sustainability, and reduction in food subsidies. And lastly, the eastern and the rain-fed areas of the central region, which have the highest potential for increases in productivity, would be the focus of attention during the 10th Plan."

The financial health of the central and state governments being poor, the beneficiary farmers as mentioned above may have to do without any input subsidy for water, electricity, fertilisers, etc. in the years to come. This appears inevitable for the sake of sustainable agricultural development by the state. The cooperation of the farmers in sharing the financial burden in agricultural developmental activities would be vital from now on. Private sector should also construct more storage godowns to store surplus foodgrains to prevent wastage due to open storage.

In the industrial and infrastructure sectors like power, coal, steel, petroleum, roads, railways, airways, ports and communication, etc. public sector was given a major role in India's development strategy. Banks and Insurance Companies too were nationalised in the mid-60s to regulate and control flow of finances in tune with the planned development. These sectors constituting "the commanding heights of the economy" were dominated by the PSUs. The private sector however (as mentioned earlier) was not totally ousted. It owned all small and medium size industries in addition to practically all major textile, leather and jute mills, etc. Commerce and trade too were left in private hands. The PSUs of the Central and State Governments had occupied the central stage for industrial development in all key areas till about the end of 80s. By then the many inherent problems and shortcomings of the PUSs, as in other socialist and communist economies, came to notice in India also. These related to inefficient, wasteful or uneconomic uses of financial resources, over-employment, poor work culture, rampant corruption, political and administrative interference in management, etc. These led to lower productivity and production in many PSUs both quantitatively and qualitatively. Many of the PSUs also became perpetually loss making and financial burdens on the state and central public exchequers. Soon enough it was realised that the policy of equitable economic growth and development through PSUs needs rethinking and restructuring (like the Russian "Parestroica").

Interestingly this was also the experience of most other socialist and left oriented economies. There has therefore been a general trend to privatise the PSUs from 1975 onwards. The economic pendulum from then on started moving from the direction of "nationalisation" to the direction of "privatisation." In the 50s the socialistic thinking was that the state should be the sole agency for key developmental activities. That was the era of "collectivization" or "nationalization." The new thinking since 90s onwards is that "to be in business is not the business of the state." Economic liberalisation or opening up the entire industrial sector to the private parties—both domestic and foreign—has now become the developmental policy in India as well. To attract private investments, incentives are being given to private investors by way of nil or lower taxes for setting up new industries in different areas. Bank interests rates, custom and excises duties have too been lowered to encourage larger private investments. As a part of economic reforms, gradual disinvestment of government share-holdings in the existing PSUs in favour of private parties is now an approved policy. In pursuance of this policy some PSUs have been sold to private "strategic partners." The liberalized economic policy visualises to confine the role of Government to that of a "coordinator", "facilitator" and "regulator", of development rather than to be a direct producer of goods and services. The Approach Paper to the Tenth Plan clarified this position in para 5.4 as below:

> "In many respects, development policy in future must make a break from the past. The government had over the years taken on itself too many responsibilities with the result that it not only marginlized individual initiatives but also succeeded in imposing severe strains on its financial and administrative capabilities."

The Economic Survey 2002-03 published by the Central Ministry of Finance also emphasises the above approach in para 7.52 reproduced below:

> **"Policies for Efficiency and Productivity**
>
> "there has been a major change in the nature of industrial policy in the light of economic reforms. The essence of the reforms process has been the quest for efficiency, or the establishment of a framework of incentives whereby the highest possible value added is obtained using a given stock of labour and capital. This is expected to lead to rapid economic growth, through improvements in productivity of the old stock of labour and capital, and the best possible utilisation of the incremental labour and capital which come on stream each year. A wide variety of policy initiatives are underway, which span across many different government agencies, which foster efficiency and productivity. These areas have now become the main focus of industrial policy."

The need for foreign direct investment (FDI) has also been accepted for valid reasons mentioned below in para 7.53 of the Economic Survey.

> **"Policies on FDI**
>
> "Foreign direct investment (FDI) directly impacts on output growth in India by augmenting the available investible capital. However, a far more important impact of FDI is through externalities leading to higher efficiency and productivity. FDI typically serves to increase competition in markets, bring new technology into India, and foster skill acquisition amongst domestic labour. FDI by international corporations is also central to the process of India being utilised as a platform for global production chains, which would pave the way for strong exports growth."

Development of the infrastructure sector like roads, railways, airports, telecom, ports, power, etc. should however continue to have some focus of the public sector. Private sector too can play a sufficient developmental role in this sector. Government, for some years to come may not be able to withdraw wholly from the above infrastructure areas of economic activities. Though the private sector has been allowed entry into these areas as a part of economic liberlisation, their operations would still be somewhat modest and subject to government regulations. The role for regulation, as stated in the Economic Survey (para 9.2) "is to protect the interests of consumers, obtain conditions of competition, and foster the institutional framework." The ultimate goal of infrastructure development policy has been stated to be "to effectively deliver infrastructure services of high quality and at low prices to households and firms in the country. (para 9.3)

Development in the social sector, i.e. health, education, water supply, sanitation, housing, welfare of the SCs/STs and OBCs as a matter of policy will have to, as in the past, receive sufficient attention of and fund allocations by public authorities. The justification for this as the Economic Survey 2002-03 says in para 10 is that:

> "The ultimate objective of all development endeavours is human development, encompassing the quality of life, the level of well-being and access to basic social services. The emphasis on the achievement of higher economic growth

along with social justice is manifest in the renewed focus on development initiatives in the social sectors."

It has also been stated in the Economic Survey that expenditure in the social sector has been increasing since 1986-87 as per cent of GDP. Figures of expenditure as given in Table 10.03 of the Survey being relevant are quoted below:

Total Expenditure of General Government on Social Services (Combined Centre and States)

Items	*1986-87*	*1990-91*	*1995-96*	*1996-97*	*1997-98*	*1998-99*	*1999-00*	*2000-01*	*2001-02*	*2002-03*
					Actual				RE	RE
					As % of GDP					
Total Expenditure	29.4	26.8	24.2	23.4	24.2	25.4	26.6	28.1	29.5	29.6
Social Services	5.8	5.4	4.9	5	5.2	5.5	5.7	6.3	6.5	6.2
Education	2.9	3.1	2.7	2.7	2.8	3	3.3	3.1	3.1	3.1
Health	1.3	1.2	1	1	1.1	1.2	1.2	1.3	1.4	1.4
Others	1.6	1.2	1.2	1.3	1.3	1.3	1.2	.8	2	1.8
					As % of Total Expenditure					
Social Services	19.6	20.3	20.4	21.5	21.4	21.6	21.3	22.4	22	20.9
Education	9.8	11.4	11.3	11.6	11.5	11.9	12.3	11.2	10.5	10.3
Health	4.4	4.3	4.3	4.5	4.6	4.6	4.4	4.8	4.8	4.6
Others	5.4	4.6	4.8	5.4	5.3	5	4.6	6.4	6.7	6
					As % of Expenditure on Social Services					
Education	50	56	55	54	54	55	58	50	48	49
Health	23	21	21	21	21	22	21	21	22	22
Others	27	23	24	25	25	23	21	29	31	29

Note: 1. 'Health' includes Medical, Public Health, Family Welfare, Water Supply and Sanitation.

2. 'Others' includes other social Services except Education and Health.

Source: RBI Annual Reports.

In spite of the above higher levels of social sector development expenditure for some years India's global rank on human and gender development is as low as 124 among of 173 countries according to UNDP's Human Development Index (HDI) for the year 2000.

Vast number of people still continue to suffer from poverty even though their number has come down from 321.3 millions in 1973 to 260.3 millions in 1999-2000 (Table 10.6 of the Economic Survey 2002-03.)[1] The number of unemployed has however increased from 20.13 millions in 1993 to 26.58 millions in 1999-2000 (Table 10.8 of the Economic Survey 2002-03). Of those employed the estimated number of working children is as high as 10.4 millions (para 10.28 of Economic Survey 2002-03). Though the literacy rate has appreciably risen from 18.33 in 1951 to 65.38 in 2001, it is still quite low as over one-third of our people are even now illiterate. To improve the general quality of life, population growth has to be brought down to the targeted level of 2.1 fertility rate (TFR) from the current level of around 3.2 per cent. Added to this are the other no less important obstacles to development like all-pervasive corruption, in sensitive administrative machinery, lack of transparency and accountability of the governmental system and above all the large scale entry of criminals into politics and positions of power.

Since poverty eradication, employment generation, improving agricultural productivity, infrastructure development, and fiscal consolidation are the developmental priorities of government it should play its new role of facilitator, regulator and coordinator of development more effectively. It is necessary that laws for population control, environment protection, soil, forest, water and mineral conservation are updated and enforced effectively to achieve the desired goals. Opening up the economy to the private sector as a policy would no doubt go a long way to accelerate the pace of development.

The Indian state has the constitutional obligation to look after the well-being of "we the people of India" in their totality. To bring about all inclusive development and growth should therefore be the main objective of the state. It must ensure "justice" to all the people even in its new role. For this purpose some basic conditions for development have to be ensured. These are—*(i)* an environment of peace and security with minimum problems of law and order; *(ii)* political stability with public spirited leadership; *(iii)* a corruption free and efficient administrative machinery; *(iv)* sound financial management capable of preventing wastages of public funds; *(v)* fiscal consolidation in order to find adequate financial resources for development; *(vi)* transparency and accountability in raising and spending of public funds; and *(vii)* public credibility and confidence in the entire system of governance and its personnel.

To bring about better and all-inclusive development both the public and the private sectors could play important roles. Numerous private sector associations of the civil society like those of trade, commerce and industrial bodies, labour unions, welfare associations of residents, organisations of women and housewives, professional bodies of doctors, engineers, teachers, etc. and other NGOs could play an active role in highlighting and promoting sound policies and programmes of development in their respective areas of interest.

NOTE

1. The definition of the "Poor" and their estimates keep changing. The latest estimate of the poor according to the 2009 Report of the Committee of Suresh Tendulkar (Chief of PM's Economic Advisory Council) is that around 38 per cent of the population (taking 2004-05 as the base year) belong to the BPL category. Numerically the BPL now will thus be well over 400 millions.

18

INDIA'S WATER RESOURCES: SOME ISSUES OF CONCERN

The two most serious and somewhat inter-connected problems that the world community will face in the near future are: (1) global warming leading to adverse climatic changes; and (2) the related problem of acute shortage of water worldwide which may even lead to water-wars between different countries. The World Development Report (2010) on Development and Climate Change (p. 137) has drawn attention to these emerging problems as below:

> "Climate change will make it harder to manage the world's water. People will feel many of the effects of climate change through water. The entire water cycle will be affected. While the world as a whole will get wetter as warming speeds up the hydrological cycle, increased evaporation will make drought conditions more prevalent. Most places will experience more intense and variable precipitation, often with longer dry periods in between. The effects on human activity and natural systems will be widespread. Areas that now depend on glaciers and snowmelt will have more fresh water initially, but supply will then decline overtime. The shifts may be so rapid and unpredictable that traditional agricultural and water management practices are no longer useful."

Global warming is on the rise due to large and uncontrolled emission of carbonized gases by many countries, specially the industrialised countries like the USA, UK, and Japan, etc. The recent global Copenhagen Conference debated on this issue to reduce and limit the emission of greenhouse gases by major countries. Even though no positive solutions could be found, the urgency of the problem was duly recognized and hopefully some satisfactory steps will be taken soon enough to mitigate the causes of global warming.

The water scarcity issues have been debated by the UN from time to time. But global cooperation for its solution is still lacking. Therefore, to begin with each country should find its own solution for its water scarcity problems.

The issues discussed here are with regard to India's water scarcity problems and how to find ways and means to tide over these.[1]

As Secretary, Irrigation and Power to the State Government of Orissa (1968-70) the author had to deal with the Krishsna-Godavari river water dispute with the States of Andhra and Karnataka since river Indravati with its large catchment areas in Southern Orissa was a tributary of river Godavari. The Government of Andhra had been objecting to any major irrigation or power projects in Orissa drawing water from river Indravati on the ground that these will reduce water availability to Andhra. I had to prepare Orissa's case for its proper water share from Indravati. The state's claim was justified on the basis of its total water contribution to the Krishna-Godavari river basin and for being a backward state its greater and pressing need for development. Ultimately the state government got its full share of Indravati water as was claimed.

Study of the water related problems of the country in connection with this case made me to realize that the inter-state water dispute cases may be many more in course of time and these disputes may also become more aggressive and bitter unless timely solutions are found through rational policy decisions. At the same time there has to be greater emphasis on water-conservation and economy in uses.

Some relevant facts and figures on the subject quoted below are taken from official reports of the Central Ministry of Water Resources, the Planning Commission, The National Commission for Integrated Water Resources Development Plan, 1999 (NCIWRDP) and the National Water Policy. To discuss water availability and water issues on a global basis it has to be noted that three-fourth of the earth's surface is covered with water but most of it is in the oceans and seas. Earth is accordingly known to be "water planet." But only about 2.7

1. Extracts from the author's editorial in the Indian Journal of Public Administration Special Issue: July-September, 2003.

per cent of this water constitutes Fresh Water (or useable water) of which again about 75.2 per cent lies frozen in Polar regions and around 22.6 per cent is present as ground water. Thus the quantum of water effectively available for consumption and other uses by mankind is a very small fraction of the total water on earth. It is hence a precious but scarce wealth. This useable water is found mostly in rivers, lakes, ponds, tanks and underground aquifers. A tiny portion of world's water is regularly renewed and made fresh by nature's solar-powered water cycle through the process of evaporation, condensation, and precipitation – or rainfall, and snowfall. Fresh water is thus not infinite but is finite and limited to what comes as rainfall, and snowfall. Accordingly, there is no more fresh water on earth to-day than what was available say 2000 years ago when the human population was only 3 per cent of the current population level. This large growth in population over the centuries has significantly reduced the per capita availability of fresh water globally giving rise to the present acute water-scarcity. A per capita annual availability of 1000 Cu.m of water is considered as the threshold value to avoid water-stress situation. This situation would keep worsening as population keeps growing.

India has 2.45 per cent of the world's land, 16 per cent of the world's population but roughly 4 per cent of the world's fresh water resources. The average annual rainfall in India is about 1170 m.m. and may not be considered to be low or inadequate. There are, however, certain negative aspects in the pattern of rainfall which considerably reduce its net value in spite of it being reasonably satisfactory in terms of quantity. The most important negative aspect is that the rainfall is not evenly spread over the entire country. There are both temporal (or time-wise) and spatial (or area-wise) variability. Some areas have "harmful abundance" or heavy rainfall resulting in floods and some other areas have meagre rainfall resulting in acute scarcity and drought. For example, average annual rainfall is around 100 m.m. in Western Rajasthan and 11000 m.m. in the North Eastern region. More than 50 per cent of precipitation or rainfall takes place in about 15 days and in less than 100 hours during the four rainy months of June to September. The rain days may be about 5 in the desert of Rajasthan areas and about 150 in the North-East. Due to this peculiar pattern of rainfall about 40 million hectares of agricultural land is flood-prone, and about 108 million hectares, or nearly one-third of the country is drought-prone. 90 per cent of the annual run-off in Peninsular rivers and more than 80 per cent in the Himalayan rivers occur during the months of June to September. Presently about 80 per cent of this river run-off goes to the sea un-utilised and is thus a waste.

Although the country receives about 4000 Billion Cubic Metres (BCM) of rainfall and snowfall the average annual run-off is around 1869 BCM. Due to hydrological, topographical and geological constraints only 1122 BCM of the above run-off can be utilized comprising of 690 BCM of surface water and 432 BCM of replenishable ground water.

The National Water Commission (NCIWRDP) has estimated that the total water requirement of the country in the year 2050 would be about 973 BCM on the lower side and 1180 BCM on the upper side depending upon the actual population growth. The Union Ministry of Water Resources, however, on the basis of other studies has estimated the country's water requirements to be around 1093 BCM for the year 2025 and about 1447 B CM for the year 2050. The present extent and pattern of water utilization is as under:

Purpose	*Utilisation Pattern (b.cu.m.)*
Irrigation	501
Domestic	30
Industrial	20
Energy	20
Others	34
Total	605

Since the total water requirement of the country mentioned above barely match or may even exceed the available utilizable water resources, there is need for both water conservation and augmentation of useable water resources. It is in this context that the Prime Minister, Dr. Manmohan Singh had sometime back appealed for water conservation. Conservation would include both efficiency and economy in the various uses of water i.e. drinking, other domestic uses, irrigation, hydropower generation, industrial, health, sanitation, and navigation, etc.

Since irrigation for agricultural purposes claims major part of available water around 68 per cent (nearly 51 per cent of irrigation is ground water based) there has to be greater efforts in economy and efficiency of water use in this sector. The attempt should be to grow more crop per drop of water. Every unit of water has to be made more productive. The present system of flooding fields for irrigation need to be replaced by drip and sprinkler methods of irrigation. In Israel water is used like "eye drops" for agriculture and yet productivity per hectare there is more than in India. Suitable cropping patterns too have to be devised for water scarcity areas. The present irrigation efficiency in the country is estimated to be between 30 to 40 per cent and can improve to around 65 to 70 per cent with improved agricultural patterns and practices. To economise on water for agriculture, reasonable water charges would have to be levied. Free or highly subsidized water and electricity for agriculture is leading to large wastages of both. Ill maintained irrigation canals and other structures too are causing huge water losses. There is need to provide sufficient funds for maintenance of irrigation works by levying reasonable water charges on the beneficiary farmers. These should be neither too high nor too low.

The industrial sector, using around 5 to 7 per cent of total useable water can also economise by suitably improving the various industrial processes so as to recycle and reuse water. Industrial wastes and effluents need to be treated and cleaned for prevention of water pollution and re-use of the same. Only make-up water of around 10 per cent could be made available for industrial purposes the rest being recycled water. Water use for drinking and other domestic purposes is estimated to be around 7 to 9 per cent of the total used water. The norms of 200 and 150 litres of water per capita per day for the urban and rural areas respectively proposed by the National Water Commission is considered by some experts to be on the higher side. One of them (Peter Gleick) thinks that the basic water requirement for human needs (drinking, sanitation services, bathing, cooking and kitchen) should be around 50 litres per person per day. While any wastage of water has to be avoided, economy in water use in the domestic front should give due importance to sanitation and health. To bring about economy in municipal water demands reasonable water charges ought to be levied. These should at least meet the cost of water supply services and maintenance of waterworks. Water losses due to leaking pipes and ill-repaired supply systems are estimated to be as high as between 30 to 40 per cent of the water supply and could be checked with proper maintenance. Not to levy any charges for such services is to be "penny wise and found foolish." Water being one of the basic needs of life and for being scarce need to be used most economically. It would accordingly be wise to impose suitable charges for its various uses.

Water pollution is another important area for attention and corrective action. Pollution of river waters and other sources of surface and ground water is very large. This reduces the quantum of usable water significantly. In addition the worrisome problem is that polluted and contaminated water is posing serious health hazard to large sections of the people. Suitable and effective strategies need to be adopted to check water contamination and pollution. Many schemes for river cleaning (like that of Ganga and Yamuna) had been undertaken in the past but somewhat half-heartedly to be effective. More serious efforts are needed to keep rivers unpolluted. The general public also need to be made aware of this for getting their cooperation. Educational text books should also emphasise the need for keeping our rivers (like Ganga, Yamuna and Godavari, etc.) which have sacred and divine status in the minds of the people pollution free. The future generation need to be sufficiently made aware of the growing water scarcity and the importance of various water conservation measures.

By and large there is unanimity to practice utmost economy and efficiency in various water uses as a part of demand management approach to meet the emerging water scarcity problem. But even after all the economy measures are adopted there will be still large gaps between demand and supply of water in the years to come due to massive population growths. Accordingly, some supply side solutions for augmenting "useable water resources" would be necessary. Here the professionals, environmentalists, human right activists and water specialists differ in finding practical solutions. One line of thinking is to depend more on local rain water harvesting and watershed development in preference to construction of large storage dams on rivers. According to this viewpoint "what is available in nature is rainfall, not just river flows; and while storing river water behind a dam doubtless converts available water into 'useable' water, so does *in situ* rain water harvesting (i.e. catching the rain drop as it falls) and local watershed development. According to this viewpoint large storage dams should be the last option as "these have serious impacts and consequences, environmental, social, and human, not all of which can be remedied or mitigated or compensated for, or even foreseen fully."

The other viewpoint is to build water storage dams wherever feasible depending on adequate river flow and proper sites for dams and storage reservoirs. According to this line of thinking "non-development of water storage projects is not a viable or available option due to large temporal variations in river flows in Indian monsoonic climate." Water harvesting or smaller water resources development projects cannot substitute the need for large water storage reserviors but can at best complement the larger projects. Now 80 per cent of river flows go unutilized to the seas in matter of days. These need to be impounded during rainy season and stored at suitable locations for use during the water scarcity months and in water scarcity areas. Most of our rivers dry up during summer months. Again river flows vary from river basin to river basin. This necessitates storing of river waters wherever technically and financially feasible. According to this view any controversy of the large versus small dams is irrelevant. There is place for both. For the reasons we maintain large stocks of foodgrains to meet scarcity situations, for similar reasons we must build large river dams for storage of surplus water during the rainy season to meet water needs for irrigation and other purposes during the non-rainy months.

In the early post-independence period some large multi-purpose water storage dams like Hirakud, Bhakra, Damodar Valley, Nagarjun Sagar etc. were built. These moderated floods, irrigated vast areas of agricultural lands and generated power. These multi-purpose dams have immensely proved their utility for the economic growth of the country and for meeting our huge foodgrains requirements. Hydropower is cheapest, and environmental friendly. Protagonists of large dams say that these help in conversion of waste lands into agricultural land and facilitate higher foodgrains production . Bhakra Dam's Rajasthan Canal is cited as the shining example in transforming the arid western Rajasthan into a vast agricultural region. Large water availability and the spread of agriculture and grass fields in many parts of the state have halted and prevented the spread of Thar desert to the adjoining areas of Panjab and Haryana. Thus water being a most valuable asset must not be allowed to go waste as unused river flows into the seas.

The existing water storage capacity of all the large dams completed and under construction in India is reported to be 252 BCM (2004). The future planning of the Central Water Resources Ministry is to raise this to 400 BCM to meet the water requirements of our bulging population. Those favouring large dams say that the controversies concerning the rehabilitation of persons displaced by dams have muddied the entire debate on the utility of water resources projects and caused much harm to the national economy and well-being of the people at large by delaying completion of some on going projects. The figure of affected people from 2784 dams for which "broad assessment" was conducted by the Central Water Commission is reportedly 6 to 7 millions only as against the "exaggerated" figures of around 70 millions claimed by the opponents of large river dams.

There are other issues of water resource management like privatization of water resources for different purposes, need to levy higher water charges for agriculture, domestic and other uses, disputes relating to inter-state rivers; inter-basin transfer of water or inter-linking of Himalayan and Peninsular river basins, water markets, desalination of sea water to increase fresh water availability, recharging of ground water, etc. which need to be suitably addressed keeping in mind their importance and urgency.

The National Water Policy laid down by the Central Government has very rightly emphasized that development and management of water resources of the country need to be governed by national perspective. Rivers and underground aquifers often cut across state boundaries. Water, as a resource of the country, is one and indivisible. Inter-basin transfer of water from the surplus to the deficit basins and inter-state river water disputes have to be viewed in the overall national perspective. The requirements of equity in various water uses has necessarily to be observed to avoid hardships to any region of the country or to any section of society. Water being a natural resource of the country as a whole has to be shared nationally for its socio-economic development.

Making available safe drinking water to rural and urban areas fully has to be the first charge on national water resources. It is indeed a matter of shame that even after more than six decades of economic planning and development our rural women in many parts of the country continue to walk miles in hot summer and cold winter to fetch a few pots of water for their families. They suffer from water scarcity the most. In most towns and cities of the country including the National Capital Delhi long queues for water is a common sight. Large concentration of urban population in mega cities do need water storage facilities of large capacities to meet their massive water needs throughout the year. Some relief could of course be found by roof-top harvesting of rain water in urban areas. Ground water acquifers also need to be recharged through rainwater harvesting measures. Currently more than 85 per cent of rural water supply is ground water based. Similarly, ground water supplies more than 50 per cent of water for urban domestic and industrial uses.

Water scarcity problems currently are not due to non-availability of enough useable water as such but due to utter inefficiency in the water supply arrangements and wastages of large quantities of water. The age-old saying "not to waste money like water" need now to be updated by the saying "use water like money." Conservation of water by practicing economy and efficiency in water uses could largely take care of the current water problems. Rain water harvesting could also provide further relief. But as a long term policy augmentation of water resources through large dams and storage reservoirs cannot be avoided. Possibility of inter-basin transfer of water too needs to be explored. Perhaps major inter-state rivers like Ganga, Yamuna, Brahmaputra, Narmada, Krishna, Godavari, etc. could be declared as national rivers and brought under the Central domain for development of their water resources. State governments lack required financial resources to take up effective flood control measures for major rivers like Brahmaputra. Integrated water resources development of major rivers also need coordinated planning and management at the Central Government level. That may to a large extent free India of its water scarcity problems. However, the connected concern for this is to ensure that our snowfed Himalayan rivers like Ganga, Yamuna and Brahmaputra etc. do not suffer from lack of flow of water on account of the melting of the Himalayan snow or glaciers due to global warming. That connected issue also requires urgent attention. The World Development Report (2010) emphasizes that allocating water efficiently and limiting water consumption to safe levels will become increasingly important with climate change." The Report also advises the policy makers and water managers of the country as below (p. 140):

> "climate change will reduce the natural water storage of snow and glaciers, which will in turn affect aquifer storage and require water managers to design and operate reservoirs differently. Water managers will have to manage the entire

water cycle. They can no longer afford to concentrate on the small share of water in rivers and lakes and leave groundwater and soil moisture to be managed by landowners. Many basins will experience increased demand, reduced availability, and increased variability all at the same time. Water managers in those places will have less room to maneuver if their decisions are not robust to a variety of outcomes." This report specially highlights that climate change will make applying and enforcing sound water policies even more important.

19

FROM THE OFFICIAL SECRET ACT (1923) TO THE RIGHT TO INFORMATION ACT (2005) DAWN OF "GLASNOST"

In a parliamentary democracy like ours sovereignty lies with the people and the state derives all its powers from them. The people elect their representatives to the national parliament and the majority, belonging to one or a group of political parties, form the government. People as sovereign, have accordingly the right to know how their elected government at any time is functioning and what all it is doing for their good to justify its proposals to impose taxes, duties and other levies and to enact any legislation to regulate their social or economic activities. A government's budget proposals to raise revenue and incur expenditure are of course placed before the Parliament for its approval. Similarly, laws to regulate trade, industry, social, economic and political activities etc. are also placed before Parliament for discussions, and debates. The broad features of these legislations are also published for the information of the people at large. Print and electronic media too discuss the merits and demerits of these legislations. On getting appropriate feedbacks government where necessary makes appropriate changes in them before these are approved and enacted by the Parliament as laws.

Such transparency or openness of government is however largely confined to broad policy matters and taxation laws only. In day to day matters of governance and administration, important rules, regulations and orders are approved and executed by the executive wing of the government without much publicity or public knowledge. In fact, the popular perception is that most of the government business and work are shrouded in secrecy and confidentiality which facilitate corruption, waste, inefficiency, abuse of powers and various other acts of mal-administration. There may be well planned programmes, schemes and policies of economic development, and social upliftment but due to lack of authentic, and timely information, people waste their time in running from pillar to post to know the details of these programmes and policies in order to avail of their proclaimed benefits. Often they are also compelled to take recourse to corrupt means at the behest of touts and other undesirable elements to know and derive any benefits from such programmes.

Secrecy breeds corruption, favouritism and nepotism. For example, sometime back one chief minister of a major state i.e. Uttar Pradesh gifted away as much as rupees 40 crores in one year to many of his party men, relatives and journalists, etc. from his "discretionary grants" intended to financially help the genuinely needy and disadvantaged people. No information was placed before the state legislature or disclosed to the media regarding the names of individual beneficiaries and the justification for doling out to them large amounts of public money. Only when a change of government took place and there was public outcry about the wrongful disbursement of public funds in the name of helping the poor it came to notice that large amounts of the discretionary funds were gifted away to undeserving persons for personal services or political gains. This kind of expenditure revealed the prevailing climate of nepotism, favouritism and reckless waste of public funds. Undoubtedly there would be many more similar cases of wasteful and malafide expenditure of public funds in other states as well. There is therefore need to legally compel publication of names of all beneficiaries of public funds under any scheme. Their disclosures may help to check cases of uncalled for favouritism so that the really needy and deserving persons get the benefit. Publication of similar information regarding any allotments made out of the discretionary quotas of any kind to individuals should also be made legally compulsory. Allotment of seats in medical, engineering and other vocational institutions from any earmarked quotas for any category of people should also be published in the press giving complete information regarding the propriety and legitimacy of such allotments. There were often rumours in the past that many dealerships/agencies of the PSUs e.g. gas agencies, dealerships of automobiles, cement, fertilizers, petrol pumps and other sales outlets were clandestinely given to the friends and relations of persons in power. In one such scam there were reportedly allotment of 3800 petrol pumps, LPG and kerosene agencies of public sector oil companies to friends and relations of the MPs/MLAs of the then ruling BJP without any public information. Due to public outcry and uproar in both Houses of Parliament on the rumours of such allotments these had to be cancelled by government. In another similar case Capt. Satish Sharma, Petroleum Minister of the Congress Party Government at the Centre allotted a few petrol pumps out of his "discretionary" quota to some of his personal staff members without public information. Similarly, Mrs. Sheila Kaul, Minister for Housing of the Congress Government allotted some houses/residential plots to her relations and friends without assigning any reasons. Both these cases of abuse of power reached the Apex Court through PIL petitions. The court not only cancelled the allotments but also awarded heavy financial damages on the ministers (these financial damages were later cancelled). The Apex Court also directed that the Government should formulate a fair and transparent system of allotment rather than allow arbitrary powers of allotments to any minister through any "discretionary quota" without prior public knowledge. Openness and public knowledge of such transactions was considered essential to minimize favouritism, corruption and nepotism.

MPs in the past had been given quotas for allotting to the people in their constituencies gas and telephone connections which were then in short supply. The MPs were however not required to furnish names of persons to whom they distributed the quotas and the reasons for the same. Due to secrecy in making such allotments there was understandably criticism and even allegations of corruption and nepotism. The scheme was later withdrawn but after it had damaged the reputation of several MPs. If scarce consumer items are distributed through such VIP quotas it may in all likelihood benefit only some privileged and well to do persons who have easy access to those VIPs. It may also breed corruption and cause popular resentment for not providing essential supplies and facilities to the deserving persons in an open manner. While earmarking of some quotas could be defended for the older persons, the war-widows, the physically handicapped or other helpless categories, names of such individual beneficiaries should however be made public to check possible abuses if any. Transparency is essential to prevent abuses.

A case of wrongful "out-of-turn" house allotment to some persons by the Estate Department of the Central Ministry of Housing on the petition of some aggrieved persons had also reached the Apex Court sometime back. The petitioners had alleged favouritism in making such unjustified allotments. Had the lists of the allottees been published with good reasons for showing special considerations to each of the individual beneficiaries there may not have been any cause for public criticism and litigation. Here also the apex court found fault with the existing system leading to suspicion of favourtism and cancelled all the "out of turn" allotments.

The prevailing secrecy and confidentiality in the general functioning of the government machinery as illustrated above is under the cover of the Official Secrets Act, 1923 which is still in force. This Act is a legacy of the colonial era, when the foreign rulers kept most official transactions secret from the Indian public in order to preserve their powers and dominance and to hide wrong doings, if any, from the public. It was not considered necessary to take the people into confidence in any official matter. All unauthorized disclosure of information from official records was in fact made a punishable offence. For example, Section 5 of the Official Secrets Act, 1923 lays down that "if any person having in his possession or control any secret official code, or pass word or any sketch or plan, model, article, note, document or information — or which has been entrusted in confidence to him—or to which he has access owing to his position or as a person who holds or has held office under His Majesty—willfully communicates—the note, document, or information to any person other than a person to whom he is authorized to communicate—he shall be guilty of an offence under this Section."

This is a very wide and all-pervasive omnibus provision. It virtually prohibits all official documents and information to be communicated to any "unauthorised" person. All information available on government records is thus uncommunicable. The offence of supplying unauthorised information is punishable with imprisonment for a term up to two years or with fine or with both.

All Government documents are divided into two categories i.e. "classified" and "non-classified." Classified documents are further sub-divided into: "top secret", "secret", "confidential" and "personal"—"not for publication"—or "for official use only." Documents are classified into the above categories rather liberally and arbitrarily. No strict criteria is applied in classifying the documents in the above manner. Even the unclassified documents or information contained in them cannot be passed on to any unauthorised person or the press by any government servant except through the PIB (Press Information Bureau) or the authorized official spokesman. A government servant under the civil service conduct rules is prohibited to disclose to anyone including a fellow government servant any information acquired by him during the course of his official duties – however, innocuous the information may be. Rule 9 of the All-India Services Conduct Rules reads "No member of the Service shall except in accordance with any general or special order of the government or in the performance in good faith of the duties assigned to him communicate directly or indirectly any official document or part thereof or information to any government servant or any other person to whom he is not authorised to communicate such documents or information". Similar restrictive rules exit for members of other Central government services also. Hence most government servants by habit have become secretive. It also pleases them as it appears to enhance their status in the public eye.

Under the cover of the Official Secrets Act not only documents and information are classified indiscriminately to render them non-discloseable, even many areas and places are declared "prohibited" to disallow access to unauathorised persons. Thus during the Narmada Dam Project agitations entry to rehabilitation sites and even villages of resettled persons were declared "prohibited" to prevent outsiders and the media to see these places and listen to the grievances of the settlers. This kind of cover operations lead to avoidable harassment of the people at the hands of lower level government functionaries. Many avoidable adverse criticism and rumours thus get into circulation due to lack of authentic information.

Undoubtedly there is need for secrecy and confidentiality in some areas of government functioning. These should however be well defined and very much restricted to delicate and sensitive matters like security, defence, Intelligence gathering, matters of foreign relations, investigation of crimes, commercial transactions and budgetary matters etc. There is no need to indiscriminately make all government records, papers, data and reports secret or confidential. Many of these give useful information to the public. Their publicity and public knowledge in fact may spare government from unnecessary criticism.

Openness of government operations is on the increase in most of the liberal democracies of the West. The UK had appointed a committee in 1971 known as Franks Committee to look into some aspects of their Official Secrets Act and the committee stated that it is the concern of a democratic government to see that information is widely defused; for this enables the citizens to play a part in controlling their common affairs. The Committee further observed "a government which pursues secret aims or which operates in greater secrecy then the effective conduct of its proper functions requires, or which turns information services into propaganda agencies will loose the trust of the people. It will be countered by "ill informed and destructive criticism."

There are growing public demands in countries where governments function in greater secrecy for a suitable legislation to ensure more openness and transparency of different administrative agencies. A law to ensure Right to Information had been in demand for a long time in India too. The press had been demanding such a legislation so that it could have access to all official records (save, matters concerning the State security) to expose government's malfunctioning, if any e.g. in the allotment of government lands and houses etc. In some Scandenavian countries citizens have free access to all official documents barring those concerning the security of the state, relations with foreign powers, prevention and prosecution of crimes and certain economic matters.

Sweden and Finland are far advanced in the sphere of openness of their governments. In the USA also there is Freedom of Information Act which gives the citizens the right of access to official information save with regard to certain delicate and security matters which are listed as exceptions to the general rule of openness.

The Universal Declaration of Human Rights, 1948 in Article 19 states: "Everyone has the right to freedom to hold opinions without interference and to seek, receive, and impart information and ideas through any media regardless of frontiers".

This right is of course subject to certain reasonable restrictions like *(a)* respect of the rights of others; and *(b)* protection of national security or public order or of public health or morals.

In India the Supreme Court in *S.P. Gupta* vs. *President of India*, made a strong plea for open government. Mr. Justice Bhagavati speaking for the majority said that "open government is the new democratic culture of a society towards which every liberal democracy is moving and our country should be no exception" (AIR 1982 SC 149).

The myth of Official Secrecy has been in practice in India far too long and has done considerable disservice to the citizens and the state. After India became a democratic republic it was legitimate and necessary to take the people into confidence and share all official information with them. The greatest blow to the Indian democracy has been the diminishing credibility of government due to ever rising corruption, wasteful expenditure, acts of nepotism and favouritism and other malpractices. These were facilitated under the cover of the Official Secret Act. A government of the people in its true sense should not hide anything of general interest from the people.

The need to have a law to allow access to all government files, records, reports, etc., to the public had been the popular demand for many years in India. Public pressure was for greater "Glasnost" or openness in governance to suit the new culture of democratic governments world over. The overwhelming view has been that well informed people alone can prevent the occurrence of financial scams and scandals and other acts of maladministration. If under the Consumer Protection Act, 1986, the consumers have the right to be informed about the quality, quantity, potency, purity standard and prices of goods why there cannot be a similar Act i.e. The Right to Information Act which compels government to give information on all matters of public importance–particularly those relating to availability and allocation of scarce public services, supplies, facilities and benefits. The grounds and justification in taking decisions by government in all such matters should be made known to the public by lawfully allowing them access to relevant official records. Secrecy or confidentiality ought not to come in the way of informing the public with regard to decisions concerning them. If a right or facility is denied to an applicant for which he was eligible he must know why he was denied the same and why some other person similarly placed got it. Equality of treatment and non-discriminatory dealings with every one by government agencies would be ensured if there is openness and transparency through mandatory legal provisions. After realizing the importance of transparency the government at last agreed to enact the Right to Information Act. In justification of this Act passed in 2005 it was highlighted that since the Constitution has made India a democratic Republic and since democracy requires an informed citizenry there was need for such a law. As the Official Secret Act, 1923 has not yet been formally repealed Section 22 of the RTI Act specifically provides that it "shall have effect notwithstanding anything inconsistent therewith contained in the Official Secret Act, 1923." Thus the RTI Act virtually eclipses or overrides the Official Secret Act in keeping the citizens informed about all government transactions of general public interest.

Under Section 7(1) of the RTI Act any information under the control of public authorities as and when required by a member of the public barring some exempt categories, are to be made available "as expeditiously as possible", and in any case within thirty days of the request. Procedure and forms of application for getting such information have been laid down in the Act and rules. For the proper and effective enforcement of the Act it provides for the constitution of a Central Information Commission for the Centre and similar separate state level commissions for the states. These are to be multi-member bodies each headed by a Chief Information Commissioner (Section 22 of the Act). The manner of their appointments and the terms and conditions of their service are such as would enable them to function as independent bodies like other independent institutions i.e. the Central Election Commission, the Comptroller and Auditor General of India, and the Central Vigilance Commission, etc. Under Section 5(1) of the RTI Act every public authority is required to designate as many officers as the Central/State Public Information Officers in all their administrative offices as may be considered necessary to facilitate timely disclosure and communication of information required by the interested applicants. Any other rule, regulation, practice or shortage of staff are not to come in the way of furnishing timely information to the citizens under the RTI Act.

Categories of information that are exempt for being given to any applicant have also been laid down in Section 8 of the Act which *inter-alia* include the following:

8(1) "Notwithstanding anything contained in this Act, there shall be no obligation to give any citizen:

(a) information, disclosure of which would prejudicially affect the sovereignty and integrity of India, the security, strategic, scientific or economic interests of the State, relation with foreign State or lead to incitement of an offence;

(b) information which has been expressly forbidden to be published by any court of law or tribunal or the disclosure of which may constitute contempt of court;

(*c*) information, the disclosure of which would cause a breach of privilege of Parliament or the State legislature;
(*d*) information including commercial confidence, trade secrets or intellectual property, the disclosure of which would harm the competitive position of a third party, unless the competent authority is satisfied that larger public interest warrants the disclosure of such information; and
(*e*) Cabinet papers including records of deliberations of the Council of Ministers, Secretaries and other officers.

The Act also does not apply to certain Intelligence and Security organizations listed in the Second Schedule (Section 24).

However, information pertaining to the allegations of corruption and human rights violations are not excluded under the Act.

To facilitate speedier availability of information to all citizens the Act (under Section 3) wants all public authorities to:

> "Maintain all its records duly catalogued and indexed in a manner and the form which facilitates the right to information under this Act and ensure that all records that are appropriate to be computerized are, within a reasonable time and subject to availability of resources, computerized and connected through a network all over the country on different systems so that access to such records is facilitated."

Section 6(2) of the Act provides that an applicant seeking information is not required to give any reasons for the same. In fact the Act under Section 4(2) wants all important information of public interest to be periodically published by way of keeping the public informed. It says:

> "It shall be a constant endeavour of every public authority to take steps—to provide as much information *suo motu* to the public at regular intervals through various means of communications, including internet, so that the public have minimum resort to the use of this Act to obtain information."

The Act also wants particulars of recipients of concessions, permits or authorizations granted by a public authority to be published. This provision would help in checking acts of nepotism, and favouritism, etc.

It may be seen that whereas the Official Secret Act, 1923 generally debarred to disclose any official information to the public, the Right to Information Act, 2005 on the other hand wants and directs public authorities to periodically publish un-exempted category of information of general interest *suo-motu*. Any public authority which delays or withholds information required by an individual has been made answerable, accountable and punishable where necessary. Thus the emphasis has now shifted from secrecy or darkness to openness in government work. Government functioning is no longer to be a closed door affair. Now the citizens have been legally empowered to seek any information from the public authorities including file notings so long the information sought is not of the exempt category. This is indeed a revolutionary change. It really tantamounts to scrapping of the old Official Secret Act of 1923 and turning government to be a government of the people in the real sense.

If the provisions of the RTI Act are faithfully carried out "glasnost" or openness of Government will become a reality. Hopefully to a good extent this should facilitate good governance by preventing or at least reducing to a good extent corruption, favouritism and nepotism in government dealings. Red-tapism too should be considerably reduced. However, much will depend on the alertness and vigilance of the citizens themselves. They have to assert their legal rights and remain vigilant on the activities of the public authorities. In the present times when the greed for money is all pervasive in every public and private organisation laws of ethical nature for good governance alone may not suffice unless the citizens themselves are vigilant and assertive of their legal rights. The RTI Act will of course enable the citizens to keep a proper watch over the day to day functioning of the government and its administrative machinery. At the same time people should cooperate in maintaining confidentiality in certain spheres specified in the RTI Act in the larger public interest. The prayer to God in the sacred verse (*Tamso ma Jyotirgamaya*) to lead mankind from darkness to light may be to some extent fulfilled with regard to the functioning of the public authorities because of the RTI Act. The public knowledge about the transaction of work in public offices would very much improve. It would be a march from darkness to light. Already due to this Act light is being thrown on some matters which were treated as confidential in the past. For example, the members of the higher judiciary have, because of the RTI Act, agreed to disclose their financial assets for general information. Such disclosure of assets would undoubtedly help to prevent corruption in the higher judiciary. The sense of accountability and responsibility of all public authorities would hopefully increase because of the RTI Act. The citizens have been sufficiently empowered under the RTI Act to seek any information from any public authority regarding any of their decisions, which may appear to be unfair, questionable or unclear . No such information can any longer be held back on grounds of secrecy as in the past except those of the exempted category under the Act. This Act hopefully will prove that "good government is an open government".

In seeking "information" the citizens too have to observe certain necessary restraints. The exempt category of information listed in the Act should be kept in mind. The most important of these is the one of a general nature which prohibits giving of such information "disclosure of which would prejudicially affect the sovereignty and integrity of India. The security, strategic, scientific or economic interests of the state, relation with foreign state or "lead to incitement of an offence." [Section 8(1)(a) of the Act.] Larger national interest has to be given due regard. Maintaining secrecy of certain types of government work and transactions is unavoidable for the safety and security of the state and information on these matters should not be asked for. It is necessary to observe some discipline and prudence in seeking information from official records so that larger national interest is not compromised.

20

WHY AND HOW TO VOTE FOR DEMOCRACY

India is a "Democratic Republic" as stated in the Preamble of the Constitution of India. The head of the Indian state is accordingly the President of India. However, being indirectly elected by the Members of both Houses of Parliament and the members of all the State legislatures the President is only a ceremonial head or a figure head. This means while the governance of the country is carried on in his name the real or effective power of governance is exercised by the Council of Ministers or the Cabinet headed by the Prime Minister of India. This is for the reason that the Members of Parliament from whom the Council of Ministers is chosen are directly elected by the people of India in the case of the Lok Sabha and indirectly in the case of Rajya Sabha. Each adult citizen enjoys the right to vote in Parliamentary and state legislature elections. Under Article 74 of the Constitution therefore the President is required to act only on the "aid and advice" of his Council of Ministers.

In a democracy the effective power of governance should necessarily be with the popularly elected members of the Parliament out of whom the Council of Ministers is chosen on the basis of Parliamentary majority in the Lok Sabha of any one political party or a combination of them if no single party has the majority. The leader of the majority party or a group of allied parties is appointed as Prime Minister by the President. The Prime Minister thereafter selects other members of the Council of Ministers.

At the state level, similarly, the state Council of Ministers comprises of the elected members of the legislature with the Chief Minister as the head. The effective power of governance lies with this Council of

Ministers. The head of the state at the state level is the Governor a Presidential appointee. He holds his office at the pleasure of the President. Like the President the Governor is also only a ceremonial head. He acts with the "aid and advice" of his Council of Ministers.

The governmental power in our democracy like in any other genuine democracy is derived from the people. They are the "sovereign" from whom power flows to other agencies and institutions of governance. It is they who elect members of State Legislatures (MLAs) and Members of Parliament (MPs). Such popularly elected governments exercising sovereign power of the people are the essence of democracies. To look after the development and well-being of the people has to be the primary aim of any good government and more so of a democratic government. Hence a democracy is known to be "government of the people, by the people and for the people." The other forms of government like "monarchy" and "dictatorship" suffer from various shortcomings. A monarchy generally being hereditary and not being elected by the people may or may not look after the genuine welfare of the people. The quality of a monarchical rule depends on the character of an individual monarch. Historical experiences have shown that kings and emperors generally, barring some honourable exceptions, were despotic and indulged in exploitation of the people. Their main focus was to keep their own grandeur and enjoy luxurious life style at the cost of the people. People could do nothing to get rid of any bad or despotic ruler except to revolt against their misrule when these became too intolerable. Prolonged exploitation and extreme cases of despotism had led to bloody revolutions like the French Revolution of 1789 and the Russian Revolution of 1917. These great historical Revolutions resulted in the beheading or killing of the autocratic rulers concerned of France and Russia by the people of these countries. In fact these two Revolutions brought about an end to monarchical rules all over the world. Monarchies were either abolished and replaced by Democratic Republics or wherever retained these became mere ceremonial institutions. Effective powers were exercised by the democratically elected popular governments.

Dictatorial regimes wherever these came into being also did not generally bother about the welfare of the people. A "dictator" after he usurped power illegally showed very little concern towards public good or public opinion. His sole concern generally remained to perpetuate his rule somehow or the other. Public money was spent to safeguard the dictator's own security. Even in the few currently existing "dictatorships"—military or otherwise, well-being of the people are not their main concerns. After all a military dictator derives power not from the people but from the barrel of his guns.

In comparison the positive aspects of a democracy are that power is exercised by the popularly elected leaders and that too for fixed terms. Fresh elections are required to be held on the expiry of the earlier term. Thus no one has the right to indefinitely continue to be in power without seeking fresh approval of the people at fixed intervals. The rulers in a democracy thus are repeatedly reminded that their power is derived from the people and they have to justify their continuance to them by seeking their fresh mandate on expiry of the earlier term wherever constitutionally more than one term is permissible. In some countries like the USA its democratically elected President can stand for election to the office only for two terms of four years each and no more. This is a desirable provision so that no single individual remains in power for too long to be harmful to the basic ideas of democracy.

To make such democratic governments a success, people have to be necessarily careful and vigilant in exercising their voting rights. For as has been rightly said "vigilance is the price of liberty." To ensure good governance the people need to exercise their valuable political right of vote properly so that persons of honesty and integrity and those who believe in democratic values and public service alone are elected. If persons with questionable backgrounds manage to get elected they in all probability would abuse governmental powers for their own well-being and aggrandisement. Sadly of late politics in India is becoming the playground of growing number of criminal and anti-social elements and the number of honest and public-spirited persons is rapidly declining. More and more persons charged with heinous crimes like murder, rape, smuggling, large-scale corruption etc. are now able to get elected, some even with thumping majority. For their electoral victories they make use of their money power, caste and communal loyalties of the voters and at times of their muscle power and their underworld mafia links. Most political parties too have been found to be harbouring and supporting such persons of dubious characters because in the present socio-political environment chances of winning elections by such persons are considered to be far better. It is seen that the main focus of the political parties has narrowed down to the winning of elections and to grab political power to serve their own ends. Development of the country and the welfare of the people occupy secondary place if at all in their thinking. Large number of financial scams and scandals reported frequently are the proof of the malafide motives of some of the elected representatives of the people for occupying the seats of power. This is happening mainly because in electing their representatives the people are no longer showing sufficient vigilance, and foresight. Caste, creed, and race identities of the candidates are being given more importance than their good character and capacity for public services. For example, a Jat or a Rajput voter would generally prefer to vote for a Jat or Rajput candidate even if the individuals concerned may have criminal backgrounds and their rivals of other castes may be comparatively more meritorious and more deserving. Minority communities similarly generally prefer to vote for minority class candidates irrespective of their suitability or otherwise. Democracy has thus started suffering from caste and communal divisions. Money and muscle powers too are increasingly vitiating "free and fair" elections which are the hallmark of a true democracy. Even upright voters are finding it difficult to vote "freely" according to their own individual choices. All kinds of unhealthy caste, communal or other pressures are brought upon them to cast their votes in favour of candidates who may not be considered suitable by them.

According to recent (2009) reports in the media more than half the MLAs in Uttar Pradesh face criminal charges and nearly a third of Maharashtra MLAs are crorepaties. Fifty-nine of the 81 MLAs of Jharkhand elected in the recent Assembly elections (2009) are reported to have criminal records. The Jharkhand Chief Minister Shibo Soren who took office after the 2009 election is himself an accused in three murder cases and was in jail as an under-trial. 17 out of 18 MLAs of his ruling Jharkhand Mukti Morcha Party (JMM) have reportedly criminal cases pending against them. Several elected MPs of the present Lok Sabha (2009) are also reported to be "history sheeters." A government comprising of, or supported by such criminal elements can hardly be called a true democratic government. For such a government is unlikely to be sympathetic or close to the vast multitude of India's poverty afflicted people. The true representatives of the people ought to be such "common" men/women who live with them, share their sorrows and sufferings and know where the shoe pinches them. A government of such true representatives of the people alone can understand their problems of poverty unemployment, and lack of food, clothing and shelter and try to solve these with greater sense of urgency and speed. Such elected representatives would be the genuine "fellow travellers" to stand by the people in their times of need.

Another serious problem haunting the present day democracy in India is the tendency of every ruling party to remain in power continuously for long years, if necessary by adopting foul means during election times. A kind of unhealthy vote bank politics is seen to be dominating electoral battles. Such vote bank politics is playing a divisive role being caste or communal oriented in seeking the votes of the people. As a result often the same individual of any ruling party or his/her close family relations manage to keep occupying seats of power for years. It is not their spirit of self-sacrifice or good records of public service that endear them to the people. On the other hand they manage to win elections by employing unethical means or by playing on their dynasty, caste or communal identities. The general perception accordingly is that electoral results no longer reflect "vox-populi" or the voice of the people. This is because people are either misled or hood-winked or even tempted with payment of money to get their votes. Thus often criminal or otherwise undesirable candidates, some even while lodged in jails as under-trials are able to win elections. Another unfortunate trend damaging true democracy, or government of the people, is the emergence of few families in some states who monopolise the powers of the state. For example, as reported recently in the media in Punjab the Akali Party leader Prakash Singh Badal is the Chief Minister (2009), his son Sukhvir Singh is the Deputy Chief Minister and his nephew Manpreet Singh is the Finance Minister of the State. In addition, few other close family relations are also members of the Badal Cabinet. This really amounts to family rule, and not a true democratic rule where power is shared and exercised by a wider sections of the people. Punjab type developments are also visible in some states like Tamil Nadu. Even among some important political parties, like the SP of U.P. and INLD of Haryana there seems to be political dominance of one family in these Parties. The "Party High Command" of SP, for example, consists of members of Mulayam Singh's family only as disclosed by Shri Amar Singh recently (2010). He was a top SP leader but was forced to quit and later expelled from the Party due to internal differences and distrust. Similarly, in the INLD Party of Haryana, Chaudhary Devi Lal's son Om Prakash Chautala succeeded him as the Party Chief. Now (2009) Chautala's two sons Abhaya Singh and Ajay Singh have been elected to the Haryana Assembly as party candidates of INLD. Thus Chautala and his two sons (all MLAs) are the Party "High Command" of INLD. If this party comes to power after winning elections at any time in Haryana these three members of Chautala family and may be a few others are likely to hold key ministerial posts on the lines of the present Akali Party regime of Badal in Punjab.

These examples show how democracy is getting damaged, distorted and weakened. The situation needs to be suitably reversed if democracy is to mean "government of the people, by the people and for the people." Real democracy may not survive if it is allowed to be dominated by one or a few powerful families only. That may degrade democracy into feudalism or "oligarchy" meaning "Government of the few by the few and for the few." It requires serious thinking to debar by law more than one member of the same family or close relations from holding specified seats of power at the same time. That would make democracy and democratic government more broadbased and not the monopoly of one or a few families.

To keep our democracy active and alive the citizens at large have to be alert and vote during elections in favour of honest and deserving persons irrespective of their caste, creed or family affiliations. Persons with criminal backgrounds or of questionable antecedents have to be prevented by the citizens from getting elected with their vote support. There is sufficient truth in the observation that "people get a government they deserve". Better governance cannot be expected from persons of criminal background or of doubtful integrity. If good persons are marginalised so would be good governance. To protect and preserve democracy and to enjoy its advantages such as "liberty, equality and fraternity", the people must exercise their right to vote in a responsible manner. Recognised political parties at national and regional levels too can preserve and sustain democracy by selecting the right type of party candidates for elections. The elected candidates should represent diverse groups and classes of people. Their choice should not be limited to a few castes or a few powerful families but should be well distributed to represent large sections of the people. Media is another strong pillar to support and safeguard democracy.

The media has to scrutinise the character and antecedents of the candidates standing for elections and bring to the notice of the voters black sheeps if any among them. Even after governments are formed following the elections, the media must keep vigilant watch over their activities. All suspected acts of corruption, favouritism and nepotism by any government functionary ought to be brought to light if necessary after obtaining correct and authentic information through the RTI Act. Freedom of the press thus could be a very valuable weapon to strengthen and sustain democracy.

In brief the constitutional provisions for democratic rule in India can be effective only if the people show genuine interest in the making and functioning of the democratic governments. We need to bear in mind that to attain any high and cherished aims necessary efforts have to be put. We take pride in saying that India is the "largest democracy" in the world. Our pride would be more justified if we can also say that the Indian democracy is the "most genuine democracy" as it reflects the true voice of all its people.

21

CASTE CENSUS: "NOT ONLY FOLLY BUT DISASTER"

Among the few great and memorable personalities of recent Indian history the name of Pt. Jawaharlal Nehru, the country's first Prime Minister shines like a luminous star for the high ideals he kept in view in the governance of the country. Protecting the dignity of the individual, preserving the unity of the nation and maintaining its secular character were given special importance by him. He was totally against casteism and any caste-based socio-economic policy in governance of the country. When socially divisive caste-based reservation demands for the "Backwards" started gaining strength for services in the states, Pt. Nehru thought it necessary to advise, and in a way warn the State Chief Ministers in a letter he wrote to them (dated 27th June 1961 copy in the Annexure) saying: this way lies "not only folly but disaster." He reminded the CMs in his letter that in a meeting held with them to consider national integration it was decided to identify the Backward people "on economic considerations and not on caste lines." Earlier Pt. Nehru had outright rejected the March 1955 Report of the first Backward Class Commission headed by Kaka Kalelkar for job reservation for persons belonging to 2399 Backward Castes as listed by the Commission. In the Government order rejecting caste based reservation in the central services it was stated that the caste system has been the greatest hindrance in the way of India's progress towards a secular and egalitarian society. "Caste" was accordingly not given any official recognition for any policy formulations except in the case of the "scheduled castes" notified under Article 341 of the Constitution. They had greatly suffered from social ill-treatment and deprivation for centuries and accordingly deserved special care and affirmative action as part of "social justice" by the state for their advancement. Suitable constitutional provisions had therefore been made for this purpose for them under different Articles of the Constitution. The Constitution did not recognize the caste identity of any other class of people. On the other hand Article 14 provides "equality" before the law and "equal protection of the laws" to every person in the country. Similarly, Article15(1) of the Constitution provides that "the state shall not discriminate against any citizen on grounds only of religion, race, caste, sex, place of birth or any of them."

While presenting the final draft of the Constitution before the Constituent Assembly Dr. Ambedkar had no doubt expressed fears about the possible revival in the future of what he called "our old enemies in the form of castes and creeds." He had also feared the likelihood of "many political parties with diverse and opposing political creeds" coming into existence in the years to come. Accordingly the thought that troubled him was: "Will the Indians place the country above their creed or will they place the creed above the country?" Unfortunately the fears of Dr. Ambedkar came to be true rather too soon when in 1989 the report of the second Backward Class Commission (headed by B.P. Mandal) recommending job reservation for persons of as many as 3743 Backward Castes listed by this commission (as against 2399 Backward Castes listed by the earlier Kaka Kalelkar Commission) was accepted by the V.P. Singh Government. This Commission was appointed by the short-lived Janata Government of Morarji Desai which submitted its report on 31st December 1980. Indira Gandhi had come back to power around that time after defeating her non-Congress rival parties and had to take a decision on this report. She however, neither accepted nor rejected the Mandal Report but in a way put it in the cold storage to allow caste politics to cool down before taking any decision. She was against casteism, but thought it politically inadvisable to reject the Mandal Report straight away. Her successor Rajiv Gandhi too considered caste oriented reservation policy a serious challenge to national unity and integration and allowed the Mandal Report to continue to lie in the cold storage. The author was Secretary in the Central Ministry of Personnel & Administrative Reforms at that time (from 1982-85) dealing with civil service policy matters and knew well why the decision on Mandal Report was deferred indefinitely by Prime Minister Indira Gandhi. The Report had been discussed at great length in a Committee of Secretaries of which the author was also a member. The general view was against caste-based reservation but it was decided to defer decision till the views of the state governments too were obtained. However, after the non-Congress Government of V.P. Singh came to power in 1989 its very first act was to immediately accept the Mandal Report in its totality without any more discussion and debate. The main purpose in deciding to accept the Mandal Report by V.P. Singh in such great haste was to gain political mileage by pleasing the powerful caste politicians who were his supporters. He did not bother to apply his mind to the short and long-term adverse implications of the Report pointed out in the earlier discussions held during the regimes of Smt. Indira Gandhi and Rajiv Gandhi. As a fall out of V.P. Singh's decision which came like a bolt from the blue, the country faced large scale caste-turmoils and disturbances leading to the death of several young persons who apprehended their future to be gloomy on account of 27 per cent job reservation for certain castes classified as OBCs in addition to the existing 23½ per cent reservation for the SCs/STs. By his decision on the Mandal Report V.P. Singh in a way strengthened and revitalized caste and caste-based politics in the country. By his retrograde step V.P. Singh reversed the policy followed by Pt. Nehru, Indira Gandhi and Rajiv Gandhi to ignore and down play caste in governances and administration. Their goal was to make India a casteless, egalitarian and a truly secular state. The state was kept above caste and caste-based politics. V.P. Singh's acceptance of the casteist Mandal Report very much harmed social harmony and the feeling of fraternity among "We the people" of India. He degraded the secular democracy of India so carefully planned and structured by out great leaders and the framers of the Constitution of free India.

The caste-based reservation policy based on Mandal Report was legally challenged in the Supreme Court through writ petitions of the aggrieved parties. In a nine-judge bench the Apex Court considered all the OBCs reservation issues in a detailed and comprehensive manner and in its verdict the court significantly diluted the casteist approach of the Mandal Report. This historic judgement (known as the Mandal judgement) ***inter-alia*** decided that caste cannot be the only or the sole basis for the identification of the "Backward Classes" for reservation purposes. It laid down that to qualify to be of "Backward" class the low nature of occupation of an individual (e.g. of being a rickshaw puller, hawker, or daily wage earner, etc.) his poor quality of residence (e.g. shanty or slums etc.,) and lack of education etc., would have to be no less relevant in addition to his low caste. No one belonging to any backward caste will *ipso facto* get reservation benefit as an OBC unless the other important conditions of "backwardness" laid down by the Supreme Court too were satisfied. The "creamy layer" or the advanced sections of any backward caste will have to be specially excluded from reservation benefits as they will not qualify to be "backward". Job reservation was thus not made solely caste-based to benefit every member of any caste classified as Backward. The Apex Court also decided that there will be no reservation in promotion to maintain efficiency of administration and that the upper limit of reservation is not to exceed 50 per cent of the vacancies in a year so that the general provision of "equality" in the Constitution is not unduly breached or violated leading to reverse discrimination. The Court also held that since all the people of Backward Castes may not qualify to be "backward" reservation for the OBCs need not be proportionate to the percentage of their population. Thus much of the mischief of casteism of the Mandal Report was removed by the Apex Court.

After independence India having become a Secular Republic caste was not given any official recognition by recording a citizen's caste in the ten yearly census. The last caste based census was held in 1931 and discontinued thereafter as it was found by the then British administration that the caste data collected during census was hugely faulty, inaccurate, confusing and unreliable. This happened because during census enumerations many persons of lower castes tended to declare themselves to be of higher castes for getting higher social status in official records. It was not possible to verify their true castes by the Census enumerators who were generally primary school teachers or other lower category government officials not fully in know of the Indian caste system and its confusing complexities. Caste names and their social rankings also varied from place to place. Often the same caste was known by different names in different areas. In some places a low caste was treated to be of higher social status and in some other places it was the reverse. The census enumerators recorded the caste of an individual as declared by him as they had no way to check or verify its correctness.

Since such faulty caste records served no useful purpose it was decided not to have caste based census after 1931. Now, also the situation remains more or less the same so far as variations in caste names, social status of different castes and other caste complexities are concerned. It may be noted, as pointed out earlier, that Kaka

Kalelkar Commission had listed 2399 castes to be "backward" and a few years later the Mandal Commission listed them to be as high as 3743 in number. Obviously there is confusion in the identification of higher and lower castes because of variations in their names and social status from place to place. Further the OBCs cannot be identified by their caste names alone. Several other important conditions as laid down by the Supreme Court in its Mandal Judgement have to be fulfilled for such identification. It is seen that presently the tendency for many groups and persons is to claim to be of lower castes because of the vested interest to get reservation benefits. Earlier the tendency for lower castes was to declare themselves to be of higher castes for getting higher social status. Any caste data collected during census now may not therefore be wholly correct or reliable as was the case earlier. There is also the possible danger of some backward castes on such wrong caste data claiming separate reservations for them on finding their representation in government jobs to be low. Thus all kinds of uncalled for caste disputes and demands for separate and higher reservation quotas may arise and further weaken the social fabric of India if caste census is reintroduced.

It is argued that caste is a "social reality" and cannot be ignored for devising and implementing appropriate social development schemes for the backward castes. We may not forget that there were other harmful "social realities" too in the past, like burning the widow of a dead person along with him (Sati-dah); forbidding widow remarriage; prevalence of child marriage; forbidding girl education, loss of caste on going abroad or on crossing the high seas by any one; etc. etc. With the march of time, spread of education, urbanization, and efforts of great social reformers most of the pernicious social evils have become things of the past. Government too had played a positive role in legally forbidding some of these harmful "social realities." In the present era of incredible technological advances and globalization every country for its progress has necessarily to keep pace with the new world culture, ideas, and forward movements in diverse spheres. Quite a few young men and women astronauts of India of different castes and creeds have made awe inspiring space journeys (with fellow foreign astronauts) to make India proud. Narrow caste ideas or outlooks did not deter them from trying to reach the moon or other planets, leave alone crossing the seas. India itself is making its moon vehicle (Chadrayan) to land on the moon. When the world has become a launching pad to reach other planets of the universe and a "global village" India should cultivate the modern outlook and take note of the new realities in all fields of human activities. India can no longer afford to be the same old casteist country holding on to its primitive caste burqa which disallowed Indians to cross the seas. A major world power like India with its scientific and technological progress can ill-afford to live in its medieval caste cell ignoring the new realities of the new world order. There has to be free mixing and full social equation among all the Indians, to march forward shoulder to shoulder in order to successfully compete with others in the new "brave world". Slowly, but certainly, this change is fortunately taking place as millions of Indians of all castes are now ignoring such of their caste beliefs and practices as are found to be of no social utility but are a hindrance to progress. Many of them do not even know their castes. Caste-based occupations are no longer sacrosanct for members of any caste. The four *Varnas* of Manu Smriti: such as Brahmins (teachers, scholars and priests), the Kshetriya (kings and warriors), the Vaishyas (agriculturists and traders) and Shudras (artisans, service providers) are not of much relevance now. It may be seen that now there are Brahmin tailors, Kshetriya hoteliers, Vaisya school and college teachers and Shudra doctors and engineers etc. There are no more caste barriers to follow any profession or vocation of ones choice. Caste has thus been ignored or marginalized for all purposes, save perhaps marriage. But inter-caste marriages too are taking place though not in large numbers. However, sooner or later theses may not remain to be exceptions but become quite normal. Government should accordingly take no notice of an individual's caste for any official activity or for official records. In the national interest government should ignore caste which will amount to abolishing caste officially.

With the march of time in place of caste bonding there are now professional and occupational bonding among the people which are far more stronger and uniting. This in a way is the "Karma" (work activities, occupations, etc.) and "Guna" (talent, ability, etc.) theory of the original caste system as explained in the Gita by Lord Krishna. Caste system originally was not hereditary but flexible as it was based on an individual's talent, capacity and work. It was self-acquired and not a family heritage.

People of all castes and communities in their urban habitats now live in the same areas and also in adjoining apartments of the same building. Many of them lunch and dine together without bothering about their castes or creeds. Caste does not stand in the way of their free mixing and socializing. There are doctors of all castes treating patients of all castes. Similarly there are teachers and children of all castes in the same schools and colleges engaged in teaching and learning. There is no desire, inclination or motivations for any one to know each other's caste. Hopefully, in not too distant a future, caste may wither away or disappear altogether like a dry leaf falling from a tree and blown away by the wind. However, if power-loving and caste oriented politicians or the caste leaders like that of the Khap Panchayats are allowed to have their way without any control or check over them they will try to strengthen and revitalize the caste system in order to maintain their hold on power and their caste leaderships. It is they who keep saying that caste being a "social reality" cannot be ignored. The deciding factor should however, be whether this "social reality" is beneficial or harmful to society and the country. The old caste system which degenerated in course of time does not appear to have any social utility now. In old days it was an indicator of occupation, social standing and intellectual ability. It had thus contributed to some kind of social order in that distant past. But after it became hereditary it lost its importance. Caste is now seen to be socially divisive, harmful and derogatory. Our great leaders like Mahatma Gandhi, Pt. Nehru, Sardar Patel and Dr. Ambedkar, etc., were therefore, totally against the existing caste system. Accordingly this so-called "social reality" should be officially ignored for being "socially undesirable", save in the case of the SCs for reasons mentioned earlier. The least that the government could and should do now would be to accord no official recognition to caste by enumerating it in the 2011 Census. Moreover, since the caste data collected during census, for reasons mentioned earlier, would be faulty, inaccurate and unreliable it will not help in devising any meaningful upliftment schemes for the "backwards". Further, rationally speaking there are no good reasons to formulate caste or creed based development projects when millions of Indians of all castes and creed equally suffer from poverty, illiteracy and ill-health. "Caste and creed" being our "old enemies" as stated by Dr. Ambedkar should not be promoted or championed by the state in any way. If Government cannot legally abolish caste as it did to constitutionally abolish "untouchability" it should at least take no official notices of caste by enumerating it in the 2011 census. For once caste of an individual is mentioned against his name in the official census records, in course of time every one wishing to join the public services may be required to declare his caste. Once that is done there will be demand to get information about the number and percentage of public officials of different castes. If in such caste related information the representation in public services of any caste is found to be comparatively low there may be demand for separate reservation for such castes. That will lead to reservation within reservation for several castes and make India more casteist. The main beneficiaries of OBC reservation now are not more than a dozen or so castes or the "forward" groups among them. They are in fact the strongest supporters of caste-based census. But they may on the basis of wrong census data face hostile opposition from other genuine OBCs with lower representations in government jobs. They will demand separate job reservations for them. Thus the supporters of caste-based census with the hope of getting more reserved jobs are not only harming the unity and social stability of the country but are also in a way digging their own graves by creating situations for separate job quotas for the more backwards among them.

Another matter of concern relating to cast census is that its wrong and inflated backward caste population figures may lead to demands for raising the present 50 per cent upper limit of job reservation. As a result the country may again face caste fights and violence. Government may also get deeply involved in solving caste problems and reservation issues leaving nil or little time for it to pursue the more important goals of economic development. From all angels therefore introducing caste–census may turn out to be "not only folly but disaster" in the words of Pt. Nehru.

As was wisely stated by Dr. Ambedkar, let the country be placed above caste politics and not caste politics above the country. In the long-term interest of the country India must discard its caste "Burqa" officially and give no heed to the fatwas of the caste Mullahas of politics. There are good reasons to hope that the present top leaders in charge of governance of the country will follow the footsteps of Pt. Nehru and other great leaders by rejecting caste and caste based policies. The great harm done by V.P. Singh to national integration and social harmony by revitalizing the caste division of the Indian society in accepting the Mandal Commission Report for his political gain ought not to be repeated by introducing caste census for the 2011 census for the political benefit of a few political parties. To do so will be a historical blunder.

ANNEXURE

Pt. Nehru's Letter to the State Chief Ministers dated 27th June, 1961

I have referred above to efficiency and to our getting out of our traditional institutions. This necessitates our getting out of the old habit of reservations and particular privileges being given to this caste or that group. The recent meeting we held here, at which the Chief Ministers were present, to consider national integration, laid down that help should be given on economic considerations and not on caste. It is true that we are tied up with certain rules and conventions about helping the scheduled castes and tribes. They deserve help, but even so I dislike any kind of reservation, more particularly in services. I react strongly against anything which leads to inefficiency and second-rate standards. I want my country to be a first class country in everything. The moment we encourage the second-rate, we are lost.

The only way to help a backward group is to give opportunities of good education, this includes technical education which is becoming more and more important. Everything else is provision of some kind of crutches which do not add to the strength or health of the body. We have made recently two decisions which are very important: one is, universal free elementary education that is the base; and the second is scholarships on a very wide scale at every grade of education to the bright boys and girls, and this applies not merely to literary education, but, much more so, to technical, scientific and medical training. I lay stress on the bright and able boys and girls because it is only they who will raise our standards. I have no doubt that there is a vast reservoir of potential talent in this country if only we can give it opportunity.

But if we go in for reservations on communal and caste basis, we swamp the bright and able people and remain second-rate or third-rate. I am grieved to learn how far this business of reservations has gone based on communal considerations. It has amazed me to learn that even promotions are based sometimes on communal or caste considerations. This way lies not only folly, but disaster. Let us help the backward groups by all means, but never at the cost of efficiency. How are we going to build the public sector or indeed any sector with second-rate people?

—Jawaharlal Nehru, Letter to Chief Ministers, 27 June, 1961.

Index